The airport business

In the 1950s and 1960s airports were seen as just another, fairly inconsequential arm of government. Over the past 20 years, however, it has become obvious that airports can actually be run as highly successful and profitable businesses. Despite this success the industry has, until now, had no defined economic theory to base itself on. The aim of *The Airport Business* is to change this. Working on the basis that airports can and should be run as successful businesses, Professor Doganis sets the airline business as a whole within a conceptual framework.

The book opens with an overview of the airport business, examining patterns of ownership and control of the world's largest airports. The author considers the key issues which will affect airport managers during the 1990s, such as privatization, the growing shortfall in airport capacity and the need to develop new and innovative sources of finance. Another important aspect of the book is cost strategy. Professor Doganis analyses the traditional cost and revenue systems that have developed for aircraft landing fees and passenger charges. He goes on to compare this with more recent strategies, such as marginal as opposed to average cost pricing. The author also discusses the need for a commercial strategy and goes on to show how to maximise airport revenue from the various activities at the airport. Because of the unique system practised in the US a chapter is devoted to the performance of American airports. Likewise, there are difficulties peculiar to the Third World, which are also examined in a separate chapter. As the airport industry continues to grow *The Airport Business* offers an insight into how to overcome the major economic and financial problems that airports will have to confront in the 1990s.

The airport business

Rigas Doganis

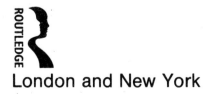

ROUTLEDGE

London and New York

First published 1992
by Routledge
11 New Fetter Lane, London EC4P 4EE

Simultaneously published in the USA and Canada
by Routledge
29 West 35th Street, New York, NY 10001

Reprinted 1996

Routledge is an International Thomson Publishing company I(T)P

© 1992 Rigas Doganis

Typeset by Witwell Ltd, Southport
Printed and bound in Great Britain by
Mackays of Chatham PLC, Chatham, Kent

British Library Cataloguing in Publication Data
A catalogue record for this title is available from the British Library

Library of Congress Cataloguing in Publication Data
Doganis, Rigas.
      The airport business / Rigas Doganis.
          p.   cm.
      Includes bibliographical references and index.
      1. Airports. 2. Airports–Management. I. Title.
    HE9797.D64   1992
    387.7'36–dc20   91–44797
                                                                            CIP

ISBN 0–415–07877–6 (hbk)
ISBN 0–415–08117–3 (pbk)

Contents

Figures

Tables

Acknowledgements

The book is based on and draws extensively on research work undertaken over the last twenty years by the author and others within the Transport Studies Group at the Polytechnic of Central London. So many people made contributions to that research that it is difficult to name them all, but special thanks are due to Dr Grahame Thompson, Geoff Myers and Heini Nuutinen. Also to Anne Graham who in recent years has co-ordinated much of the airport research at the Polytechnic. Her assistance in preparing this book has been invaluable and she has, of course, contributed the important chapter on United States airports. I am indeed indebted to her.

The research work at the Polytechnic was supported for several years by the then British Airports Authority. One is indeed grateful to the BAA and to Sir Norman Payne who, as Chief Executive at the time, responded so willingly to requests for financial support for academic research. Others within the BAA have also contributed to the development of thinking on airport economics and management notably Michael Maine, Michael Poole, Stan Maiden, Michael Toms, John Phillips and Martin Booth. From the UK Civil Aviation Authority both Stan Abrahams and Tom Bass have made important contributions. Finally one should not forget the fact that many airport managers from other countries have also helped develop our understanding of the airport business. I can single out Utz Heinzelman of Frankfurt airport, Sigi Gangl at Vienna and Guntram Brendel of the Weitnauer Group. Over many years these three and others mentioned above have given me the benefit of their extensive airport experience. I wish to thank them all. This book owes much to them.

It is difficult to understand the airport business unless one is close to it. I have been fortunate enough either as a researcher or a consultant to visit a large number of airports particularly in Europe and South East Asia. I have benefited considerably from the openness with which airport managers have received me. A further source of insight has been provided by talking to the participants at the annual Airport Economics and Finance Symposium held in February at the Polytechnic of Central London. This draws each year a small select group of airport managers from around the world and provides a unique forum for the open and frank discussion of key issues affecting airports.

Introduction

The airport business is taking off. During the last twenty-five years the airport industry has been transformed from being a branch of government into a dynamic and commercially oriented business. The change has come about as the close ties between governments and airports have been progressively loosened. At the same time airport managers in many countries have been given greater freedom to operate commercially in order to produce profits or at least to reduce their deficits. Yet there has been much uncertainty as to how such commercial freedom might be used. In most countries, up to the mid- or late 1970s, airports had been thought of as little more than an insignificant arm of government and little attention had been paid to them. As the pressure to become commercially oriented grew, so it became increasingly apparent that little was known about airport economics or the airport business. Independent airport managers had no body of public knowledge or economic theory to call on to aid them in turning subsidized airports into profitable companies.

Numerous articles and conference papers have appeared in recent years dealing with particular aspects of airport management. But there has been no coherent attempt to place the airport business as a whole within a conceptual framework. That is the prime aim of the present book. It starts with the premise that airports, the larger ones at least, can be operated as successful businesses. Whatever their form of ownership, they should be able to at least cover their full costs, including capital charges, from their revenues. If they set out to do so, they should also be able to generate substantial profits.

The focus of the book is the economic and financial aspects of the airport business. It is concerned with providing a sound understanding of the economics of that business placing particular emphasis on revenue generation from both aeronautical and commercial activities. Airport managers face a unique problem. They must plan and undertake huge capital investments in large and immovable assets, which have no alternative use, to satisfy a demand over which they have little control. It is the airlines and not the airports who decide where and how the demand for air transport will be met. Maximizing revenue generation in such a situation is a particularly demanding task.

The book starts with an overview of the airport business identifying what the business is about and highlighting its sparkling financial performance in recent years. It examines the patterns of ownership and the relative importance of the world's largest airports (Chapter 1). This is followed by an examination of the key issues which will affect airport managers during the 1990s such as privatization, the growing shortfall in airport capacity and the need to develop new and innovative sources of finance (Chapter 2). An analysis of the cost and revenue structures of airports (Chapter 3) leads on to a detailed review of the traditional pricing policies and structures which have been developed for aircraft landing fees and passenger charges (Chapter 4). In recent years some congested airports have moved away from the traditional approach and have considered marginal as opposed to average cost pricing. Alternative pricing strategies are discussed in Chapter 5 as is the question of selling or auctioning runway slots. Discussion then shifts to airports' commercial activities and the need to develop a clearly defined commercial strategy (Chapter 6). The major problem facing airport managers in the 1990s will be how to maximize airport revenues from the various activities and concessions at the airport which are operated by others. This is considered in detail in Chapter 7. In operating their airports as business, airport managers will need constantly to monitor various aspects of their performance. The development of useful airport performance indicators is, therefore, of some importance (Chapter 8).

Much, though not all, of the analysis and many of the examples used in the book relate to European airports and experience. While the analysis is relevant to airports worldwide there are two groups of airports that have unique characteristics which merit more detailed analysis. The first of these are the United States airports. These have their own particular system of funding which in turn creates particular revenue and cost structures and poses different management issues. These are compared briefly with European experience in Chapter 3 but are discussed in greater detail in Chapter 9. Finally, airport managements in developing countries face particular problems arising largely from economic and institutional factors in their own countries (Chapter 10).

There can be little doubt that the airport business will be one of the financial success stories of the 1990s. Its financial performance should continue to outstrip that of its major customers, the airlines. To share in that success individual airport managers must face up to and understand the major economic and financial problems that will emerge. This book attempts to provide an insight into some of those key issues. Read on and take off.

Chapter 1

The airport business

IMPROVING FINANCIAL PERFORMANCE

Airports are big business. The public flotation of the British Airports Authority in the summer of 1987 for £1.3 billion focused attention on a much neglected and often maligned sector of air transport. In the latter part of the 1980s inadequate runway capacity, congested terminals and air traffic control delays generated poor publicity for airports in Europe, the United States and, to a lesser extent, Asia. But adverse press and public comment obscured the sparkling financial performances of many European and other airports.

The 1970s and 1980s saw the transformation of airports from what were previously little more than central or local government departments to commercially oriented enterprises capable of generating substantial profits. Moreover, as the financial performance of airports improved they were generally cushioned from the adverse economic factors affecting airlines. Thus most large airports continued to make profits in 1980 and 1981 when many of their airline customers were plunging into huge losses. In the decade that followed airports continually improved their profitability even in years when airline profits faltered or declined.

Among European airports financial results have improved dramatically in recent years and profits have risen sharply. In the five years between 1983 and 1989 profits at eighteen of Europe's major airports more or less quadrupled (Table 1.1). Of the two airports that reported losses in 1983 one was profitable six years later.

It would be valuable to assess airport financial performance in terms of the returns on the assets employed. However, in practice it is very difficult to arrive at the true asset value of airports in different countries. An easier alternative is to use a Revex ratio, an indicator also used in the airline industry. This shows revenue as a proportion of expenditure before tax (Table 1.2). Many European airports have Revex ratios that are surprisingly high and would be the envy of most airlines. As a group airports in the British Isles (shown in capitals in Table 1.2) have particularly high Revex ratios, though it should be borne in mind that the ratios for the British Airports Authority

Table 1.1 Reported surplus or deficit of major European airports 1983 and 1989

	Surplus or deficit[1]		
	1983 £'000		1989 £'000
London Heathrow[2]	50,307		145,000
London Gatwick[2]	5,829		54,900
Manchester	13,791		29,834
Frankfurt	7,615		56,008
Dublin[2,3]	5,765		17,631
Amsterdam	951		14,199
Glasgow[2]	2,475		12,400
Nice[4]	2,679		5,979
Rome		−4,953	6,308
Copenhagen	832		4,953
Belfast	988		3,367
Milan	91		1,140
Birmingham	1,393		4,848
Vienna	2,435		5,721
East Midlands (UK)	1,999		2,238
Marseilles		−287	−142
Geneva	524		965
Basle-Mulhouse	153		584
Total (18 airports)	92,587		365,933
Change 1983 to 1989			+299%

Notes: [1] Converted to pounds sterling using OECD purchasing power parities. Figures are after tax.
[2] No interest charges included.
[3] Depreciation not charged.
[4] Loan redemption included instead of depreciation.

(BAA) airports have been calculated before the inclusion of interest charges. Dublin's very high Revex ratio is partly due to the fact that no capital charges are borne by the airport.

Another aspect of airports' growing profitability is that their financial results are less affected by the downturn in air travel than are those of the airlines. Thus in 1980–1, when many scheduled airlines made substantial losses because of falling demand and higher fuel prices, most airports that were already profitable continued to make profits. The same phenomenon was apparent in 1990 and 1991 following the invasion of Kuwait. The traffic and profits of many airlines nosedived. While airport traffic levels also declined few faced serious financial difficulties as a result. In the financial year 1990–1 the airports owned by BAA Plc registered no traffic growth but pushed up their profits by almost 10 per cent (BAA 1991).

The improving financial performance of European airports has been

Table 1.2 Revex ratio for major European airports 1988

	Revex ratio[1]
LONDON HEATHROW[2]	1.69
GLASGOW[2]	1.59
LONDON GATWICK[2]	1.49
DUBLIN[2,3]	1.47
Nice[3]	1.38
BIRMINGHAM	1.33
MANCHESTER	1.30
Belfast[3,4]	1.23
EAST MIDLANDS	1.23
Marseilles	1.15
Amsterdam	1.12
Frankfurt	1.12[5]
Copenhagen[4]	1.10
Vienna	1.10[5]
Basle-Mulhouse	1.07
Milan	1.04[5]
Rome	1.02[5]
Geneva	1.01

Source: Transport Studies Group, Polytechnic of Central London.
Notes: [1] Revex is ratio of revenue to expenditure (excluding taxes and extraordinary items).
[2] No interest charges included.
[3] Depreciation not charged.
[4] 1989 data used.
[5] Airport authorities with major involvement in passenger, baggage, or freight handling.

mirrored by similar improvements in some other parts of the world, notably East Asia and the Pacific (Table 1.3). While many of the larger United States airports have been profitable for many years, the airport-use agreements which some US airports have with their airlines prevent them from earning large profits. Several do little more than break even as a result. Though many airports around the world, particularly medium-sized and smaller ones, continue to operate at a loss, the general picture is one of improving financial results. How has the airport industry managed to sustain an ever-improving profit record?

In the first place, airports have benefited from relatively high traffic growth. In the ten years up to and including 1990 passenger traffic at UK airports grew at an average of 6.1 per cent per annum despite two years from 1980 to 1982 when traffic stagnated. Most European airports also enjoyed an annual growth of around 5 to 6 per cent during this ten-year period. Growth was more rapid at North American airports, partly as a result of airline deregulation, but was most rapid among Far East airports. In the East Asia and the Pacific region annual growth at many airports was 10 per cent or more. Airports unlike airlines benefit from marked economies of scale. As

Table 1.3 Reported profit or loss for selected airports 1989

	Profit or loss (US$ millions)		Terminal passengers (millions)
Los Angeles	51.0		45.0
Washington Dulles/National	18.8		24.6
Toronto	18.8		18.6
Tokyo Narita[2]	82.5		15.3
Madrid		−18.1	14.2
Detroit	4.3		13.8
Bangkok	74.4		12.2
Palma de Majorca	4.3		11.5
Mexico City[1]	42.5		11.1
Cincinatti	14.2		8.7
Barcelona		−10.1	8.1
Vancouver		− 1.1	7.3
Calgary		−12.8	4.7
Bogota[1]	14.7		4.4
Tehran[1]	15.7		4.3
Guadalajara[1]	10.8		3.1
Belgrade[1]	1.9		2.8
Montreal Mirabel		−28.8	2.3
Prague		− 9.5	2.0
Medellin (Colombia)[1]	2.3		1.6
Barbados	2.0		1.4
Nadi (Fiji)	0.5		0.6
Mahe (Seychelles)		− 0.6	0.3

Sources: ICAO 1989a and airport annual reports.
Notes: [1] Inadequate or no provision for depreciation.
       [2] 1988 data used.

traffic builds up, the runway and terminal facilities are better utilized and their fixed costs are spread over larger numbers of aircraft or passengers. Unit costs go down, unless an airport invests too much or too soon in new facilities. In the year 1974–5 Gatwick's single runway handled 73,000 commercial aircraft movements and 5.1 million passengers, yet the same runway fifteen years later handled more than twice as many aircraft movements and 21 million passengers though with additional terminal space. Clearly there are marked scale economies. (See pp. 46–54 for detailed analysis of airport cost structures.) We thus face an interesting paradox. The more congested, crowded and uncomfortable an airport the more likely it is to be highly profitable.

Second, airports all over the world have taken advantage of changing government attitudes towards airports. Progressively the view that airports were a quasi-public utility to be run and financed by local or central government in the same way as roads or public transport has been abandoned. It has been replaced in many countries by the view that airports could be and should be run as commercial enterprises. This change in attitudes was exemplified in the United Kingdom by the 1978 Government White Paper on *Airports Policy*. Written by a Socialist government, it stated categorically that 'there can be no general justification for subsidizing airports and air services . . .' (HMSO 1978). The UK government's attitude was mirrored by similar developments in other countries.

As a result of these changing attitudes, the ties and links between airports and governments have been loosened in most of Europe. There are notable exceptions as in Greece or Belgium where most airports are still run in effect by government departments. In other parts of the world also the links with government were progressively loosened. In numerous cases this has involved the creation of autonomous airport companies or corporations able to operate as independent commercial enterprises while remaining under government ownership. The success of the British Airports Authority, set up orginally in 1966 to run a group of airports around London together with one in Scotland, led to similar developments elsewhere. The Nigerian Airports Authority, the Airports Authority of Thailand and the International Airports Authority of India set up in the late 1970s or early 1980s are examples of this. More recently in January 1988 the Federal Airports Corporation was established in Australia. Elsewhere, individual airport directors, while still nominally under central- or local-government control, have been given greater commercial freedom in operating their airports, and have been put under pressure to break even or to produce profits thereby reducing the need for government financing.

The third factor which has enabled many airports significantly to improve their financial performance has been their monopolistic or quasi-monopolistic supply position. This is particularly true of airports designated in the bilateral air services agreements as international gateways. Airlines operating international services have had no option but to fly into such airports. There may well have been competition for longer-haul flights between airports in relatively close proximity, such as Brussels or Amsterdam, but generally such competition has been at the margin. When given the freedom to do so airports have been able to increase or change their landing fees or other charges with little fear that they would lose traffic as a result. The development of 'hubbing' in recent years may now be making competition between airports more acute – but more of that later.

Thus, using their new-found commercial freedom and exploiting the monopolistic position they often enjoyed, airports pushed up their earnings rapidly especially from duty-free concessions and other non-aeronautical sources. This was made easier by the rapid traffic growth being experienced.

NOT ALL AIRPORTS EQUALLY PROFITABLE

While the financial results of many airports have been steadily improving in recent years not all airports are equally profitable (See Table 1.3). Moreover, while the capital-city or largest airports in many countries appear to be making profits, many of the secondary or regional airports are loss-makers. This is the case for instance in Canada, Australia, Sweden or Malaysia. But the published financial results of the larger and apparently profitable airports may in many cases mask the true economic performance even of those airports. This may be so where an airport's costs have been underestimated for one of the following reasons:

(a) At many airports, particularly those still run by government departments, grants received from international aid agencies or even the airport's own government may not appear as a cost in the airport accounts. Assets financed from such grants may not be charged a depreciation cost, as was the case until the mid-1980s at municipally owned British airports.

Furthermore, such grants may be interest free. The failure to allow fully for capital costs, depreciation and interest is a feature of many airport accounts especially where airports are still operated as little more than government departments. At least six of the airports listed in Table 1.3 have inadequate or no provision for depreciation. Their apparent profitability would be significantly reduced if full and proper depreciation were charged. Another shortcoming in accounts may arise where government grants or subsidies are used to cover annual operating losses and no interest charges are borne by the airports for such 'overdrafts' or 'loans'.

(b) Where services at an airport are provided by other government department, for instance runway maintenance by the Public Works Department, the airport may in some cases not be charged for such services. These costs may well not be reflected in the airport's accounts. This is most likely to happen with the costs of building, taxiway or runway maintenance, with fire services, and with airport policing and security.

(c) Finally, there is the tricky question of air traffic control, notably the aerodrome approach and control services provided at an airport. Since these facilities are an integral part of an airport, should their costs and revenues not be included in the airport accounts in order to assess an airport's overall profitability? Where airports themselves provide such services, as at several UK airports, this is exactly what happens. But in many instances such airport-approach air traffic control is operated at a loss by the respective civil aviation departments. Including such losses in airport's accounts would reduce or eliminate many apparent profits.

In short, the true economic performance of many airports, after allowing for all real costs associated with the provision of airport services, may be somewhat worse than their published financial results might indicate (See Table 1.3).

WHAT IS AN AIRPORT?

Airports are complex industrial enterprises. They act as a forum in which disparate elements and activities are brought together to facilitate, for both passengers and freight, the interchange between air and surface transport. For historical, legal and commercial reasons the actual activities within the airport for which an airport owner or manager is responsible vary between countries and often between airports in the same country. Thus the airport business can, in some instances, cover almost everything that goes on at an airport, while elsewhere it may encompass only a small part of the total airport activity.

An airport is essentially one or more runways for aircraft together with associated buildings or terminals where passengers or freight transported by the aircraft are processed. Around the world the majority of airport authorities own and operate their runways, terminals and associated facilities, such as taxiways or aprons. But there are exceptions, notably in the United States where many terminals are owned by airlines, and in France where the ground facilities are sometimes owned by the government rather than the local Chambers of Commerce who run the airports.

Within the overall airport umbrella a wide range of services and facilities are provided which can be divided into three distinct groups: essential operational services, traffic-handling services and commercial activities. By examining how these services are dealt with among European airports it is possible to assess both the range of activities that go on at an airport and the varying degree of involvement in them by airport owners.

Essential operational services and facilities

Such services are primarily concerned with ensuring safety of aircraft and airport users. They include air traffic control (ATC) services provided at the airport to facilitate the approach and landing of aircraft, meteorological services, telecommunications, police and security, fire and ambulance services including those for search and rescue, and finally runway and building maintenance.

These facilities and services are normally provided by the airports themselves or by local or central government departments. But even when the airport operator is responsible for their provision, that operator may have relatively little discretionary control over them because their provision may be heavily influenced by government policies or national or international regulations. For instance, in recent years the level of security provided at British airports has not been at their descretion but has been determined by the relevant government minister.

At the majority of European airports *air traffic control* (ATC) and the associated meteorological and communication services are undertaken by government departments. The costs of such provision are handled in two ways. First, at many airports such as the BAA airports (Heathrow, Gatwick and Glasgow), Amsterdam, Frankfurt, Geneva, Milan, Rome and Vienna the costs associated with these activities are not passed on to the airports. Nor do the airports themselves levy any charges on users for ATC, though the civil aviation authorities may do so. So there is no revenue generated for the airport. For example, though ANA, the Portuguese government body responsible for Lisbon airport, also runs the ATC services, the airport and the navigation services are kept completely separate and the airport administration itself does not incur any ATC costs or revenues. Second, at other airports where ATC services are provided by the government, the airports are actually charged for such services. They therefore include an ATC or navigation service charge in their own airport charges in order to recoup this expense. In Europe such airports include Birmingham, Copenhagen, Geneva and Manchester. Their accounts show a cost figure arising from the provision of ATC. This is also the case with a third and much smaller group of airports who operate the ATC services themselves. These include East Midlands, Jersey and Stockholm airports.

With the increase in hijacking and terrorism, *policing and security* is nowadays an airport service of considerable importance. Apart from the normal police duties required at any large public place, specialist staff are now also needed for passenger search, baggage search, access control and so on. These latter services are sometimes defined as security rather than policing activities but the distinction between the two is very blurred and so they are considered together.

Dublin is one of the few airports which provide all their own policing/security and incur all the costs. Belfast, in Northern Ireland, is similarly in charge of all these activities but subcontracts some security work to private companies. It receives grants from the government to cover the extra measures needed because of Belfast's additional security problems. At Geneva and most UK airports (except Jersey), a combination of state police, airport employees or private companies are used with the airport paying the total costs. Similarly responsibility for security rests with more than one body at Amsterdam, Copenhagen, Düsseldorf, Frankfurt and Lisbon but in these cases the state police are provided free of charge. Finally all policing/security at the French and Italian airports, at Vienna and at several other European airports is undertaken by the state with minimal or no costs being passed on to the airports.

Air traffic control services and policing/security are the major operational areas where the most important discrepancies arise in their treatment by different airports. Differences associated with the other main operational activities, namely apron services, fire and ambulance services, cleaning and maintenance, are likely to be far less significant. Apron services such as 'follow me', marshalling, snow clearance and so on are nearly always undertaken by airport employees. Similarly fire rescue activities are provided by the airport authorities themselves at all but a few airports. At the Italian airports this service is provided free of charge by the state whilst at Marseilles, Bordeaux and Lisbon the airport authority pays for a specialist company to provide the service. The larger airports also have their own ambulance services whilst the smaller airports tend to rely on local state services. The responsibility for airport cleaning and maintenance often lies wih employees of the airport authority, although the more specialist the work required the greater likelihood of these services being subcontracted out or provided by a government department.

Handling

A variety of handling activities take place at airports. Some are associated directly with the aircraft itself and include cleaning, provision of power and loading or unloading of the baggage/freight hold. This is sometimes referred to as ramp handling. Other handling activities are more directly traffic related and cover the various stages of processing of passengers, baggage or freight through the respective terminals and onto the aircraft. Various parts of the handling process may be the responsibility of different authorities.

At about half the larger European airports the airport authorities have no involvement in any of these activities, which are provided by airlines or specialist handling agents. This is the situation that exists for instance at Amsterdam, Copenhagen, Dublin, Gatwick, Geneva, Heathrow, Marseilles and Nice. The airport authorities of some other UK airports, of Bordeaux, Lisbon and Stockholm provide a limited range of handling services required at an airport.

But there are several airports that are very heavily involved in providing such services. These include Düsseldorf, Paris, Frankfurt, Milan, Rome and Vienna. At the German airports and Vienna all the ramp handling is provided by the airport authority. Passenger and freight handling is undertaken by both the airport authority and the airlines at Frankfurt whilst at Düsseldorf and Vienna the authority itself provides freight handling. Passenger handling at Vienna is undertaken by both the airlines and the airport authority (who in fact subcontract Austrian airlines to carry out some of this work). Handling at many Italian airports is provided by the airport authorities.

Commercial activities

At most of the European airports commercial facilities are provided by concessionaires, who will be specialists in their own field of business. The airport authorities will collect concession fees or rents from these companies.

But there are a few airport authorities who are themselves directly involved in running some or virtually all the commercial outlets. Aer Rianta, the Irish Airport Authority, operates the duty-free shops at all its airports including Dublin. In Rome the duty-free shop and the restaurants are operated directly by the airport authority whilst the other shops and bars (commencing in 1983) are provided by concessionaires. At Düsseldorf the airport authority only operates the duty-free shop. At Amsterdam all the catering outlets are provided by a company which is in fact partly owned by the airport authority. The only commercial service which a significant number of airport authorities provide themselves is car parking. Amsterdam, Dublin, Düsseldorf, Frankfurt, Geneva, Lisbon, Manchester, Nice, Rome and Vienna are among those that run their own car-parking facilities whilst the rest of the European airports use concessionaires to do this.

In addition to the usual shops, restaurants, bars and car-hire kiosks, some of the larger airports provide an extensive range of other services for their customers both within the terminal buildings and on airport land. The most notable example here is Frankfurt airport where the additional commercial activities include cinemas, bowling alleys, a discotheque, hairdressers, supermarkets and a conference centre and hotel. These are normally rented out as concessions.

As the above European examples show, one airport authority or operator can be very different from another and yet they are both in the airport business. Differences arise because most of the facilities and services previously mentioned may be provided by the airport operators themselves or they may all be provided by third parties, such as central or local government departments, airlines, specialist agents or private companies. Nearly every airport in Europe seems to be directly involved with a different mixture of services. At the one extreme airports such as Copenhagen, Geneva, Marseilles or Nice almost play the role of a landlord with very little direct participation in most of their airport activities. In the United States too airport authorities are largely landlords. This can be contrasted with Rome, where the airport itself provides and operates most of the facilities and services mentioned above.

The extent of an airport authority's involvement in the various functions of an airport will obviously substantially affect the cost and revenue structure of each airport. It will influence the overall employee levels just as significantly. Moreover differences between airports will be further compounded if the airport authority is not charged the full cost of any service provided by a third party. This is most likely to occur when separate government departments or agents provide some of the essential services such as policing or fire and rescue. Differences in the functions performed by the airport owner or operator clearly pose comparability problems when assessing and comparing airports. These are compounded where airport owners are conglomerates with substantial non-airport activities, such as BAA Plc or the Port of New York Authority.

PATTERNS OF OWNERSHIP

Public (state) ownership with direct government control

While the functions carried out by airport operators differ widely, so too do the forms of ownership and management. But the majority of airports around the world are directly owned and operated by central or local government. This is normally done in one of two ways.

In many countries a single government department, usually the Civil Aviation Department which is part of the Ministry of Transport or sometimes the Ministry of Defence, operates all or most of that country's airports. The same government department will frequently also have responsibility for related services such as air traffic control or meteorological services. In most of the Third World, airports are run by civil aviation departments. But this form of management is also found elsewhere, as in Greece, Sweden or Norway. In most countries, even if the Civil Aviation Department runs the majority of airports, there will be a few airports open both to civilian and military use which are owned and sometimes managed by the military authorities.

An extreme example of direct government operation of airports is in Canada, where the federal government through Transport Canada owned and operated more than 130 airports including all the major ones except Edmonton-Municipal. Most were unprofitable apart from two or three. In 1987 the government decided to allow local governments to take over their airports if they wished to. By early 1991 a few had agreed to do so including Calgary and Vancouver. That still left around 130 airports under federal management!

The alternative to centralized government control is localized ownership. In a few countries it is local governments, either regional or municipal, who own the airports. This means that instead of a single government department running all the airports, each airport, or sometimes a group of two or three airports, is owned by one or several municipal or regional authorities. This form of local public ownership is particularly widespread in the United Kingdom, Germany and the United States. Within the USA, municipally or county-owned airports have a range of operating entities. Many are run by a division or a department of aviation ultimately responsible to their city councils. For instance, Baltimore, Chicago and Houston are run by departments of aviation. Some cities have airport commissions to run their airports, as in Los Angeles or New Orleans. Elsewhere the city council operates the airports directly but with the help of an advisory board as happens at Atlanta.

Public ownership through an airport authority

Some governments and municipalities, while maintaining ownership of their airports, have felt that they could be better operated and managed if those airports had greater autonomy. This has been achieved by setting up airport authorities with a specific brief to manage one or more airports. The precise legal form of the airport authority varies from country to country. But its primary aim is generally to set up an administration with greater professional skills able to undertake and implement long-range plans while central or local political control is exercised only at the strategic policy level. In some cases, as with the larger municipal airports in Britain or Germany, the legal form of the airport authority may be a private or limited liability company but with all the shares being held by one or more municipal or regional governments.

Airport authorities have been a common form of airport management in the United States for many years but have become widely adopted elsewhere only in the last fifteen years or so. Such authorities have been set up not only at the national or regional level to operate several airports but also at a local level to run individual airports.

The British Airport Authority (BAA), established in 1966, was one of the first autonomous national airport authorities. Even though it initially took over only four government-run airports, three in London and one in Scotland, it subsequently acquired another three in Scotland. More recently, in 1990, it also bought Southampton airport south-west of London. It quickly developed a corporate identity and a level of profitability which became the envy of other airports. Its success provided an example for other governments to follow and several did so. In the late 1970s and in the 1980s several national airport authorities came into being, some modelled on the BAA as it was prior to privatization. The Airports Authority of Thailand, set up in 1979, the Israeli Airports Authority, the Mexican Airports Authority and Aer Rianta (the Irish airports authority) are all examples of national airport authorities, though Aer Rianta was set up before the BAA. In a few cases governments set up national authorities to run not only their airports but also all the civil aviation infrastructure within their countries. This happened, for example, with the Civil Aviation Authority of Singapore, established in 1984, and with that of Fiji set up in 1979.

In a number of countries one finds regional rather than national airports authorities each running a group of airports within its own region. This is the case with the Aeroport de Paris, which operates four airports around Paris, and with the Port of New York Authority and Massport in Massachusetts. In the United States, four states have each set up their own airport authorities to run the state's airports. These are Alaska, Connecticut, Hawaii and Pennsylvania.

Much more widespread are airport authorities set up by central or more usually local or municipal governments to run individual airports, though in some cases there may be a smaller local airport or much smaller general aviation airports within the same authority.

Such individual airport authorities usually have a single owner, the local municipality or government. This is the case among others with Amsterdam, Düsseldorf and Frankfurt in Europe and Cincinatti or Tampa airports in the United States. A somewhat more complex form of ownership is one where the individual airport authority might be owned by a consortium of other government-owned agencies. For instance, Vienna airport is owned jointly by the central government (50 per cent), the government of Lower Austria (25 per cent) and Vienna City Council (25 per cent), while the Port of New York Authority is a joint venture by the states of New York and New Jersey. Birmingham airport in Britain is owned by a consortium of six district councils. An interesting oddity is Basle-Mulhouse airport on the French-Swiss border jointly owned and administered by these two governments.

In a few cases authorities have been set up to run not only airports but also other transport facilities. One of the first was the Port of New York Authority, which in 1947 was given the task of running New York's airports in addition to the port facilities it already managed. There are several such multipurpose authorities in the United States (Massport in Massachusetts which operates Boston airport is another example), but they are relatively rare elsewhere. Belfast airport is such a case. It is run by a state-owned company which owns other transport undertakings in Northern Ireland.

Mixed public and private ownership

A few airports are operated by authorities or companies with ownership split between the public and private sectors. This is so at some of the larger Italian airports which are managed by companies, holding an operating concession, with both private and public shareholders. In the case of Aeroporti di Roma close to 56 per cent of the company's shares were sold to Alitalia which is itself 30 per cent privately owned. Alitalia also holds shares in the airports of Genoa (15 per cent), Florence (10 per cent), Naples (5 per cent) and Turin (1 per cent).

A feature almost unique to the United States is the private ownership and management of terminals within an otherwise publicly owned and operated airport. This is usually done by airlines as with the major terminals at New York's J.F. Kennedy airport. This form of split ownership is unusual outside the United States but is beginning to spread.

A rare long-standing example can be found at Zürich in Switzerland. Although the Canton of Zürich is the legal owner and operator, a private real-estate company, Flughafen Immobilien Gesellschaft (FIG), has taken over much of the work from the Canton. Though the Canton maintains a 50 per cent shareholding in FIG, the remaining shareholders are private and it operates as a private company. FIG constructs the great majority of the buildings and maintains, manages and rents out all landside facilities. The airport authority, set up by the Canton, is responsible for the operation of airside facilities. Thus, for example, duty-free and other airside concessionaires pay fees to the airport authority, whilst landside tenants pay fees and rents to FIG. FIG also pays ground rent to the airport authority, which in turn pays rent for airside building space to FIG.

A number of airports are beginning to experiment with private investment in airport terminals as a way of reducing the capital financing requirements of the airport owners. One of the first was Transport Canada which in 1987 brought in a private consortium headed by a property development company to finance, construct, own and manage the new third terminal for Toronto's international airport. In Britain in 1989 a company was set up to build a new £60 million European 'hub' terminal for British Airways at Birmingham Airport. The company has six major partners, namely Birmingham Airport (25 per cent shareholding), British Airways and National Car Parks (21.4 per cent each), John Laing Construction (11.9 per cent), local district councils (14.3 per cent) and the hotel company Forte (6 per cent). Airline and other private participation in airport development will inevitably spread during the 1990s.

Private ownership

Hitherto totally private ownership of airports has been restricted both in number and in scope, being generally confined to smaller airports. It has of course been much more widespread among general aviation and aeroclub airfields. In the United States a few of the smaller scheduled-service airports are privately owned, such as Rochester in New York State. In Europe fully private airports were even fewer. In Britain they include Belfast-Harbour airport and London City airport in London's docklands, opened in 1987.

A big breakthrough in private ownership came with the privatization of the British Airports Authority in 1987 together with a commitment by the Conservative government of the time to eventually privatize Britain's larger regional airports. At a stroke with the flotation of BAA Plc seven airports were privatized, including London Heathrow, Europe's largest airport and the fifth largest in the world in terms of passengers handled. Further airport privatizations are sure to follow.

MEASURING AIRPORT OUTPUT

Air-transport movements

In managing an airport it is important to have some clear indication of its output. The earlier analysis (see pp. 7–10) suggested that an airport's functions are quite heterogeneous. Can output then be measured in anything other than total revenue generated? In order to assess an airport's performance one must surely try to do more than this.

An airport's primary function is to provide an interface between aircraft and the passengers or freight, including mail, being transported by air. Thus output could be measured in terms of numbers of aircraft movements handled (a movement is a landing or departure) or the volumes of passengers or freight embarked and disembarked. But each of these measures of output relates primarily to only one part of an airport's infrastructure and activity.

Runways, taxiways and associated facilities are related to the number of aircraft movements, while the size and nature of terminal facilities are dependent on the number of passengers or the volume of freight and mail handled.

Output is important essentially as a measure of revenue and profit-generating potential. Therefore a choice could be made between airport output measures in terms of their relative economic importance, in revenue and cost terms, to the airport. On the airside a logical step is to exclude all non-commercial flights such as general aviation or training flights since they generate very little revenue in proportion to their number. This means measuring the throughput of an airport's runway facilities in terms of commercial air-transport movements (ATM).

If one considers the worlds' top forty airports in terms of commercial air-transport movements (excluding general aviation), the dominance of the United States airport industry is clearly apparent (See Table 1.4). Of these top forty airports, thirty-three are in the United States, two are in Canada and five are European. There are no Asian, South American or African airports in the group. Moreover, the largest non-American airport, London's Heathrow, is ranked only eleventh overall. If one were to include general aviation and business-aircraft movements then the dominance of the United States airports would be further reinforced.

Passengers and freight handled

Commercial air-transport movements (ATMs), however, tell one relatively little about an airport's revenue or profit potential since much of both the revenue and the costs are generated from handling passengers and freight. Thus one should also evaluate airport output in terms of passengers or freight.

In terms of passengers handled in 1989 (Table 1.5) the dominance of United States airports is overwhelming but not quite as marked as when considering commercial ATMs. Of the forty largest airports twenty-five, including the four largest, are in North America. Nine are European while another six are Asian. There are no South American or African airports represented. European and Asian airports are ranked significantly higher in terms of passengers handled than in terms of aircraft movements. In other words relatively fewer aircraft are needed at these airports to handle a given number of passengers than at United States airports. This is due both to larger aircraft being used, especially at Asian airports, and to higher passenger-load factors.

It is only when one turns to cargo handled that one finds a South American

Table 1.4 World's top forty airports 1989 in terms of commercial air-transport movements (ATMs)

	North American	*European*	*Annual ATMs ('000s)*
1	Dallas Fort Worth		691
2	Chicago O'Hare		643
3	Atlanta		640
4	Los Angeles International		584
5	San Francisco		393
6	Las Vegas		385
7	St Louis		380
8	Boston		371
9	Pittsburg		370
10	Phoenix		358
11		London Heathrow	345
12	New York Newark		343
13	Miami		327
14	New York LGA		323
15	Seattle		322
16	Chicago Midway		320
17	Philadelphia		318
18	Denver		314
19		Frankfurt	305
20	Baltimore		303
21	Toronto		300
22	Minneapolis		299
23	Salt Lake City		296
24	New York JFK		293
25	Vancouver		282
26	Detroit		274
27	Cincinnati		263
28	Nashville		263
29	Honolulu		259
30		Stockholm	254
31	Memphis		242
32	Charlotte		235
33	Houston Intercontinental		225
34	Cleveland		223
35		Paris CDG	204
36	Indianapolis		203
37	Dayton		202
38	Kansas		199
39		Copenhagen	199
40	Washington National		192

Sources: AACC 1990, BAA 1990.

airport, São Paolo, in the top forty (Table 1.6). North American airports also appear less dominant with only eighteen of the top forty airports. This reflects the inland location of many US airports and the availability of good surface

Table 1.5 World's top forty airports 1989 in terms of terminal passengers

	North American	European	Asian	Terminal passengers (millions)
1	Chicago O'Hare			59.2
2	Dallas-Ft Worth			45.6
3	Los Angeles International			45.0
4	Atlanta			43.3
5		London Heathrow		39.6
6			Tokyo Haneda	36.5
7	New York JFK			30.3
8	San Francisco			29.9
9	Denver			27.6
10		Frankfurt		26.7
11		Paris Orly		24.1
12	Miami			23.5
13	New York LGA			23.2
14	Honolulu			22.6
15	Boston			22.3
16		London Gatwick		21.2
17	Toronto			21.0
18	New York Newark			20.9
19	Phoenix			20.7
20		Paris CDG		20.3
21	St Louis			20.0
22	Minneapolis			19.4
23			Osaka	18.5
24			Tokyo Narita	17.6
25	Orlando			17.2
26	Pittsburgh			17.1
27	Las Vegas			16.7
28			Hong Kong	16.2
29	Houston Intercontinental			16.0
30		Rome		15.6
31	Charlotte			15.3
32		Amsterdam		15.3
33	Seattle			15.2
34	Philadelphia			14.8
35	Washington National			14.4
36		Madrid		14.2
37		Stockholm		14.1
38	Detroit			13.8
39			Singapore	13.0
40			Bangkok	12.7

Sources: AACC 1990, BAA 1990.

transport especially by road. Conversely surface transport in Asia is relatively poor and many international cargo movements involve a water crossing where air transport's speed advantage is reinforced. In addition East Asian countries are major exporters of low-bulk, high-value products which lend themselves to export by air. As a result the relative importance of several Asian airports as cargo hubs is much greater than their ranking in terms of passenger traffic. This is particularly true of Tokyo (Narita), Hong Kong, Singapore, Seoul, Taipei and Bangkok. Eleven of the top forty cargo airports are in the Asian/ Australasia region, all but one along the Pacific Rim. Among European airports Frankfurt is pre-eminent as a cargo centre while another nine feature in the top forty.

Considering the passenger-output measure by itself, it is evident that the costs and revenues associated with different types of passengers can vary considerably, the most notable example being international as opposed to domestic passengers. Unit costs tend to be greater for international passengers since this type of traffic needs substantially more terminal space for customs, health, immigration, etc. and also spends on average more time in the terminal. Conversely more revenue is generated since these international passengers tend to spend more on commercial activities and the passenger fee for this type of traffic is often higher. If one were to produce a list of the world's top airports in terms of international passengers few North American airports would be included in contrast to their showing in Table 1.5. There would be only one American airport, New York's Kennedy Airport, in the top ten. The list would be dominated by European and Asian airports. But such a list would be misleading in terms of the real size and importance of different airports.

Transfer or interline passengers are another complication, especially if the transfers are taking place between two international flights. This will result in all the costs and revenues associated with these passengers being limited to the airside of an airport. A further complexity is also introduced since a transfer passenger is counted twice in airport traffic statistics but should only be regarded as one passenger when considering matters such as capacity, expenditure per head on duty-free goods, and so on.

Ideally these different types of passengers should be combined using weights associated with the relative costs that they impose on airports. In practice very few airports are able to make even an approximate estimate of the costs of handling different types of passengers, especially as there are so many joint costs which have to be apportioned. The BAA however, has carried out various studies to assist in the setting of their airport charges. Since the early 1980s the BAA have calculated their passenger charges on the basis of marginal-cost models which they have applied to their new developments at Heathrow's Fourth Terminal and Gatwick's North Terminal. They evaluated the costs associated with four different passenger types, namely Domestic, European, North American and Other. They also distinguished between peak

Table 1.6 World's top forty airports 1989 in terms of cargo traffic

	North America	Europe	Asia/ Australia	South America	Cargo Tonnes ('000s)
1	New York JFK				1,257
2	Los Angeles International				1,129
3		Frankfurt			1,084
4	Chicago O'Hare				957
5	Miami				892
6			Tokyo Narita		888
7			Hong Kong		730
8		London Heathrow			692
9			Seoul		622
10		Paris CDG			585
11		Amsterdam			582
12			Singapore		578
13	San Francisco				558
14			Taipei		549
15			Tokyo Haneda		462
16	New York Newark				400
17	Atlanta				379
18	Dallas - Ft Worth				361
19			Bangkok		349
20	Honolulu				326
21			Osaka		325
22	Toronto				309
23	Seattle				294
24	Los Angeles Ontario				285
25			Sydney		282
26	Boston				279
27		Zurich			262
28		Paris Orly			248
29		Brussels[1]			235
30		Rome			227
31	Cincinnati				224
32				São Paulo	221
33			Melbourne		215
34		London Gatwick			210
35			Bombay		209
36		Madrid			208

Table 1.6 Continued

	North America	Europe	Asia/ Australia	South America	Cargo Tonnes ('000s)
37	Philadelphia				195
38	Oakland				190
39	Denver				185
40	Indianapolis				178

Sources: AACC 1990, BAA 1990.
Note: [1] 1987 data used.

traffic-related and total traffic-related costs, since the additional capacity needed for peak passengers pushes up the costs. Off-peak passengers can continue to be accommodated within the existing capacity and hence overall costs will be lower. By indexing the cost associated with domestic passengers at 100 the BAA has found that costs related to the other three types of passenger range from 250 to 300 in the peak to just over half of these values at other times. This indeed supports the view that a passenger is not a homogeneous unit of output. Airports need to do more work in developing a methodology for allocating costs to different categories of passengers or freight.

Work-load units

The need to obtain a standard measure of output combining both passengers and freight pushed the airline industry from the early days to convert passengers into a weight equivalent, namely passenger tonnes and also passenger tonne-km. One passenger (80 kg) and their baggage (20 kg) were assumed to be equivalent to 100 kg so that ten passengers made up 1 tonne. The rationale was that an aircraft could only lift a certain payload and that a passenger and their baggage could be directly substituted by their weight in freight. Passenger and baggage weights are now assumed to be lower. Most airlines use a figure of 90 kg so 11.111 passengers are equivalent to 1 tonne.

The International Civil Aviation Organization (ICAO) used the airlines' orignal 10:1 relationship (i.e. ten passengers = 1 tonne) to produce its traffic units as a combined measure of airport passenger and freight output. An ICAO traffic unit is 1,000 passengers or 100 tonnes of cargo. Since this is difficult to conceptualize it seemed easier to use the passenger as the basic unit of output. It is for this reason that the Polytechnic of Central London in its airport studies since the early 1970s has used the work-load unit (WLU) which is equivalent to one terminal passenger or 100 kg of freight or mail. This maintains the original 10:1 relationship used within the airline industry and has been widely adopted by many airport authorities.

While such a ratio was logical for airlines in that it was based on weight which was critical for aircraft payloads, its relevance to airports is perhaps more questionable. For airports the WLU is a rather arbitrary method of linking passenger and freight throughput since the same weight of passenger and freight does not require the use of similar resources in physical or financial terms, nor does it generate the same revenue. Very detailed research would be required to establish in airport-resource terms the freight equivalent of one passenger. In the meantime, the work load unit provides a reasonable way of assessing airports' combined total output.

Ranking the world's top forty airports in terms of work-load units produces a better assessment of their relative size than the other measures used previously (see Table 1.7). When compared to the top forty airports in terms of passengers handled there is little overall change in the airports listed. The changes are largely in terms of ranking though they are not significant. The European and more especially the Asian airports all move up two or three places in the ranking reflecting their greater involvement in freight. No South American or African airports make it into the top forty.

Ultimately one would like to combine commercial air-transport movements and traffic measures, such as the work-load unit, into a combined weighted measure of total output based on the relative costs of handling aircraft and passengers or freight. The problem is that for most airports it is difficult to obtain a breakdown of the separate costs associated with these three activity areas. Such a combined measure has yet to be produced. However by looking at the shares of revenue dependent on these items it is evident that outside the United States revenues based on aircraft (i.e. landing and parking charges) are in nearly all cases considerably less than half the total revenue generated. Moreover at most airports the percentage of aeronautical revenue raised from the passenger fee has in recent years been increasing whilst the aircraft weight-based element of the fee has declined (see pp. 76–8). The bulk of the remaining revenue comes from sources related to facilities and services in the passenger and cargo terminal. In other words an output measure combining passengers and freight handled provides a better indicator of revenue-earning potential than a measure based on aircraft movements or on total weight of aircraft handled. Thus, if one wishes to use a single measure of output then the work-load unit despite its shortcomings would be the most suitable. While it only measures passengers and freight handled, it is also an indirect indicator of the total number of aircraft that would be required to move those passenger and freight volumes. In the analysis in the following chapters the work-load unit (WLU) is frequently used.

THE WORLD'S MAJOR AIRPORTS

From the preceding analysis it is clear that North American airports dominate the airport industry in that they provide the vast majority of the world's

Table 1.7 World's top forty airports 1989 in terms of work-load units (WLU)[1]

	North America	Europe	Asia/ Australasia	Annual WLU[1] (millions)
1	Chicago O'Hare			68.8
2	Los Angeles International			56.3
3	Dallas-Ft Worth			49.2
4	Atlanta			47.9
5		London Heathrow		46.5
6	New York JFK			42.9
7			Tokyo Haneda	41.1
8		Frankfurt		36.8
9	San Francisco			35.5
10	Miami			32.4
11	Denver			29.4
12		Paris Orly		26.6
13			Tokyo Narita	26.5
14		Paris CDG		26.1
15	Honolulu			25.9
16	Boston			25.1
17	New York Newark			24.9
18	Toronto			24.0
19	New York La Guardia			23.7
20			Hong Kong	23.5
21		London Gatwick		23.3
22	Phoenix			21.8
23			Osaka	21.8
24		Amsterdam		21.1
25	Mineapolis			21.1
26	St Louis			20.7
27			Seoul	20.2
28			Singapore	18.7
29	Orlando			18.7
30	Seattle			18.2
31		Rome		17.8
32	Pittsburg			17.8
33	Houston Intercontinental			17.6
34	Las Vegas			16.8
35	Philadelphia			16.8
36		Madrid		16.3
37			Bangkok	16.2

Table 1.7 Continued

	North America	Europe	Asia/ Australasia	Annual WLU[1] (millions)
38	Charlotte			15.3
39			Sydney	15.0
40		Stockholm		14.9

Sources: AACC 1990, BAA 1990.
Note: [1] A work-load unit is equivalent to one passenger or 100 kg of freight handled.

largest airports. Their dominance is most marked when one measures airport size in terms of air-transport movements, with only a handful of non-American airports ranked in the top forty (Table 1.4). When one looks at passenger or freight traffic levels the dominance is less marked with about ten European and a smaller number of Asian/Australasian airports featuring in the top forty (Tables 1.5 and 1.6). The same happens when one ranks airports in terms of work-load units (WLU) (Table 1.7).

Within North America, four airports stand out as being by far the largest, namely Chicago O'Hare, Dallas-Fort Worth, Atlanta and Los Angeles International. They clearly lead the world whatever the measure used. The European leaders are London's Heathrow airport and Frankfurt followed by the two Paris airports. In the Far East Tokyo's two airports dominate, Haneda and Narita, but Osaka, Hong Kong and Singapore airports are also major centres.

The rankings shown in the preceding tables change slightly from year to year but the overall pattern remains fairly constant. The only discernible trend is that the East Asian airports are gradually climbing up the rankings. During the last decade air-transport growth in the Asia-Pacific region has been well above the world average and has outstripped growth in all other regions. East Asian airports have enjoyed particularly rapid growth as a result. Since all long-term air-traffic forecasts predict much higher growth for Asian than for North American markets, Asian airports will continue to improve their rankings among the world's top forty.

With one exception, it is noticeable that no African, central or South American airports appear in the four tables above. The exception is Brazil's São Paulo airport which appears in the cargo rankings (Table 1.6). This reflects the relatively lower volumes of air traffic in both these continents. Though they have many large and well-developed airports, they are much smaller in terms of traffic handled than the airports listed above. Mexico City, the largest airport in Central America, generated 12 million WLU in 1989, while the most important airports in South America and Africa, Caracas and Cairo, handled well below 10 million WLU each in that year.

The case studies in the second part of this book examine in detail three distinctive groups of airports. The United States airports are one such group having unique administrative and financial features different from those in other countries. They also include a major share of the world's largest airports. Another group which merits attention because they face particular problems are airports in developing countries, mainly in Central and South America, Africa and parts of Asia. Initially, however, the financial performance of European airports is examined in considerable detail because they are the airports which have been most closely studied in the past and for which detailed financial and operational data are most readily available. It is for this reason too that many of the examples in other chapters are also drawn from Europe.

Chapter 2

Issues in airport management

OBJECTIVES OF AIRPORTS POLICY

Policy makers at central or local government level must resolve four key questions in developing an economic strategy for their airports.

First, *should airports be run as commercially oriented profitable concerns* or should they be thought of as public utilities with public service obligations? In other words, should their objective be to cover their full costs from charges of various kinds levied on passengers and other users or should their prime purpose be to provide a good level of service to current and potential users whether or not the cost of such services is covered by the revenues generated. The basis for adopting the latter objective would be that the beneficiaries of an airport's services are not only the direct users but also the community at large. In other words, it could be argued that the external benefits from an airport in a particular area more than cover any net internal costs.

Many governments still cling to the latter view of airports as public utilities as do the airlines and the International Air Transport Association (IATA) when arguing against increases in airport charges. But it is a view of airports which is in retreat.

Whatever policy one adopts in response to this first question one must also face up to the second question, namely *how should one improve airport economic efficiency* and reduce or eliminate losses where they occur? One will wish to do this even if one's answer to the first question is that airports should be primarily concerned with public service rather than profitability. It is important to ensure that the airport provides the desired level of public service as efficiently as possible and at a minimum cost to the taxpayer. To achieve this objective one needs a better understanding of airport economics and airport management.

The third question to resolve is whether any *profits from larger airports should be used to cross-subsidize loss-making smaller airports,* or should the latter's losses be met out of local or national tax revenues? In other words, should one treat all the airports in a country or a large region as a single system or as disparate and separate infrastructure elements which may in some cases be competing with each other? The response a government makes to this question will have major repercussions on the pricing and commercial policies of the larger airports as well as on their ability to self-finance their own development.

Even governments favouring a policy of commercially oriented and competitive airports may prefer a system-wide approach to one of having individual airports managed in isolation one from the other. Thus the British government in privatizing the British Airports Authority (BAA) in 1987 did not set up seven independent and competing airport companies but one parent company owning three London airports and four airports in Scotland.

The response that airport authorities make to the three questions above will clearly affect both the way in which their airports are managed and their financial performance. This is so whether the airports are owned and operated directly by government, by other public bodies or by private interests.

This leads one on to the final and currently perhaps the most critical question. *Should airports be privatized* in the real sense of being sold off to the public at large and of having their shares freely traded on stock exchanges? Those governments whose answer to the first question above is that airports should be profit-oriented commercial enterprises will also have to decide whether they should take the final step and privatize one or more of their airports. This will undoubtedly be one of the crucial issues facing the airport industry throughout the 1990s.

Clearly individual airport managements will each face their own particular problems and difficulties related for instance to staffing or to some of the economic questions, such as pricing policy, discussed later in this book. But there are in addition a number of more general issues that the airport industry will face throughout the 1990s. One already mentioned is whether or not to privatize. Another will be how to cope with an increasing level of demand for airport facilities and especially for runways, which in many parts of the world is rapidly outstripping the supply available. Providing the facilities which will be needed by the year 2000 will require huge investment. How to finance such large-scale airport expansion is another key issue. Finally, European airports have to face up to the uncertainties generated as Europe moves towards closer integration in the period both before and after the creation of the single European Market on 1 January 1993. Careful consideration of these issues provides a necessary background to the more detailed micro-economic analyses which follow.

TREND TO AIRPORT PRIVATIZATION

For many years a number of airports around the world have operated as private companies, such as, for instance, most of the larger German airports and the airports of Vienna and Milan. In nearly all such cases the shareholders have been one or more central or local government departments or other government organizations. Such airports, while being private in a legal sense, did not have the commercial freedom which a truly privately owned company would have.

The British government was the first to tackle airport privatization in the real sense. For the UK government the issue of airport privatization was resolved as long ago as June 1985 in a White Paper on *Airports Policy* (HMSO 1985). This re-emphasized the government's commitment to non-subsidization of airports and air services, but went much further in saying:

(a) that airports should operate as commercial undertakings and
(b) that airports policy should be directed towards encouraging enterprise and efficiency in the operation of major airports by providing for the introduction of private capital (HMSO 1985).

The 1986 Airports Act followed the White Paper. In pursuit of these objectives, the act first of all turned the BAA into a limited company, BAA Plc, which was subsequently floated on the Stock Exchange in the summer if 1987. It was launched as a single company owning seven airports, each of which became subsidiary companies.

Second, under the 1986 Airports Act the bigger regional United Kingdom airports, those with an annual turnover exceeding £1 million, also had to be set up as public limited companies run at arms length from the local government authorities who were their owners. By early 1989 sixteen airport companies had been set up, each owned by one or more local governments. The UK government's intention was that they would eventually be sold off to private shareholders. The local authorities resisted this and the government did not have the necessary powers to force them to sell their airports. However, the government did have one rather persuasive argument. In Britain municipally owned airport companies are subject to public-sector borrowing controls. So if they want to borrow money for investment they must obtain government approval. If this is not readily forthcoming privatization may well be the only way to escape the need for government loan approval. Since most of the sixteen airport companies are profitable they would have little difficulty in raising loans from the capital market if they moved into the private sector. In the spring of 1991 there were suggestions that if the Conservative party won the forthcoming general election it would introduce legislation to force the privatization of the airport companies. However, the Conservative manifesto later that year did not make any such promise.

Meanwhile, early in 1990, Luton, a London area airport but outside BAA ownership, set out to be the first of the British municipally owned airports to be sold to the private sector, largely because the local town council could not iteself fund the £100 to £150 million capital needed for further development, nor could it obtain government approval to borrow such large amounts. Luton Borough Council, the local government authority owning the airport, had been expecting to raise £30 to £45 million from its sale by the end of 1990. While the collapse of the UK charter market during that year seriously undermined the prospects of a good sale, a change in the political composition of Luton Borough council in May 1991 made the privatization of the airport unlikely.

Earlier, in May 1990, the local government authorities jointly owning

Liverpool airport, in the north-west of England, sold a 76 per cent share to British Aerospace, the aircraft manufacturer, which planned to develop it as a major hub. The pattern has been set. More and more of Britain's municipal airports are likely to be privatized during the 1990s.

An interesting and innovative development in 1987 was the opening of an entirely new airport in London's docklands which was built, financed and owned by the private construction company Mowlem. If this venture ultimately proves a success despite substantial losses in the early years and difficulties in getting initial permission to operate jet aircraft, it may encourage further private investment in new airports.

Outside the UK, airport privatization has been actively considered in several countries. In April 1988 New Zealand's three largest airports were turned into separate individual corporations each jointly owned by consortia of central and local governments with a view ultimately to injecting private capital through the sale of the shares owned by the central government. Early in 1989 the Singapore government hired consultants to examine the feasibility of privatizing Singapore's Changi airport, while the Austrian Finance Ministry was examining the legal and economic consequences of selling off the government's 50 per cent shareholding in Vienna airport.

Undoubtedly pressures to privatize airports are spreading, largely because governments are increasingly reluctant to go on funding airport development themselves when they feel that airports have the financial strength to raise and pay for their own capital investment. In June 1989 the Malaysian Transport Minister summed up the financial pressures on governments when, in announcing that airport privatization was being put off, he stated: 'Earlier, the Cabinet considered privatization of the airports because it did not want to pour so much money into the modernization, expansion and upkeep of these airports especially with the economic slowdown' (*New Straits Times* 30 June 1989). A year later, in 1990 the Malaysian government proposed the creation of the Malaysian Airports Corporation to take over twenty airports from the Department of Civil Aviation. The short-term aim was to operate the airports more commercially as a business so as ultimately to privatize them. However, the formal establishment of the corporation was delayed at least until 1991.

BENEFITS AND RISKS OF PRIVATIZATION

Privatization may be the ultimate step in setting airports free. While several European and other airports already operate as private companies, their shareholders are normally one or more government bodies. A few, Milan among them, have private minority shareholders. Of the larger airports the BAA is the only fully privatized airport company whose shares are traded freely on the Stock Exchange. It is the BAA which exemplifies the potential benefits but also the risks of privatization.

Easier access to investment funds is clearly a major potential benefit. Prior to

1987 the BAA's capital expenditure was controlled by government fiscal policy and was constrained by limits on public-sector borrowing. Privatization has freed the BAA from such financial constraints. It is now able to fund its development using normal commercial sources. Michael Toms, BAA's Economic Regulation Manager, stated in 1988 that the company's short-term borrowings

> are now catered for by a £200 million seven-year multi-option facility with a consortium of thirty-five banks. Flexibility is enhanced by a commercial paper programme of up to £100 million, which can further reduce short-term borrowing costs, and by a facility with the European Investment Bank for £150 million (BAA 1988)

By 1990 the commitment from the European Investment Bank had risen to £350 million of which £150 million had been used to fund the North Terminal at Gatwick Airport, a £100 million facility had been signed for Gatwick while a further £100 million was available for Stansted or Glasgow airports (BAA 1989b).

Other constraints have also been lifted. In many countries government-owned airport companies are limited as to the range of commercial activities they can engage in. As a state-owned authority the old BAA was limited to operating airports. As a privatized company it has the freedom to expand the scope of its activities. In particular, it can set about realizing the full commercial value of its large land assets. The BAA diversified rapidly after privatization in 1987. It began developing three hotels on its own land. For a time in 1988 it considered buying a stake in the international operations of Ramada Hotels, though this was subsequently abandoned. But BAA Plc continued to look at other possible acquisitions in the hotel sector and announced plans to create a chain of two-star hotels in the UK and Europe (BAA 1989a). In February 1990 it opened its first hotel at Ghent in Belgium. Its three airport hotels, one at each of its London airports, opened in the second half of 1990, while another three new hotels were opening during 1991. It signed an agreement with British Rail jointly to build and operate a new £300 million rail link to Heathrow airport. In 1988 it bought a major property development company, Lynton Property and Reversionary Plc, valued at approximately £220 million. The BAA used its airport expertise to win contracts to manage shopping facilities in hospitals. By 1990 it had eight such contracts. The company also set out to become more closely involved in the expanding air-cargo business at its airports. In February 1989 the BAA bought Scottish Express Ltd, a rapidly growing freight forwarder and road haulier, and two months later it took over a firm handling bonded cargo at Gatwick and Heathrow. Finally, the company expanded its consultancy work and won several airport management contracts including some overseas. In the summer of 1990 it also acquired its eighth UK airport at Southampton. All this in the first three years after privatization in mid-1987.

Apart from greater freedom of action, a further advantage of privatization, some would claim the most important advantage, is improved efficiency. This view is based partly on the political belief that privately owned utilities are likely to be run more efficiently than if publicly owned. It may well be that as far as airports are concerned freeing them from civil service constraints while giving them total financial responsibility does focus and sharpen management irrespective of the form of ownership. This is certainly the view of many airport managers.

Privatization also entails some risks. Most large airports enjoy a substantial degree of monopoly, which may well increase as traffic growth outstrips the provision of new facilities. Given this, many governments will be loath fully to privatize airports without maintaining powers to prevent abuse of dominant positions. Such abuses may occur in a number of ways. Airport managers may reduce space for passenger and cargo shippers in order to maximize revenues from a variety of commercial activities. They may introduce totally unrelated activities, such as discotheques, into terminal buildings even when space is short. Airports might also enter into cosy monopolistic arrangements with particular suppliers of services such as passenger or baggage handling, duty-free shops, freight handling or car hire by granting only one concession so that the concessionaires can extract monopoly profits from airport users. These can then be shared by the concessionaire and the airport authority through the concession-fee arrangement made between them.

The UK government was aware of the dangers. The 1986 Airports Act imposed some tight controls on BAA Plc and the new airport companies. In the first place, airport companies are required to produce much more detailed accounts than is normally required under the Companies Acts. Revenues and expenditures must be presented in some detail and must be transparent. Second, airport charges at the three largest airports, Heathrow, Gatwick and Manchester, and at Stansted are directly regulated by the Civil Aviation Authority (CAA). Other airports may subsequently be included. During the first five years after 1986, aeronautical charges, that is aircraft landing and passenger fees expressed as revenue per passenger, at the three London airports were allowed to rise each year by an amount equivalent to no more than the increase in the retail price index (RPI) minus 1 per cent. In other words, average increases had to be a little below the rate of inflation. This was known as the 'RPI 1' formula. Manchester airport also had a similar maximum permitted increase. These and other airports may also be examined every five years by the UK Monopolies and Mergers Commission. Finally, the CAA can investigate complaints against airports of discrimination or abuse of dominant position when made by airport users of so-called 'relevant activities' (i.e. air-service related). In some ways these controls on what privatized airports can charge and do are more onerous than the ones they replaced.

The full impact of government price controls on the privatized BAA was felt in the spring of 1991. Following its statutory quinquennial review of BAA activities the Monopolies and Mergers Commission recommended that for the next five-year period from April 1992 the permitted charges formula should be changed from the existing RPI minus 1 per cent to RPI minus four per cent. But the CAA, the ultimate regulator of the BAA's aeronautical charges, proposed that they should be held down to an annual increase of 8 per cent less than the RPI (i.e. RPI minus 8 per cent). But the BAA, through its charges, could recover up to 85 per cent of any additional security costs plus a full recompense for the loss of intra-Community duty-free sales when these were phased out. The CAA believed that even with the minus 8 per cent price constraint the BAA's London airports could still produce a 7 per cent return on investment. BAA Plc's immediate reaction was that this dramatic limitation on its pricing freedom forced it to review its plans to build a fifth terminal at Heathrow and the Heathrow rail link. A compromise was eventually agreed.

In addition to pricing or other regulatory constraints, governments which privatize their airports may also impose other limitations on them. They may need to insist when the privatized companies are set up that there can be no change of use for airport land without government approval. Governments may also reserve the right to take over private airports in the event of war or some other national crisis. Finally, they may limit the size of any individual shareholding (as in the case of BAA Plc, where it is 15 per cent) to prevent takeover battles and resultant instability. While having such constraints placed upon them, private airports may in addition find it increasingly difficult to meet public or local-community opposition to their developments if they are no longer owned and supported by local or central governments.

Another problem for airport managements once privatized is that they become over-sensitive to fluctuations in their share price. Managers' decisions may well be influenced by this. For instance the BAA has become much more secretive since privatization because of concern that any information may have an impact on its share price. Its annual reports in fact became much less informative after it was privatized than they had been before.

Others have also been assessing the implications of privatization. The International Air Transport Association (IATA) believes that an independent review system for airport charges will become essential when airports become privately owned and motivated primarily by the profit motive. The European Commission has also looked at the possibility of the abuse of dominant position. It is particularly concerned with the monopoly franchises for ground-handling services. In July 1988 such monopoly agreements were exempted from application of the Community's competition rules but only on condition that there was no discrimination between carriers and that the buyers of such services were not required to sign exclusive contracts. In time the Commission will look into other potentially monopolistic practices.

Any constraints on airports' pricing freedom with regard to airport charges once privatized may accelerate moves towards diversification. It would also push airports to generate more revenue from concessions and other commercial activities where pricing controls are unlikely.

Diversification, such as that pursued by BAA Plc, has its dangers too. The non-airport businesses may be volatile and more subject to economic cycles than is the core airport busines. Thus in its financial year 1990-91, BAA Plc managed to increase the operating profit on its airport business by 9.8 per cent to £275 million despite the downturn in air traffic following the 1990 invasion of Kuwait and the subsequent Gulf War. This was offset by a net loss of £28 million from property and other non-airport activities because of the economic downturn (BAA 1991). The downturn in property values required provisions of £36 to £37 million to be made against profit at the Lynton property subsidiary while the newly opened hotels also lost money. In short, diversification away from the airport business has proved highly risky for BAA Plc. As they move into other activities such as property development, which may potentially be very profitable but which are subject to greater fluctuations, senior management energies may well be dissipated. Airports that are part of conglomerates may lose their flexibility and speed of response.

The ultimate aim of privatized airports must be increased profits. Jeremy Marshall, BAA's then chief executive, stated the case bluntly in 1988: 'Let us be absolutely clear about our main strategic objective, with no beating about the bush: Profit' (BAA 1988).

Too rigid a pursuit of such an objective may bring airports into conflict with airlines, passengers or other airport users who have yet to make the jump from thinking of airports as public utilities to seeing them as profit-oriented private companies. The privatized BAA's attempts to squeeze revenue out of every area of activity shows this clearly. Taxi drivers at first refused to serve Heathrow when the BAA introduced a charge for taxis using their taxi compound. In the spring of 1988 bus and coach operators serving the London airports were told that as from January 1989 they would have to pay a fee to the BAA for picking up airline passengers from Heathrow or Gatwick. It was claimed that fees for some operators would rise from £1,000 to £180,000 per year (*Flight International* 20 May 1989). The proposal was postponed while the Office of Fair Trading considered this and other wide-ranging complaints about BAA operations including car-parking charges, duty-free prices and restrictions on competition. The BAA gave way. In January 1990 it agreed that car-parking charges would not increase faster than inflation and gave other undertakings. As a result the Office of Fair Trading in February 1990 abandoned plans to ask for a Monopolies and Mergers Commission investigation of the BAA's trading practices.

The BAA's aggressive pursuit of increased profitability from all its activities led in 1989 and 1990 to growing public and press criticism. As a state-owned corporation the BAA had been looked upon as one of the most successful nationalized industries which was both profitable and responsive to the needs of its customers. As the privately owned BAA Plc it increasingly gave the impression of a rapacious monopolist out to squeeze the last penny from its customers and users as evidenced by the proposed bus charges. The worsening public image clearly led to a clash within the BAA Board of Directors, and Jeremy Marshall suddenly and unexpectedly vacated the post of chief executive on 28 August 1989. It seems conflict had arisen within the board between the pursuit of short-term profit and the more long-term business approach of the traditional airport management.

The BAA experience highlights a difficult problem facing any privatized airport management, namely how to pursue a profit objective more vigorously without worsening its relationships with its customers, whether airlines, passengers or freight shippers.

GROWING RUNWAY SHORTAGE

Few new runways or airports

In recent years, it has become increasingly apparent that the rapidly growing demand for air travel has been outstripping the supply of infrastructure both in the air and on the ground. The late 1980s were uncomfortable years for airport users. In both 1988 and 1989 congestion of airspace and of airport runways meant frequent and lengthy delays for passengers especially at peak periods. Delays were particularly bad in Europe but also at certain Asian and North American airports. In Europe at least the problems of 1988 have led to a massive investment in improving air trafffic control facilities, in training many new controllers and in improving the interfaces between various national air traffic control authorities.

But little has been done to increase the availability of runway capacity. In 1987 the Association of European Airlines in a study of west European airports found that under a medium scenario of growth thirteen airports already had or would have insufficient runway capacity by 1995 and another twelve would prove insufficient by the year 2000. If as a result of airline liberalization and the creation of the single European market in 1993 traffic growth were to accelerate, the number of airports running out of runway capacity would be twenty by 1995 and a further eleven by the year 2000 (AEA 1987). Three years later an IATA-sponsored study of Europe's twenty-seven larger airports found that eleven would have inadequate runway capacity by 1995. This figure would rise to sixteen airports by the year 2000 while another four would have runway capacity only marginally in excess of projected demand (SRI 1990). But this is a world-wide problem not just European. Runway capacity is also inadequate to meet future needs at many North American and several Asian airports. The Federal Aviation Administration has also predicted growing congestion and delays at US airports with close to thirty airports having unacceptable levels of delay by 1996.

All the various long-term forecasts produced in 1989 and 1990 agreed that passenger traffic world-wide would more or less double by the year 2000 and that, in some parts of the world notably the Asia/Pacific region, it would double much sooner (ICAO 1989a and McDonnell Douglas 1989). There will be a less than proportional but still very significant increase of 45–50 per cent in the number of additional aircraft to be handled. Estimates suggested a net increase, after retirements, of between 4,000 and 4,500 jet aircraft by the year 2000 compared to the 1989-90 fleet levels. Much additional runway capacity and apron space would be needed to handle these aircraft. The Gulf crisis and subsequent war early in 1991 led to a dramatic downturn in traffic in many markets but by mid-1991 long-term forecasts, such as that produced by Airbus Industrie in June 1991 (Airbus 1991), were predicting that within a couple of years traffic-growth rates would be back to the levels forecast in the late 1980s. This confidence rested on the basic premise that growth in air travel was, and is, closely linked to developments in the world's major economies, and prospects for these looked good (Airbus 1991).

Yet by early 1991 few new airports were being built or planned. In Europe the only entirely new airport under construction, at Munich, was due to open in 1992. There were firm projects for new airports for Athens, planned to open in 1997, and Oslo and for one or two additional runways, notably at Lyons in France and Manchester in England, but little else. In Asia, a new airport was under construction in Osaka Bay and at least one additional runway was planned to be inaugurated at Tokyo's Narita airport by 1993. A new airport was also under consideration for Seoul in Korea. The decision to build a new US$7 billion airport on Lantao island to serve Hong Kong was bedevilled by political uncertainty until September 1991. By then the building of a new airport in nearby Macao was already under way. In July 1991 the Airports Authority of Thailand invited tenders for the master planning phase for a new Bangkok airport with construction due to start in 1993. In the United States many new runways were also needed. Seventeen sites were being evaluated in Southern California for a new airport to relieve congestion at Los Angeles. Several other projects were under consideration including a new airport for Chicago, its third. In 1989 Denver had decided to go ahead with a mammoth new airport with a capacity of six to twelve runways. But by 1991 this was the only new major airport in the United States on which a firm decision had been taken, though the project appeared to be facing financing problems.

All such projects, however, cannot by themselves come anywhere near to coping with the projected increase of demand. Thus in Europe four or five new runways or airports may be built, but twenty-five to thirty or so airports will suffer serious runway congestion by the year 2000.

In the 1960s many new runways were built but in the following two decades the emphasis switched to terminal building. Why are so few runways being built or planned at the present time? The reason seems to be that airport planners and governments became complacent about future requirements. This was, first of all, because of environmental oppostion in the 1970s and early 1980s to runway building, often very violent as in the cases of Frankfurt and Tokyo/Narita. Many airport authorities put their heads in the sand and hoped that the problem would go away.

One saw this very clearly with the then BAA when in 1974 it decided not to safeguard land needed for a second runway at Gatwick but to build the second terminal on it instead. The BAA claims that at the time its hand was forced by a 1971 government decision that a second runway would not be needed. But the BAA went a step further. In 1979 to secure planning permission for converting a parallel taxiway into an emergency runway for use when the main runway was closed, the BAA entered into an agreement with West Sussex County Council undertaking not to construct a second runway for forty years! This was clearly shortsighted as many experts, including a former BAA chairman, were then predicting that a second runway would be needed. Subsequently the second terminal was built on the land earmarked for such a runway.

Many other airport authorities followed the same kind of complacement thinking. They were also lulled into a false sense of security by the low growth rates of the early 1980s, which suggested that the problem could be put off, and also by the belief that the increase in air travel would be absorbed by larger aircraft and higher load factors. But by the end of that decade a number of parallel developments made the prospects for runway capacity much bleaker.

Adverse trends

In the latter part of the 1980s demand for air travel particularly on international routes rose more rapidly than had been predicted earlier. In 1987 international passenger traffic grew by 14 per cent. It grew a further 11 per cent in 1988 and 8 per cent in the following year, yet annual growth rates of about 6 per cent had been forecast for this period. Growth slowed down in 1990 and 1991 as a result of the economic downturn in several major countries and the Gulf Crisis after August 1990. However, the expectations were that by 1992 or 1993 demand would again be rising rapidly particularly in the East Asian and Pacific markets. Such rapid growth can be catered for by more flights, larger aircraft and higher load factors or some combination of all three. The more that can be absorbed through increasing the size of aircraft and operating them at higher load factors the lesser is the need to increase frequencies and thereby put runway capacity under pressure. But the trends have not been favourable.

First, as a result both of airline liberalization, which led to hubbing and an increased emphasis on high frequencies, and the introduction of smaller long-range aircraft, average aircraft size has stopped growing. In the United States it continued to grow for a year or two after deregulation but after 1981 average aircraft size remained static or declined. One saw the same pattern in Europe, where average aircraft size grew rapidly in the 1970s and peaked in 1981–2. Since then the average size of aircraft used in European operations has remained largely unchanged (Figure 2.1). There is little evidence to suggest any significant increase in the medium term.

In 1988 aircraft manufacturers and others were predicting that average aircraft size would rise from 170 to 175 seats in 1986 to around 210 to 220 by the year 2000. But between 1987 and 1989 orders for over 2000 new aircraft were placed, most of which were medium – or smaller-sized twin jets.

Analysing the spate of orders and manufacturers' plans, one long-term forecast, that of *Airline Monitor*, predicted that average aircraft size would only be 188 seats by 2000 compared to 176 in 1989 and 1990 (*Airline Monitor* 1989).

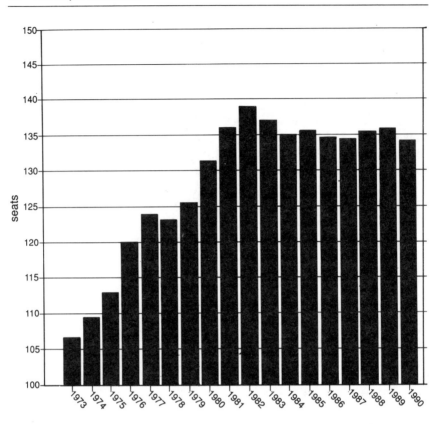

Figure 2.1 Average aircraft size of Association of European Airlines (AEA)
members (European and domestic services)
Source: Compiled by the author from AEA data.

The second adverse trend has been in terms of passenger-load factor. There is a
real danger that load factors in Europe and on long-haul international air services,
which have traditionally been high, may fail to rise further and may actually
decline as a result of liberalization. Certainly in the deregulated US domestic
market most US airlines have been unable to push up their passenger load factors
above 62 to 63 per cent, while in the more capacity-controlled markets of the rest
of the world average load factors have climbed steadily to around 67 per cent and
for many airlines they are over 70 per cent. As airline liberalization spreads in
European and other markets the existing high load factors may well decline. In
other words, it will become increasingly difficult in liberalized airline markets to
achieve the high load factors that airport planners were forecasting ten or even
five years ago.

Smaller than predicted aircraft and lower load factors mean that more flights

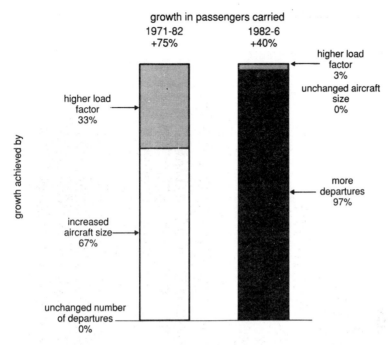

Figure 2.2 Accommodation of passenger growth on US domestic services
1971–86
Source: Compiled from Boeing data.

will be needed to handle the forecast passenger volumes, thereby increasing the
pressures on existing runway capacity.

Another unfavourable development is that operational changes associated with
greater airline competition are adversely affecting airport capacity by increasing
demand at peak periods. This happened in the United States with hubbing. This is
because the essence of hubbing is that you have a complex or a group of flights
coming into an airport, all arriving within an hour of each other, and then a
complex of departures occurring within the following hour. There may then be a
four-or five-hour gap, and then another bunching of arrivals and departures.

In Europe hubbing is beginning to be implemented, but another development
will also adversely affect runway capacity. That is the phasing out of inter-airline
revenue-pooling agreements. One consequence of the pooling agreements was
that, since airlines were not in effect competing in terms of capacities and timings,
they were able to agree to spread their frequencies through the day. After 1987,
following pressure from the European Commission, airlines, like British Airways,
KLM, Air France or SAS, which previously were frequently operating in a pool,
abandoned such pools. One result has been that some flights that were previously
spread through the day are increasingly bunched at peak times.

The potential pressures on airport runway capacity can be summed up by

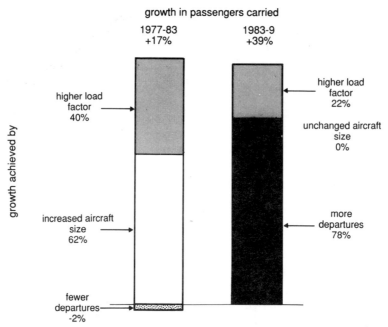

Figure 2.3 Accommodation of passenger growth by AEA member airlines 1977–89 (European and inter-continental services)
Source: Compiled by the author from AEA data.

examining how growth in demand was accommodated by United States airlines before and after deregulation (Figure 2.2). In the period 1971 to 1982, the average annual growth in the number of passengers in the US was 5.2 per cent. According to Boeing, much of this growth was absorbed through increases in aircraft size and load factors. But from 1982 to 1986 when annual growth accelerated to 8.8 per cent the situation changed dramatically. The increase in demand was met very largely by increases in frequency and only marginally by increases in aircraft size and load factors. The same pattern was repeated in Europe in the period 1977 to 1989 (Figure 2.3). In the six-year period up to 1983 growth among European airlines was largely through increases in aircraft size and higher load factors while frequencies actually declined. In the six years after 1983 as liberalization slowly spread there was no increase in aircraft size and three-quarters of the passenger growth was catered for by significant increases in the number of departures.

Which of these alternative growth scenarios are more likely in the 1990s as airline liberalization becomes more entrenched in Europe and spreads to other continents? It could be argued that the market will adjust to the absence of capacity. In other words, airlines faced with airport and ATC congestion will ignore the tendencies outlined above and will start buying larger aircraft and flying them at higher load factors in order to overcome the shortage of runway slots. While a few airlines may be doing this, an examination of the new aircraft on order in 1990–1 would suggest that this could not happen quickly or widely enough significantly to reduce the demand for more runway capacity.

There can be little doubt that shortage of runway capacity will be the major problem facing managers at many European, North American and Asian airports throughout the 1990s. Airport congestion will become increasingly severe. There will be growing public, media and government pressure on airport authorities to increase runway provision. Some short-term responses are needed since the provision of more runways, which must be the ultimate long-term solution, will require eight or more years for planning and building.

Short-term solutions to runway shortage

In the circumstances, many airport managements will inevitably have to consider short-term solutions to runway-capacity problems.

The first might be to make better use of existing runways by relaxing night restrictions or night bans. Airports are the only key industry whose major productive assets are switched off for a third or a quarter of the day. Night restrictions at London's Heathrow and Gatwick airports limit them to about 70 per cent of their potential runway capacity. As early as 1988, the CAA in the UK had expressed the view that a larger increase in night flights by quieter aircraft should be allowed (CAA 1988). Making greater use of night hours would require additional actions on the part of governments, airports and airlines. One is to convince the public that aircraft are actually getting quieter. Not enough has been done in that respect. Greater expenditure is also required on research into making aircraft even quieter and on sound-proofing and noise-alleviation measures. Finally, passengers using scheduled flights have to be persuaded to travel at night and earlier in the morning, that is to change their travelling habits. The charter services already use the night hours and their passengers seem to accept the idea of flying at night. Passengers are also prepared to fly at night in the long-haul markets. Those airports that do not have night bans, Paris for instance will undoubtedly have greater potential for growth than those that do.

The second short-term solution is for governments or airports to introduce traffic-distribution rules that discourage smaller aircraft, such as business jets, or non-passenger flights from using airports where there is runway congestion. This may mean excluding all-cargo aircraft or general aviation or taxi flights at periods of peak runway demand. Already in Britain in 1986 following a consultation process the CAA recommended to the government that all-cargo and general aviation flights should only be allowed to operate at London's Heathrow and Gatwick airports at peak periods after receiving prior permission (CAA 1986). The government accepted this recommendation as a traffic-distribution rule thereby creating uncertainty about the long-term future of all-cargo flights at these airports. In 1989 and 1991, in giving advice to the UK Secretary of State for Transport, the CAA again recommended that this traffic-distribution rule should be maintained though others could be abandoned (CAA 1989b and CAA 1991). As pressure on runway capacity at London and other airports becomes overwhelming it seems inevitable that all-cargo and other non-passenger flights will be forced to more remote airports. This will also happen at other congested airports.

The third short-term solution which may be forced on airport management is the introduction of some kind of pricing mechanism to allocate runway capacity or slots between potential users when demand is far in excess of supply. Slot-allocation methods and more particularly the possible use of slot pricing will become a major issue in airport management as demand outstrips supply (see pp. 99–111).

Finally, congestion and runway shortage at the larger airports will mean that growth at secondary and regional airports will be faster than predicted as airlines switch to more direct flights and develop alternative hubs at airports where runway slots are readily available. This may require the re-negotiation of many bilateral air-services agreements if routes to specific regional airports are not already allowed for. While regional or secondary airports may have unused runway capacity they may become short of terminal capacity if growth suddenly outstrips their traffic projections. This was the thinking behind British Airways' decision in 1989 to part finance a new terminal at Birmingham airport in central England designed to facilitate hubbing of air services from regional points throughout Europe.

In the longer term one must build more new runways and more new airports. But where should these be? They must be in areas which are environmentally acceptable and that means away from congested urban or semi-urban areas. This may well push one towards the American concept of 'wayports'. These are remote junctions or interchange hubs for air passengers and air freight which are intended to relieve the pressure on existing airports by diverting transit and interline traffic away from the latter. For example, in 1989 the Texan cities of Midland and Odessa jointly presented a proposal to use federal funds to develop Midland airport, 450 km west of Dallas, as a wayport with up to eight runways capable of handling 150 million passengers a year. There were other potential candidates too.

To conclude, the complacency of the airport planners and governments of the 1970s and 1980s means that the demand for runways and to a lesser extent terminal facilities will far exceed supply, and that the imbalance will become progressively worse. Dealing with it will be the major headache for airport managers in this decade.

FINANCING AIRPORT EXPANSION

Not only will runways be in short supply but so will airport terminals. But these pose a less acute problem because it is easier to find space for additional terminals than for new runways. Worldwide, many new terminals were due to be completed in the early 1990s while many more are planned. Among the former one may include the new terminals at Singapore-Changi, Frankfurt, Manchester, Karachi,

Calcutta, Philadelphia, New York La Guardia and Toronto. Despite much new terminal building, bottlenecks and congestion will continue at many airports if traffic growth doubles as predicted during the 1990s.

In the short term increased runway and/or terminal congestion will push up airport profits to record levels as facilities become more intensively used. If quieter aircraft and growing congestion induce governments to relax or abandon night restrictions there will be a profits boom. In the longer term congestion will necessitate additional investments in new terminals and ultimately in more runways and new airports. In some cases these can be financed partly if not largely in internally generated funds as airport profits increase.

Elsewhere internally generated funds are unlikely to be sufficient to fund the investments required, many of which will be quite massive especially where entirely new airports need to be built as at Athens, Lisbon or Hong Kong. Thus another key question, in terms of long-term strategy, is how are these investments going to be financed? Up to now, in most parts of the world airports have been financed essentially by local or central government funding. That system will no longer be able to cope with the large investments required, and increasingly airports are going to have to turn to commercial money markets for capital finance. In turn, that may well mean a move to the privatization or part-privatization of airports. It will also mean the introduction outside the United States of the American practice of direct airline involvement in terminal financing. This was seen for the first time in Britain in 1989 with British Airways' decision to part finance a second terminal at Birmingham airport. A trend to external funding can also be seen in the new third terminal at Toronto airport opened in 1990. This terminal costing US$381 million was the first major airport complex outside the United States to be developed, owned and operated by a private company, the Airport Development Corporation, set up specifically for the venture by a consortium of firms led by a Toronto property development company. In July 1991 the Greek government launched a tender process to find a private consortium to finance, construct and operate the new Athens airport which was expected to cost about US$1.5 billion. The Greek government wanted to be a major shareholder in the company created by the consortium but was not expecting to provide any of its own finance other than the provision of the airport land.

It is evident that airport authorities will need to be innovatory in order to gain access to private financing of airport projects. But in many countries there are institutional barriers to the use of such finance. Thus in the United States the single largest barrier to private-sector finance is that public-airport entities have access to tax-free debt through the revenue bonds. This makes such debt relatively cheap though it may be limited. In some other countries the institutional structure of their airports makes the introduction of private finance difficult or even impossible, for instance if the airport is run by a government department. Inevitably if airports or governments are to look to private finance for airport projects they may first have to implement institutional changes in the legal framework of airport ownership or tax regulations and so on. But such changes, aimed at overcoming institutional barriers to private finance, are difficult and slow to bring about.

EUROPEAN AIRPORTS AND 1993

European airports have faced and continue to face additional problems arising from the growing political and economic integration of the European Community (EC). In the early 1990s while planning for new capacity most west European airports have had to deal with the uncertainties of the creation of the internal market by 1993. This entailed the removal of political and commercial frontiers between the twelve member states of the EC. It would create havoc for airports. Yet even by early 1991 they were barely in a position to grapple with the problems because so much uncertainty existed.

In the process of removing internal frontiers by the end of 1992, intra-community traffic previously international would be reclassified as domestic and would need to be handled through each airport's domestic channel. At London's Gatwick airport, domestic traffic, hitherto 6 per cent of the total, would shoot up to nearly 60 per cent. The existing domestic facility could not cope, so the international facilities would have to be redesigned at a cost of about £30 million. All EC airports faced the same problem. It could only be solved through substantial capital expenditure, a reduction in terminal capacity, at least in the medium term, and possibly a deterioration in passenger service standards. According to Juan Rosas Dias, Chairman of Aeropuertos Espanoles, speaking in June 1991, this was exactly what would happen at Madrid airport. Existing international facilities would be switched to intra-EC, and new facilities for non-EC passengers would need to be built at a cost of US$450 million (AACI 1991). At Milan's two airports the cost of conversion was estimated at $34 million (AACI 1991).

But while the European Council of Ministers had taken the decision on the removal of passport controls, individual governments were slow to decide how to implement it. While some were prepared to accept free movement of intra-EC travellers, others notably the UK government wanted to maintain some systematic checks to combat drugs, terrorism or immigration of non-EC nationals.

By early 1991 with little time to go uncertainty still reigned, yet airports needed some time to redesign and reconfigure their terminals. In the summer of 1991 the Council of Ministers agreed in principle on the removal of internal passport controls at all airports from 1 January 1995. An exception was made for the United Kingdom to allow it to carry out checks on non-EC citizens entering the UK from another EC country.

The second equally disturbing effect of the 1993 internal market would be to ban passengers travelling between EC countries from buying duty-free or tax-free goods. For most European airports, especially those with a large charter share, intra-EC passengers represent the largest single component of their traffic. At Brussels or Nice they are just over 60 per cent of the total, at Amsterdam, Düsseldorf and Gatwick they are close to 55 per cent and at Heathrow 39 per cent. At a stroke, with the implementation of a duty-free ban, such passengers would no longer be able to use the duty-free shops. Dublin would be worst hit with over 90 per cent of its traffic suddenly becoming domestic.

The impact on airports' duty-free concession revenue would be dramatic. Manchester airport estimated that 83 per cent of duty-free and tax-free sales would be lost. The figure for Frankfurt was 80 per cent and Paris 33 per cent. Sir Norman Payne, then chairman of the BAA, claimed in 1988 that the BAA would lose more than half of its duty-free concession income. The effect on total airport revenues would also be significant. It was estimated that individual European airports might lose 2 per cent to 12 per cent of their total revenues from 1993 onwards depending on the proportion of intra-EC traffic they catered for and on the size of the airport. Smaller airports generally generate a lower share of their total revenues from concessions, but a higher proportion of their international passengers are likely to be intra-EC. In the longer term these sales might well be replaced by increasing sales of duty-paid and tax-paid goods. But it will take years for such sales to build up.

Here again uncertainty reigned. While the principle to phase out duty-free sales by the end of 1992 had been accepted, the method of its implementation was as yet undecided by early 1991. A vigorous campaign was mounted by airports, duty-free concessionaires and other interested parties to try to delay its implementaion. They argued that a lengthy transition period was required to allow airports to make the necessary adjustments. It was not until November 1991 that the European Community finance ministers finally decided to abolish intra-EC duty-free shopping as from 1 July 1999. This afforded the airports an unexpectedly long transition period.

Further aspects of Community policy were expected to affect European airports after 1992. One was the intention to introduce value-added tax on intra-EC air fares. If this was to go through it would have a dampening effect on travel demand and would partly counteract the stimulus to growth arising from liberalization.

In addition, a European Commission directive on consultation between airports and airlines and on airport-charging principles was likely to be enacted during 1991. It would also require airports to produce transparency in their accounts, which means that they should be clear and open. Moreover, charges for domestic and intra-EC flights would have to be similar unless there was a clear cost difference. Hitherto domestic fares had been much lower than international. If intra-EC charges were reduced to existing domestic levels there would be distinct losses of revenue. At Milan the potential loss on landing fees and passenger charges was estimated at US$27 million per year (AACI 1991). Alternatively, airports might be forced to increase domestic charges which would be unpopular. This directive might actually restrict airports' new-found commercial freedom.

It seemed certain that all the necessary measures arising from closer integration would not be both agreed and implemented by 1 January 1993. Moreover, as integration proceeds, further directives and regulations affecting airports and the way they are managed are sure to emerge from the European Commission. Thus a period of uncertainty for European airports will continue for much of the decade. For instance, the Europe Against Cancer action programme being mounted by the European Commission might result in duty-free sales of all tobacco products being abolished at European airports. Yet tobacco sales generate about a third of airport duty-free income.

Non-EC European airports may be unaffected by some of the above developments, notably the removal of passport controls and the abolition of intra-EC duty-free shopping. So from that point of view their future financial viability may be sounder. Many however are too closely bound up with EC member states to escape entirely. Moreover, several non-EC countries opened negotiations with the European Commission in 1990 and 1991 with the aim of harmonizing their air transport regulations with those of the Community. Sweden and Norway, in particular, were keen to do this because of their close political and economic links with Denmark, a member state. In March 1991 a draft agreement was concluded extending the scope of EC aviation policy to Norway and Sweden. As a result it seems, inevitably, that their airports too will be adversely affected by EC policies.

Major capital investments are going to be needed in Europe to meet both the rapid growth of traffic and the redesign of airports necessitated by the internal market. Yet at the same time a major source of airport revenue, the duty-free and tax-free shops, will be crippled by the loss of a large part of their clientele.

In the longer term airports will develop alternative sources of commercial revenue from duty-paid shops. In the short term, they may try to compensate for the lost duty-free revenues by increasing aircraft landing fees and passenger charges. Sir Norman Payne, the BAA's then chairman, claimed in 1988 that European airports would need to increase airport charges by 15 per cent to 20 per cent to compensate for lost concession income. A more recent study suggested an increase of about 25 per cent in landing fees and passenger charges at UK airports (NEI 1989). Though these are probably overestimates, growing conflict between airports and airlines seems inevitable, especially since in a liberalized and more competitive European environment the airlines will be looking to cut costs.

Chapter 3

Airport cost and revenue structures

Airport management and planning is not an easy task. Airport authorities must invest substantial capital sums in large and immovable assets that have no alternative use, to satisfy a demand over which they have little control except very indirectly. It is the airlines and not the airports who decide where and how the demand for air travel or air freight will be met. Airports merely provide a facility for bringing together airlines and their potential customers. Thus, matching the provision of airport capacity with the demand while achieving and maintaining airport profitability and an adequate level of customer satisfaction is a difficult task. It is made particularly difficult because investments to expand airport capacity are lumpy, increasing effective capacity by much more than is needed in the short term, and because they must be planned long in advance. The planning cycle from the initial conception and decision to build a new large terminal to its actual opening may be between five and ten years. Moreover, that terminal may well have sufficient capacity to meet projected demand for at least another ten years. Thus airports are planning fifteen to twenty years ahead. This clearly requires above all the use of accurate and sophisticated forecasting techniques. But airport managers also need to have a clear understanding of their cost and revenue structures both to ensure that they achieve profits or at least reduce their losses and in order to monitor the financial impact of any new investments.

STRUCTURE OF AIRPORT COSTS

Analysis and comparison of airport costs is certainly more difficult than an assessment of airport revenues because there is much less uniformity world-wide in the treatment of costs than of revenues. Airport expenditures are categorized and defined in various ways in different countries. It is, therefore, difficult to establish what the cost structure of a typical airport might be even within a limited geographical area such as Europe. However, during the 1980s researchers at the Polytechnic of Central London examined the accounts of two dozen or so western European airports over a number of years, and attempted, as far as possible, to reproduce them on a common cost basis. From this

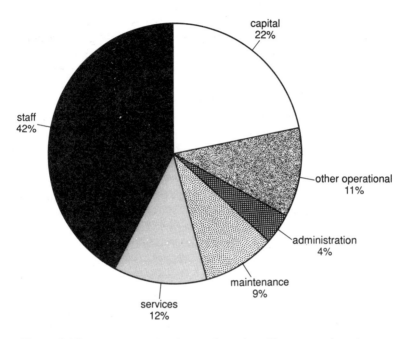

Figure 3.1 Average cost structures of western European airports
Source: Transport Studies Group, Polytechnic of Central London.

research it proved possible to identify what the cost structure of an average European airport might look like (Figure 3.1). The average distribution of costs among European airports did not appear to change much from year to year. However, it should be borne in mind that the cost structure shown in Figure 3.1 represents very much of an average and masks wide variations between individual airports.

Among western European airports, staff or labour costs are the largest single cost element, representing on average around 42 per cent of total airport costs. They are rarely below the 30 per cent level though for several airports the figure rises above 45 per cent. In a few cases staff costs may represent as much as 65 per cent or more of total costs. This is usually the case when the airport authority itself undertakes activities which at most other airports may be carried out by concessionaires or the airlines. Such activities may include passenger or baggage handling, freight handling, catering, the operation of duty-free shops or other shopping facilities. These are all areas which are particularly labour intensive. Therefore, the greater an airport authority's involvement in these areas the more likely it is that staff costs will become a higher proportion of total expenditure. Thus Milan airport's heavy involvement partly explains why its labour costs amount to over two-thirds of its expenditure.

The second major cost element is capital charges, which encompass interest paid and depreciation. While on average such charges make up about 22 per cent of airport costs, for most European airports the actual figure is generally in the range between 20 per cent and 35 per cent. For a handful of airports, however, it may be as low as 10 per cent or less, normally because of accountancy practices in certain countries. In several cases airports may have relatively low capital charges because they do not charge proper depreciation on some of their assets. Frequently this happens with assets funded through government grants or from other external sources. For example, the airports of Rome, Milan and Vienna have traditionally not charged depreciation on government-financed assets. As a result capital charges have represented well below 20 per cent of total expenditure. Where an airport has a policy of not depreciating all its assets fully thereby reducing its capital charges while at the same time being involved in many labour-intensive activities, then labour costs can represent the overwhelming share of costs. This is what happens at Milan.

Labour and capital costs taken together make up close to two-thirds of most European airports' costs. Other operating-cost elements which together total 36 per cent are less significant. The cost of services bought in (including water, electricity and so on), of equipment and of supplies together account for 12 per cent of total costs. Maintenance and repair costs, excluding the staff element, average around 9 per cent while administration accounts for another 4 per cent. This leaves a poorly defined category of other costs which on average represent 11 per cent of total costs (see Figure 3.1).

The cost structure of United States airports is significantly different from that of their European counterparts because of differences in the way they are operated and financed (see Chapter 9 for details). In the first place, at many US airports the terminals and other facilities, which in most of the world are operated by the airport itself, are rented or leased out to airlines or others. In some cases terminals may even be owned by airlines rather than the airport. Since such facilities are likely to be largely operated and staffed by non-airport-authority employees, the authority's staff costs are reduced. At the same time few US airports are engaged directly in passenger or baggage handling but leave these and other similar functions to airlines. Second, many US airports particularly larger ones have financed much of their development through revenue bonds on which they have to pay interest every year irrespective of their level of profitability. While some US airports have benefited from federal government funding through the Airport Improvement Program (AIP) it is generally the smaller airports unable to raise money through revenue bonds who have been most reliant on the AIP (see Chapter 9). In contrast to the United States, airports elsewhere have been much more dependent on financing their expansion through government grants many of which are either interest free or at very low rates of interest. Much finance has also come from internally generated funds. Commercial loans or bonds have generally played a relatively small part in airport finance outside the United States. As a consequence of the different approach adopted to financing, many US airports find that interest paid is a major part of their annual expenditure and is a much more significant cost element than for airports elsewhere. If one adds together depreciation and interest paid one finds that capital charges represent a relatively large proportion (44 per cent) of the total costs of US airports (see Figure 3.2).

The relative importance of capital charges at US airports is reinforced by the fact that staff costs are less significant as a cost element. For example if one looks at the total costs, operating plus non-operating, of eight of the largest US airports in 1989–90, one finds staff costs at six of the nine were between 11 per cent and 18 per cent (see Table 9.6 p.201). On the other hand capital charges, that is depreciation plus interest paid, accounted for a much higher share of total costs ranging from 35 per cent at Chicago O'Hare to around 72 per cent at Atlanta, an airport heavily dependent on revenue bonds as a source of finance. For the larger US airports capital charges are generally between 25 per cent and 55 per cent of total costs, and in the majority of cases they are much higher than staff costs.

The above figures contrast sharply with the European picture (see Figure 3.2) where capital costs average around 24 per cent of total expenditure and are rarely above 35 per cent, while staff costs average 42 per cent but may climb to 60 per cent or more. Another contrast with European airports relates to maintenance and repair. Because many US airport authorities act effectively as landlords renting or leasing out land and facilities, they tend to have low direct operation costs but proportionally higher maintenance and repair costs. Certainly the latter costs as a proportion of total costs tend to be much higher at US than European airports where they average around 9 per cent.

ECONOMIC CHARACTERISTICS OF AIRPORTS

The preceding analysis is concerned with the structure or composition of airport costs rather than the level of costs. One can measure cost levels in terms of the cost per unit of output which may be a passenger or a work-load unit (WLU). Unit costs at individual airports will be influenced by a whole range of factors which will vary from country to country and between airports in the same country. Some of these factors are discussed in the later chapter on performance indicators (Chapter 8). However, detailed analyses of airport costs over many years suggest that airports as business units exhibit certain economic characteristics irrespective of their cost structure or level.

The first marked characteristic is that there seem to be significant economies of scale in airport operations. This means that as an airport increases its traffic throughput the cost per unit of traffic declines. Early studies of British airports showed that unit costs fall sharply as traffic

(a)

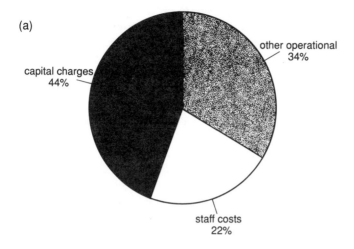

(b)

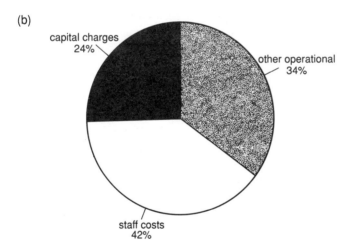

Figure 3.2 Average cost structures: (a) large US airports 1989–90; (b) European
airports 1989
Source: Transport Studies Group, Polytechnic of Central London.

throughput increases, particularly up to 1.0 or 1.5 million passengers. As traffic
grows beyond a level of about three million passengers, unit costs flatten out and
do not seem to vary much with airport size. In economic terms the long-run
average cost curve for airports takes the form shown in Figure 3.3. There is no
evidence that in the long term there are any significant internal diseconomies

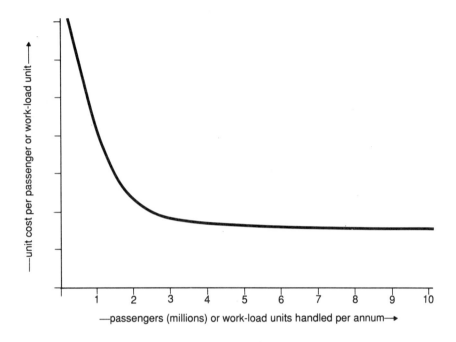

Figure 3.3 Airport long-run cost curve

of scale, as in some other industries, which would push up unit costs when airports start to get very large. There may, however, be some short-run increases in unit costs if congestion becomes excessive. In addition there may be external diseconomies in terms of noise pollution or road-traffic congestion.

The implication of all this is that smaller airports will tend to have higher unit costs. From an airport-planning point of view it suggests that concentration of air traffic within a region on a small number of larger airports will result in lower airport costs than spreading air services to a large number of relatively smaller airports, even though the latter strategy may reduce passenger access costs.

The second economic characteristic of airports is that major development programmes push up unit costs. Where airports undertake major expansion and development programmes which are too large in relation to immediate traffic needs or which are undertaken too soon, the short-term and medium-term effect is to increase their unit costs. This is not only because the airport's depreciation and other capital costs go up but also because operating costs rise. A major new terminal has to be heated, lighted, cleaned and maintained and staffed even if the number of passengers using it is well below the design capacity.

As a result unit costs per passenger rise, often dramatically, and airports having undertaken major expansion schemes often find themselves losing money. It is only when traffic builds up to make better use of the expanded facilities that profitability is likely to be restored – unless, of course, the airport embarks on a further cycle of expansion too soon. Conversely smaller airports that hold back on investment, even though they are heavily congested at peak periods, may actually achieve profitability despite their smaller traffic throughput and higher unit costs. The implications are clear. Airports should hold back investment as long as possible if they want to keep their unit costs of production low. In addition they should avoid grandiose developments which entail very large jumps in capacity in a single step. Montreal's Mirabel airport is an example of airport development on too grand a scale which has resulted in heavy financial losses. Airports by their very nature require relatively large indivisible investments in additional terminals or even runways. But where possible investment should be phased in such a way that jumps in capacity are not too large or too soon.

These first two economic characteristics of airports may appear contradictory in that there are economics of scale on the one hand, while on the other development programmes aimed at achieving these economies actually push up costs. In fact these two conclusions are reconcilable. There are a number of situations in any industry with falling long-run costs where an increase in capacity will lead to higher costs in the short term: first, if the investment in new capacity takes place too soon and demand is not in a position to grow sufficiently quickly to allow the utilization of the new capacity at a low-cost output level; second, if investments in capacity need to be undertaken in large discrete stages, implying that the short-run cost curves are far apart from each other, then the effect of a new investment programme is the same. In both cases demand or traffic throughput is too low in relation to the increased capacity to ensure low unit costs. It is clear that in many airport situations both factors often occur in conjunction. Investments are undertaken too soon and the jumps in productive capacity which result from these investments are too great. In other words there is a divergence between short-run and long-run costs.

Airports expand by building new terminals and/or additional runways. Each discrete level of capacity is represented by a short-run average cost curve as in Figure 3.4. The long-run average cost (LRAC) curve envelops the short-run curves and is tangential to them. With one terminal and one runway the airport is operating on the first short-run average cost curve (SRC^1). As throughput increases unit costs decline until at output level Q^1 they are at a minimum. If output increases beyond this point then congestion and overloading of the terminal may lead to a slight increase in unit costs. The airport has been building a second terminal however and the short-run average costs for a level of capacity with two terminals is shown by curve SRC^2. If the airport moves to a two-terminal operation when output is at say Q^2, unit costs will

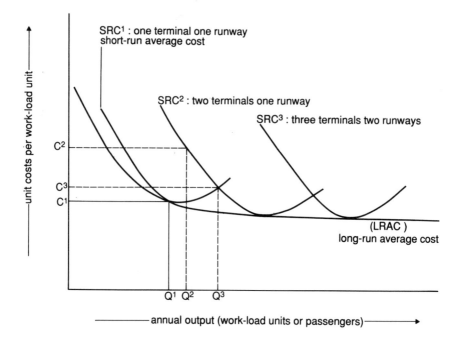

Figure 3.4 Relationship between short- and long-run average costs of airports

immediately go up from about C^1 to C^2. They will then decline over time moving down SRC^2 as throughput grows. Alternatively if the opening of the second terminal is timed so as to coincide with output reaching the Q^3 level there will in theory be no jump in unit costs. However, in the meantime, there will have been an increasing level of congestion in the existing single terminal. As traffic expands beyond Q^3 then unit costs will gradually decline along SRC^2 to levels lower than those when there was only one terminal.

A third variable which has important repercussions on an airport's performance is the proportion of international passengers within its total traffic. This has an important effect both on an airport's cost and on its revenue levels. Unit costs increase as the proportion of international passengers increases because such passengers need substantially more terminal space for customs, health and immigration and so on than do domestic passengers and also because they spend, on average, more time in the terminal. This in turn means greater space and amenity requirements. But unit revenues increase more than in proportion to the increase in unit costs. This is not only because revenue from shops and other concessions in the terminal rises dramatically as international passenger throughput increases, but also because landing fees and other aeronautical charges at many airports are higher for international than domestic flights. Thus the net effect is that an airport's chances of breaking into profit are improved as the proportion of international passengers in its total traffic increases. This is a major justification for airport managers to try to attract international air services.

SOURCES OF AIRPORT REVENUE

Airport income is generated from aeronautical or traffic-related activities on the one hand or from non-aeronautical or commercial sources on the other. *Aeronautical* revenues are those that arise directly from the operation and landing of aircraft, passengers or freight. They include aircraft-landing fees, passenger-service charges, air-traffic-control charges if ATC services are provided by the airport authority, aircraft parking and hangarage fees, and charges related directly to the handling or cleaning of the aircraft. *Non-aeronautical* revenues are those generated from non-aircraft-related commercial activities in the terminal/s and on airport land. They may arise from a whole host of sources but generally include rents for office space and check-in desks; income from shopping concessions of various kinds; car-parking fees; recharges to tenants for services such as electricity, water and so on; and revenue from catering whether this is provided by the airport or a concessionaire (see Table 3.1). This distinction between aeronautical and non-aeronautical is not always clear cut. For instance, how should one categorize fuel charges levied by an airport on each gallon or litre uplifted? Is this a traffic-related aeronautical revenue or is it a form of concession fee? Since airports normally charge rent for land and any other facilities used by aviation-fuel companies, which would appear as rental or commercial income, then the fuel throughput charge should perhaps also be treated as a concession revenue.

The greatest uncertainty and confusion arises in relation to revenue from handling of aircraft or of passengers, baggage or freight. At most airports such services are provided by airlines or handling agents. In the case of handling agents a concession fee may be charged by the airport and revenues arising would appear as non-aeronautical. If, on the other hand, the airport authority provides some of these services itself, say freight handling, it may categorize any income earned as aeronautical. In the analysis which follows fees from handling undertaken by an airport itself are treated as aeronautical while fees earned from other handling agents are identified as commercial.

Greater uniformity among airports in the treatment of revenues means that revenue analyses and comparisons of airport revenues are likely to be more accurate than when dealing with costs. Western European airports on average generate about 56 per cent of their total income from aeronautical charges and 44 per cent or so from commercial or non-aeronautical sources. The more detailed breakdown within each of these two categories is shown in Figure 3.5. In the 1970s aircraft landing fees represented by far the most significant part

Table 3.1 Categorization of airport revenue sources

Total revenues

Aeronautical or
traffic revenues

Non-aeronautical or
commercial revenues

Aeronautical or traffic revenues	Non-aeronautical or commercial revenues
Landing fees	Rents or lease income (from airlines
Airport air traffic control	and other tenants)
charges	Recharges to tenants (for
Aircraft parking, hangarage and	electricity, water, cleaning, etc.)
picketing	Concession income (from shops,
Passenger charges	catering, duty-free shops, banks, car
	parks, hotels, etc.)
	Direct sales (shops etc. operated by
	airport authority)
	Car-park revenue (if operated by
	airport authority)
Freight charges	Miscellaneous (e.g. interest earned)
Apron services and aircraft	Non-airport related activities
handling (if provided by airport	(e.g. land development)
authority)	

Fuel throughput surcharges

Passenger, freight and baggage handling

Note: [1]Individual airports may not have access to all of the revenue sources listed.

of aeronautical revenues but during the following decade airports put greater emphasis on generating revenue from passenger-related charges. By the early 1990s aircraft-related landing fees and passenger-related charges were each producing a similar share of the total revenues. The suggestion in Figure 3.5 that handling services generate on average about 13 per cent of revenue is somewhat misleading. It is an average figure based on two extreme situations. Most European airport authorities do not themselves provide any handling services at all so no aeronautical revenue is produced from this source, while airports such as Frankfurt, Rome, Vienna or Milan that are heavily involved in handling may generate 35 to 50 per cent of their total income in this way. If one excludes handling revenues then the aeronautical revenues decline to 49 per cent of the total while non-aeronautical or commercial rise to 51 per cent. Among non-aeronautical sources, concessions generate on average the largest share of revenues. Revenues from other commercial sources are fairly evenly spread.

The revenue composition of individual airports may differ substantially

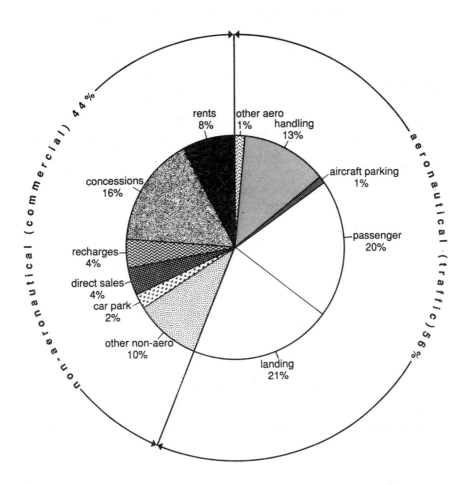

Figure 3.5 Average revenue structures among European airports 1989
Notes: [1] Handling revenues are those arising from the provision of services by the airport
authority itself.
[2] Direct sales revenue is from catering outlets or shops operated directly by the
airport authority; only a few airports do this.
Source: Transport Studies Group, Polytechnic of Central London.

from the average break-down shown in Figure 3.5 as a result of the various
factors affecting either their aeronautical or non-aeronautical revenue-
generating potential. These are discussed in greater detail later on (see
Chapters 4 and 6). However, there does seem to be a common relationship
between airport size and revenue generation. Smaller European and other
airports tend to be almost entirely dependent on aeronautical revenues which
are supplemented by some rental income (see Figure 3.6). As traffic grows
commercial revenues build up providing an increasing share of total revenues.

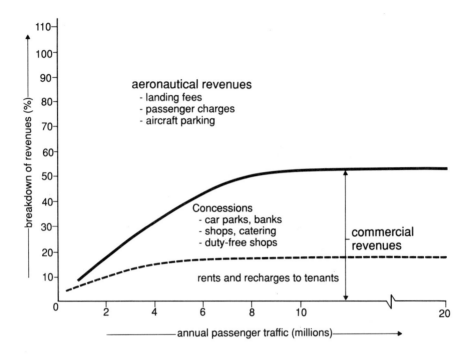

Figure 3.6 Revenue split as traffic grows among most European airports

But this growth in commercial income comes very largely through concession income arising from the expansion of shopping, catering and car-parking facilities and sales and, where available, from increased duty-free shopping. Other commercial revenues, that is rents and recharges to tenants for services provided, stabilize at around 15 to 20 per cent of total revenues. By the time airports are handling close to nine to ten million passengers or more, commercial revenues should have risen to between 50 per cent and 60 per cent of total income. For some reason, at airports outside the United States even among the larger ones this figure rarely rises much above 60 per cent.

Revenue structures of United States airports are significantly different from those of European and other airports. In contrast to the latter two groups US airports generate a much higher proportion of their income from various commercial sources. On average, around 75 per cent to 80 per cent of revenues at the medium-sized and larger-sized US airports come from commercial sources with a correspondingly small balance generally less than 30 per cent coming from aeronautical charges (see Figure 3.7). At some US airports the aeronautical charges represent little more than 10 per cent of total revenues. For example, this was the case at Los Angeles International in the financial year 1989–90 when landing and other flight fees generated only 8 per cent of

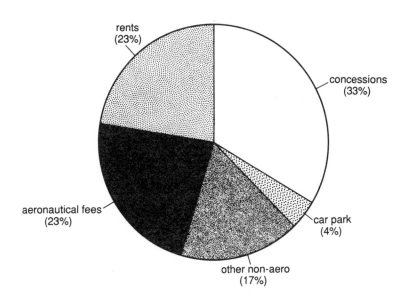

Figure 3.7 Average revenue structures of medium/large US airports 1989–90

that airport's total revenues (see Table 3.2). Until 1991 US airports were not permitted to generate revenue for themselves from a per capita passenger charge even though such a charge was widely used in other parts of the world (see pp.203–5). Thus aeronautical revenues were almost entirely composed of aircraft-landing fees. The absence of passenger-related charges is one reason why commercial revenues are so much more important than traffic or aeronautical income. Another more important factor is that the leasing out of terminal buildings, hangars and other facilities is much more widespread among US airports and is done to a greater degree than is the case elsewhere. As a result rentals and leases tend to generate a relatively high proportion of total income at most US airports. One feature particular to US airports is the very high revenues generated from car parking and from car-rental and limousine concessions. They are invariably the major single source of non-rental commercial revenue whereas among non-US airports it is normally revenue from duty-free concessions which dominates. Among US airports duty-free concession revenues are inevitably lower because for most of them international passengers are a relatively small proportion of the total. Another feature of US airports is that they appear to earn a higher share of their income from interest on short-term investments and bank deposits than do their counterparts elsewhere. The particular features of US airports discussed above can be seen by reference to one example, the airport of Los Angeles (see Table 3.2).

Table 3.2 Income structure of Los Angeles International airport (financial year to June 1990)

	(%)
Aeronautical	
Landing and other flight fees	7.5
Fuel commission[1] and miscellaneous	0.6
Total aeronautical	8.1
Non-aeronautical	
Concession income	51.4
Rentals and lease income	26.6
Recharges for services	0.9
Interest earned	12.8
Other	0.3
Total non-aeronautical	91.9
Total income (US$194.6m)	100.00

Source: Data supplied by the City of Los Angeles Department of Airports.
Note: [1]Fuel commission could be classified as non-aeronautical.

TRENDS IN REVENUE DEVELOPMENT

During the 1970s increasing pressure on airports to operate on a commercial basis led to a rapid increase in landing fees and passenger charges at most non-US airports. As a result, at many airports, especially those in the UK, aeronautical revenues grew faster than non-areonautical and their share of total revenue increased. In the subsequent decade and partly as a result of pressure from airlines, the rate of increase in airport charges slowed down and there has been increased emphasis on maximizing revenue from commercial activities.

A number of airports have tried to split their costs and revenues between aeronautical (i.e. traffic) and non-aeronautical (i.e. commercial) activities despite the problems and difficulties involved in cost allocation. These difficulties in allocating costs are especially acute because so many are joint costs. This is particularly true of costs associated with passenger or freight terminals. For instance, there are many areas and facilities within passenger terminals which are used both for passenger handling and for commercial purposes such as shopping. How does one then allocate the costs of the space used, or its heating and cleaning costs, between the traffic and commercial activities? Nevertheless, the British Airports Authority (BAA) had been doing this for many years in its annual reports prior to its privatization. Invariably such analyses showed that while aeronautical or traffic revenues failed to cover traffic-related costs, commercial activities at most of the BAA airports tended to be profitable. Particularly large profits on commercial activities at

Heathrow and Gatwick more than offset losses on air-traffic operations at most of its other five airports. These results seemed to justify placing so much emphasis on the generation of non-aeronautical revenues.

However, in its evidence to the UK Monopolies and Mergers Commission in 1985, the BAA stated that certain costs could only be allocated on an arbitrary basis between traffic and commercial operations (MMC 1985). This arbitrariness affected the extent to which the results shown were meaningful, especially as the cost allocation was biased in favour of commercial activities and this exaggerated their profitability. In fact, for a number of years the BAA had made representations to the Secretary of State for Transport asking that such tables should no longer be published but this request had been turned down.

The Monopolies and Mergers Commission also rejected the BAA view. Despite the problems posed by cost allocation, the Commission recommended

> that a distinction can and should continue to be drawn in the Authority's [BAA] accounts between the results of its traffic operations and its commercial activities at each airport. This should continue to apply if privatisation takes place, so that the extent of subsidisation of traffic operations by commercial activities and of one airport by another is disclosed.
>
> (MMC 1985)

The Commission's recommendation was incorporated into the Airports Act 1986. United Kingdom airports run as airport companies are required to break down their costs and revenues into traffic and commercial areas (see Table 3.3). They once again show losses on traffic operations being more than compensated for by large profits from commercial activities even at smaller BAA airports. In the previous financial year 1988–9 the total loss on traffic operations was much greater at £53.9 million. In contrast to the BAA, similar data for the larger UK regional airports show them making profits on both the traffic and commercial sides (see Table 3.3).

In the early 1980s economic recession and low or negative traffic growth seem to have encouraged many airports to pay more attention to the already reasonably well-developed commercial side of their operations. Airport operators are now increasingly venturing into new and sometimes totally non-airport-related activities. For example, many of the activities and services provided at Frankfurt airport, such as the huge Dorian Gray Discotheque, appear to be unrelated to the airport's main purpose.

Widespread evidence of this growing emphasis on generating more revenue from non-aeronautical sources can be found. For instance, prior to privatization the BAA had four performance targets agreed with the government and six further internal targets agreed each year between the Board and the Managing Director. None of these ten targets referred specifically to traffic

Table 3.3 Profit or loss by activity area at selected UK airports 1989–90[1]

	Airport charges[2] (traffic operations) (£m)	Other income[3] (commercial) (£m)
BAA Plc		
London Heathrow	8.5	136.5
London Gatwick	−15.7	70.6
Stansted	−10.0	4.4
Glasgow	5.0	7.4
Edinburgh	2.1	4.5
Aberdeen	− 0.6	2.3
Prestwick	− 0.6	0.9
Total BAA	−11.3	226.6
Non-BAA		
Manchester	16.4	20.6
Birmingham	1.3	7.1

Sources: Airport reports and accounts 1989–90.
Notes: [1] No interest charges have been allocated to either airport charges or other incomes. Their inclusion would further increase losses on the traffic operations.
[2] Airport charges cover those activities connected with landing, parking and take-off of aircraft including passenger charges.
[3] Other income covers retailing activities such as duty- and tax-free sales, car parking, accommodation and utility charges for airport users and aircraft-related support facilities.

revenues but three were specific to the BAA's commercial activities. The three commercial revenue targets for 1985–6 were as follows:

1 to increase duty-free and tax-free income per international departing passenger by 4.75 per cent in *real* terms;
2 to increase other concession income (excluding duty-free, tax-free and car-parking) per passenger by 4.75 per cent in *real* terms;
3 to increase gross rental income by 4.5 per cent in *real* terms.

These were annual targets and the target numbers could be changed each year. It is not known what the targets have become since privatization.

In most countries, airports have operated under government restrictions on the frequency or level of increases in aeronautical charges. At the very least any increases have first been approved by the relevant ministry. Where governments try to hold back or limit rises in landing or passenger fees higher revenues can only be generated from commercial activities. Even if privatized, airports may still face constraints on their aeronautical charging policies. As previously mentioned, the UK government in privatizing the BAA imposed a formula which limited the BAA's maximum annual increase on airport aeronautical charges. In 1987 this limit was expressed as (RPI − 1) + S where RPI was the increase in the retail price index and S was a figure to cover the increased security costs. Five years later in July 1991 the Civil Aviation Authority proposed an RPI minus 8 per cent price limit. Inevitably any limits to pricing freedom on the aeronautical side must push airports once again to expand their commercial revenues. Interestingly there were no constraints on the BAA's commercial-revenue targets, even though such revenues were targeted to increase in *real* terms, provided the company did not appear to be abusing its monopoly position.

Finally, one can see the growing emphasis on maximizing commercial revenues in the very recent trend towards establishing duty-free shops on arrival. Such shops are already established at Singapore, Kuala Lumpur, Reykjavik and one or two other airports. Arrivals shops may pose serious headaches for airport authorities because they normally have relatively little free space in the arrivals area and the provision of such space may prove costly. Airlines may also prove hostile since arrival duty-free shops will eat into in-flight sales. On the other hand there are safety and weight advantages if passengers take less duty-free goods on board. The biggest problem in Europe will be to pursuade the customs authorities to accept such shops. If they do, their revenue-earning potential is substantial. It is estimated that at Singapore up to 20 per cent of duty-free sales are now made in the arrival shop. Because of this it is likely that more and more duty-free and other concessions will in future be provided in the arrivals areas of airports.

Chapter 4

Aeronautical charges and pricing policies

IMPORTANT OF AERONAUTICAL CHARGES

While the trend world-wide is towards greater emphasis on maximizing commercial revenues, the generation of aeronautical revenues from landing fees and passenger charges will contine to be crucial for several reasons. First, because for most airports aeronautical charges will continue to generate well over half their total revenues. They are particularly important for smaller airports and airports with little or no international traffic, where commercial revenues are likely to be less significant. Second, because it is the income source that can be adjusted most rapidly to meet any increases in costs or shortfall in revenues. Concession revenues from shops or other commercial sources can only be increased very slowly as traffic throughput builds up, as contracts are renegotiated or as new facilities are built and opened. In contrast, landing fees or passenger charges can, if necessary, be increased at a stroke though ideally with some months' notice to the airlines. Thus when duty-free shopping for intra-European Community (EC) passengers is eventually phased out at European airports, the short-term solution to cover the revenue loss may well be sharply increased aeronautical charges. Over time other commercial revenue sources may be built up to replace intra-EC duty- and tax-free shopping.

Because of their continued importance airport charges and the pricing philosophies underlying them merit particular attention. It should also be borne in mind that from the airlines' point of view aeronautical charges are most critical since they impinge directly upon their own costs. A certain mythology has grown up around the belief that airport charges represent only 3 per cent of total airline operating costs. If that were so, then increases in airport charges could only have a very marginal effect on airline costs. The 3 per cent is a totally misleading world average figure which hides the major cost impact of airport charges on many airlines. This impact is particularly adverse for short-haul airlines, which pay landing fees more frequently, and for airlines based in or operating through airports where the passenger charge is paid directly by the airline rather than by the passenger on departure (see p.77).

Airport charges, that is aircraft-landing, aircraft-parking and passenger fees,

Table 4.1 Impact of airport charges on airline costs: airport charges as a
percentage of total operating costs

Scheduled airlines (1989)	(%)	Mainly charter airlines (1988)	(%)
Air UK	19.8	Air Europe	17.7
British Midland[1]	15.7	Britannia	15.5
VIASA (Venezuela)	9.3	Dan Air	15.1
Austrian Airways	9.1	Monarch	14.6
British Airways	6.1		
Cathay Pacific	5.8		
Air France	5.4		
Air India	4.5		
Ethiopian	4.3		
Egyptair	4.1		
Quantas	2.7		
KLM	2.5		
Northwest	2.1		
Olympic	1.9		
American	1.8		
Delta	1.6		
United	1.6		

Source: ICAO 1989b.
Note: [1] 1988 data used.

impact quite differently on different airlines. It is clear from the figures in
Table 4.1 that the worst affected are primarily short-haul carriers or charter
airlines especially if operating within Europe where airport charges are high.
For short-haul European airlines, such as Air UK or British Midland, and for
most European charter airlines airport charges represent around 15 per cent of
total operating costs. At the other extreme, for long-haul carriers, such as
Qantas, or for United States airlines airport charges may be as low as 2 per
cent or less of total operating costs. Nevertheless for most airlines airport
charges will continue to be a major source of concern.

TRADITIONAL STRUCTURE OF AERONAUTICAL CHARGES

A commercial aircraft landing at an airport faces a number of possible charges.
These will normally include an aircraft-landing fee and possibly one of the
following: a charge per passenger usually paid on departure, an aircraft-
parking or hangarage fee and one or more of a variety of very specific user
charges. The review below outlines the most widespread and common
approach to aeronautical charges.

Aircraft landing fee

The major single source of revenue for most airports has traditionally been revenue derived from landing fees charged to aircraft. This is particularly true of smaller airports. Since the early days landing fees have been based on the weight of the aircraft, usually the maximum take-off weight (MTOW) or the maximum authorized (or ramp) weight (MAW). At some United States airports the maximum landing weight (MLW) is used. There is a charge per unit weight (per tonne, 1000 lbs or 500 kg), and the fee basis is normally one of five kinds:

A   A fixed rate per tonne or other weight unit irrespective of the total weight. The total charge is based on the number of tonnes multiplied by the unit charge.

B1 A rate per tonne, with weight break-points, so that the rate increases in steps as total weight increases. An aircraft is charged on the basis of its weight times the appropriate rate per tonne for that weight.

B2 As for **B1**, a rate per tonne, with weight break-points, so that the rate increases in steps as total weight increases. But unlike **B1** the charge is accumulative. This means that the first, say, 15 tonnes of an aircraft's weight are charged at the rate for that weight range, the next 15 tonnes (weights 16 to 30 tonnes) and so on. At a few airports the rate per tonne actually decreases as aircraft weight rises.

C   A rate per tonne whether fixed (**A**) or with weight break-points (**B1** or **B2**) which varies by the nature of the flight. Traditionally there have been two categories of charges, one for domestic and one for international flights. In some countries, length of sector rather than the type of flight has been used to differentiate the unit charge. Whatever the basis of differentiation, the aim has been to ensure that aircraft on longer flights pay a higher unit rate.

D   A few airports have replaced the weight-based landing fee with a single fixed charge per aircraft irrespective of size. For example in 1990–91 all aircraft landing at London Heathrow during peak periods were charged at a flat fee of £400 whether small twin turbo-props or large jets (though the fee was £380 if less than 16 tonnes). This may be called a movement charge.

At most airports in the world the aircraft landing fees have normally covered the use of the following facilities:

1 air traffic control facilities used during approach and landing and also on departure; at a minority of airports a seperate terminal navaid charge may be levied (see p.68–9);

2 landing facilities (runways, taxiways, etc.);

3 parking of the aircraft on a stand or apron for some clearly specified time (usually at least two hours) after which a seperate parking fee is charged;

4 use by disembarking passengers of aircraft gates, fingers and other facilities

in the terminal building; departing passengers may be paying for these facilities through a separate passenger charge on departure;

5 take-off facilities on departure.

In the vast majority of airports the fee is paid on arrival per landing and there is no separate charge for the aircraft itself on departure.

Complex and diverse systems of *surcharges and rebates* on the basic landing fee are operated at different airports. These are usually of three kinds. They may be related to the distance or type of flight, to noise levels of the aircraft or to night landings. As previously mentioned a rebate for domestic services or for very short-haul flights is common as are rebates for training and other commercial flights. Conversely some airports impose a surcharge for international or inter-continental flights. Most European airports, other than those in the UK, have highter international landing fees. But the trend is away from international surcharges on the weight-based landing fee.

In recent years several airports, especially in Europe, have introduced noise-related rebates or surcharges to encourage the use of quieter aircraft. For instance, Amsterdam and the larger French airports have quite complex noise surcharges for different aircraft types while most German airports have simpler surcharges. Interestingly, in November 1987 a French high court declared that Aeroport de Paris' noise surcharges were *ultra vires* since they were not related to services actually provided by the airport for its airport customers.

At airports not operating on a twenty-four-hour basis there is frequently an extra surcharge on those aircraft wishing to land and take-off during the shut-down period. Even when the airport is open for twenty-four hours there may be a special fee during night hours to cover the costs of runway lights, as happens at Athens, at Italian airports and at many Third World airports. Generally, lighting charges are much less common at European or North American airports than in other continents.

A small number of airports have introduced a surcharge for landings during defined peak periods. For example at Athens Airport in 1991 landing charges were increased by 25 per cent for flights arriving between 1100 and 1700 hours in the period June to September, while at Hong Kong there is a flat fee added to the basic weight charge. The London airports have for many years had a more complex peak charging structure based on a different pricing philosophy. (This is discussed in the following chapter.)

In some countries, such as Italy or Greece, landing-fee structures and levels are uniform at all airports though sometimes with the exception of the major airport. In several countries, airports are divided into two or more categories according to the level and quality of their runway and terminal facilities, and a different level of landing fees is applied to each category. This happens in Malaysia and Brazil.

Aircraft parking and hangar charges

Beyond the free-parking period covered by the landing fee, which is generally two to six hours, aircraft must pay a charge if parked on the airport's apron, taxiways ramps or hangars. This charge can only be avoided if the aircraft is parked on apron space or maintenance areas leased to the airline or belonging to it.

The parking fee is normally an hourly charge, or it may be for a unit of hours. Frequently twenty-four hours is used as the time unit once the free period has been exceeded. In other words, whether it stays one hour or twenty-three hours beyond the free time, an aircraft is charged the same. This clearly provides no incentive to airlines to vacate parking stands once they have entered a twenty-four hour period. If airports want to ensure better utilization of parking stands so as to reduce the number and cost of stands needed, then they should have a very short free-parking period followed by a parking charge for each hour or part of an hour that an aircraft stays on the stand. A few airports are now doing this.

The parking charge is calculated usually on the basis of the aircraft's weight or less often on its area, that is wingspan times length. If based on weight, the parking charge will, in most cases, be a fixed amount per tonne or unit weight as at Dublin or Frankfurt, or less frequently the unit charge may actually decline as the aircraft's weight increases. The latter happens at Cairo and at Jordanian airports, while at Athens the unit charge goes up with weight. Another method is to express the parking fee as a percentage of the landing fee which is itself weight-based. Thus Tel Aviv charges 25 per cent of the landing fee for parking, which is unusually high, while Vienna airport takes 7 per cent. There appears to be no economic rationale other than ability to pay for basing parking fees on aircraft weight. A sounder approach is to use the area of the aircraft, as expressed by its wingspan multiplied by the length. This at least reflects the area of space on the airport apron that each aircraft uses up. Khartoum, Kuala Lumpur and Singapore are among the few airports that charge for parking on the basis of aircraft area.

Some airports provide hangar space for commercial or private aircraft. The charge for this is likely to be markedly higher than for open parking, and it is commonly based on the aircraft area (wingspan times length). This is the case at Amsterdam and Oslo airports. At other airports the parking fee may vary between different areas of the airport, with stands nearest the terminals being more expensive.

Passenger charges

Charges per passenger began to be levied after the Second World War as a source of airport revenue additional to the aircraft weight fee. Subsequently it was argued that the passenger charge was specifically aimed at recouping airports' very substantial terminal investments from those that used them. This was a strong argument in the years before non-aeronautical concession revenues were built up to their current levels.

Passenger charges, a major source of airport revenues, have been widely adopted throughout the world except at United States airports. The latter have been prevented by law from charging for passengers on a per head basis until a new passenger facility charge was approved by Congress in October 1990 as part of the 1991 Federal budget. Once the appropriate Federal regulations were in place airports would be able to charge a $1, $2 or $3 passenger fee to cover the cost of specific capital projects (see pp.203–4). It was not expected that airports wishing to do so would be able to impose the passenger facility charge before 1992.

While traditionally there have been no airport-imposed passenger fees at United States international airports, there are a series of Federal airport charges which are generally uniform throughout the country. In 1990 these charges were: per arriving passenger, $5 for immigration clearance and $5 for customs use; and, per departing passenger, $6 for the international passenger transport tax. But the revenue generated did not accrue to the airport itself but to the relevant Federal authorities.

The passenger charge is normally charged on each departing passenger only, though a small number of airports, Birmingham and Belfast in the United Kingdom among them, charge on the basis of arriving passengers. Thus while aircraft pay per landing, passengers pay on departure. Perhaps this can be justified on the grounds that terminal capacity and size is determined primarily by departing passengers who spend much longer in the terminals than arrivals who pass straight through it.

The passenger charge is levied in one of three ways:

1 it can be paid directly by the passenger to the airport authority on departure; this requires a separate collection desk or facility in the check-in area as at Manila airport;
2 it can be collected by the airline, on behalf of the airport, from passengers when they buy their tickets or check in on departure; the airline then pays it to the airport; most airports in Asia, Africa, South America or Australia use this or the previous method of levying the charge;
3 it can be levied directly by the airport on the airlines who incorporate the charge within the fare; thus no separate charge is levied on the passengers themselves; this practice is common among European airports.

The passenger charge is a major source of conflict between airlines and those airport authorities that levy the charge directly on the airlines. Through IATA, the International Air Transport Association, the airlines argue vehemently that it should be charged directly to the passenger on departure and not through the airlines who have to increase ticket prices to cover it. The airlines argue that including the passenger charge in the ticket has adverse consequences. It entails the passenger paying more than the airport actually charges because the ticket price has to be increased by a greater amount both to cover increased commission paid to travel agents on the higher ticket price and to absorb the airlines' own administrative costs of handling the airports' passenger charges. On the other hand, the International Civil Aviation Organization (ICAO) has argued that collecting a fee from departing passengers especially at large airports aggravates terminal congestion and increases the likelihood of delays.

The level of the passenger charge varies widely. Many countries exempt passengers on domestic flights or levy a lower charge on domestic than that on international passengers. In some countries, no passenger service charge is levied at less-developed airports. It is common practice to exempt infants and transit passengers.

A differential between the domestic and international fees may be justified on cost grounds because international passengers are more costly to handle in terms both of facilities and the space they require. A number of airports, including those of the BAA Plc, have estimated that the terminal costs of a domestic passenger are only about 40 to 50 per cent of those of an international passenger largely because of the lower space requirements. However, some airports have introduced different passenger charges which are purely discriminatory in the sense that they cannot be justified in any sense on cost terms. Sometimes they have arisen for historical reasons, as in the case of the very low passenger charge at Malaysian airports for passengers going to Singapore and vice versa. Or they may be an attempt to stimulate particular traffic flows. Thus at Dublin airport passengers on European flights are charged less than those on transatlantic services but at neighbouring Belfast airport in Northern Ireland the reverse is the case. At Syria's Damascus airport there is a three-tier fee structure: there is an international passenger charge; if travelling to another Arab country the charge drops to less than half of the international charge; but if the passenger going to the other Arab country is a Syrian the charge falls further to 20 per cent of the full international fee. Clearly these fee differentials bear little relationship to airport costs.

Some airports as in Italy or Israel have a cargo charge per kilogramme of freight handled through the airport but this is not common.

Other aeronautical charges

Most airports world-wide impose the three types of charge outlined above, the major exception in the past being the absence of airport-imposed passenger charges in the United States. But there are a variety of additional charges which are not universal but which are levied selectively by individual airports.

A *terminal navaid charge* is levied at a minority of airports where the cost of air traffic control services on approach and at the airport are not covered by the aircraft landing fee or are not separately funded as in the United States. In some cases the airports collect such a charge but the revenues are then passed on to the relevant civil aviation authority or department which provides the service. This happens at London's Heathrow and Gatwick airports and at major French airports.

Many airports raise additional revenue through a *fuel throughput charge*. This is in essence a royalty for the fuel concession granted in addition to the rental for the space occupied by the fuel companies. This royalty is not a percentage of the turnover, as with other concessions, but is usually a flat charge per hectolitre or gallon of fuel throughout. It is levied at a few airports in Europe and elsewhere but is very widespread at South American airports, where it generates a substantial share of total airport revenues. Thus at Mexico City airport the fuel charge generates around 15 per cent of the total revenues. Though aircraft related, it should not be considered as an aeronautical charge but as a commercial concession fee.

Airports are beginning to impose separate charges for specific facilities which may be used in the process of embarking or disembarking passengers. Such charges may include a separate *fee for airbridges, buses* or *mobile lounges*. A few airports many also impose more general charges for *apron services*, as at Birmingham in the UK, or for *terminal facilities*, as at the Canadian airports.

Some airports may themselves provide passenger-, baggage- or freight-handling services or aircraft cleaning. The range of such services provided by an airport itself with its own dedicated staff varies enormously between airports. A few provide virtually all the handling services while at the other extreme most airports leave it all to the airlines or specialist handling companies. Where airports offer any handling services they normally charge on a per passenger or per flight basis. In the latter case the charge may vary by size or type of aircraft.

Finally airport *security charges* are also becoming more widespread. While the cost of increased security is in most cases borne by governments or airlines, in a few cases a security charge is levied by the airport on a per passenger basis.

TRADITIONAL PRICING POLICIES

From the early days of air transport, the principle underlying the structure of airport charges outlined above was that airports were a public utility providing services of national importance. This belief, which was and still is strongly held by many governments and civil aviation authorities, has had profound consequences as far as airport charges and finances are concerned.

In the first place, it has ensured a willingness on the part of central or local governments to support airport development and investment and to subsidize operating losses when they occurred. Second, it has meant that airport pricing policies have been broadly based on recouping the costs of the facilities provided. Cost recovery was the basis of the charging structure. But in many instances it has not been pursued too vigorously because of the underlying assumptions that the external economic or social benefits of airport provision outweighed any internal losses and that airports were unlikely to be commercially viable anyway. Finally, since airports were public utilities of national importance it was felt that they should be freely available to all users on the same terms and that there should be no undue discrimination against particular users. The principle of non-discriminatory airport charges was enshrined in the 1944 Chicago Convention on International Civil Aviation to which most countries are signatories and in subsequent bilateral air-services agreements. Article 15 of the Convention requires airports of signatory states to be open under uniform conditions to the aircraft of all the other contracting states and not to discriminate between foreign aircraft and aircraft of its own state (ICAO 1980) (see pp.78–80).

The ill-defined objectives of cost recovery and non-discrimination led naturally to a structure of airport charges which involved, more or less, the averaging out of airport costs among the users irrespective of the costs that individual users imposed on the airport. The averaging out of costs was done initially through the weight-scale aircraft landing fee and later through the passenger charge, where applied.

Over time the fairly simple average-cost pricing approach was modified in two ways. When it became apparent that larger aircraft required longer and stronger runways and, therefore, were more costly to cater for, the basic weight fee for larger aircraft was often increased. A break-point structure was introduced whereby the fee per tonne increased as certain aircraft weight levels were exceeded. Separate charges were also introduced by some airports for use of specific facilities such as airbridges or buses.

The other concept which increasingly crept into airport pricing was that of ability to pay or of charging what the traffic will bear. It was apparent that airport charges were a smaller proportion of total airline-operating costs for longer-haul flights than for shorter flights. It followed that long-haul services and their passengers were better able to bear higher charges. Thus distance-related surcharges on the landing fee or on the passenger charge were introduced at many airports.

The pricing philosophy underlying this traditional airport charging structure was one which attempted to combine two principles, those of average-cost pricing and ability to pay. But no real attempt was made to apportion costs between users and to charge accordingly. Where the unit fee increased with weight or was higher for longer-haul or international flights, it was justified either on the grounds that such flights could bear the higher charges or on the grounds that long-haul aircraft were larger and heavier and therefore required longer and stronger runways, taxiways and aprons. The latter argument was an attempt to relate charges more closely to costs but no serious examination was made of the costs imposed on airports by the larger aircraft. Thus, the relatively higher landing fees imposed on larger aircraft were little more than an indication that those aircraft imposed higher costs. They were in no sense a true reflection of the higher costs imposed. (A more detailed critique of the current pricing structure follows on pp.80–4).

The fairly simple relationship between length of haul, size of aircraft and runway requirement which existed perhaps up to the mid-1960s no longer applies. Short-range wide-bodied aircraft, increased engine performance and improved landing-gear technology all mean that total aircraft weight can no longer be used as a simple proxy for estimating the runway costs imposed by different aircraft.

It is also clear when one looks at the various facilities whose use is covered by the landing charges that aircraft weight could never have been a very good indicator of costs imposed on each of the facilities. For instance, a large, long-haul aircraft with a high approach and landing speed would normally impose lower air-traffic-control and runway-occupancy costs than a small but very much slower aircraft. The latter would occupy the runway approach for much longer and need wider horizontal separation from larger and faster aircraft in front or behind it, yet it would pay a much lower landing fee than the large, long-haul aircraft.

Despite its shortcomings, the universality of the traditional approach can be seen in Table 4.2 which shows airport-user charges at a random selection of seven airports from the six continents. Though there are some local modifications, usually in the form of additional but relatively small charges, the basic structure for all seven airports is a weight-based landing fee plus a passenger charge on departing passengers. The similarity in charging structure around the world occurs because most countries have adopted the recommendations made by ICAO and, to a lesser extent, IATA. Both organizations have tried to achieve standardization of airport charges. Though they are in disagreement on some of the elements of any standardization, the policies of both organizations have reinforced the weight-based charging structure.

THE ICAO AND IATA VIEWS ON AIRPORT CHARGES

In 1967, the Council of ICAO produced a series of recommendations on airport charges to the member states (ICAO 1967). In outlining the principles for user charges at airports it suggested that airport users should bear their full and fair share of the cost of providing airport facilities. According to ICAO, users' capacity to pay should not be taken into account until all costs were fully assessed and distributed on an objective basis. Nor should some users be burdened by extra charges as a result of preferential charges or rebates to other users. In other words, there should be no cross-subsidization of one group of users by another.

In theory, these principles should have resulted in a cost-based charging

Table 4.2 Airport charges at selected airports March 1991

	Rio de Janeiro	Man-chester	New York JFK	Toronto	Kuala Lumpur	Sydney	Nairobi
Basic landing fee							
Basis Unit	MTOW	MAW	MTOW	MTOW	MAW	MTOW	MAW
charge per	tonne	tonne	1000lb	tonne	500kg	tonne	tonne
Increases with weight	No	No	No	Yes	Yes	No	Yes
In how many steps	–	–	–	3	5	–	11
Free parking	3hrs	2hrs	3hrs	6hrs	3hrs	2hrs	6hrs
Surcharge/rebates							
Type/distance	No	Yes[1]	No	No	No	No	No
Night/lighting	No	No	No	No	Yes	No	Yes
Noise-level related	No	Yes	No	No	No	No	
Passenger charge[2]							
Paid by	pax	airline	[3]	airline	pax	[3]	pax
Type/distance related	No	Yes	No	No	Yes	No	No
Other charges							
Separate navaid fee	Yes	No	No	No	No	Yes	No
Security charge	No	No	Yes	No	No	Yes	No
Rescue/fire charge	No	No	No	No	No	Yes	No
Airbridge fee	No	No	Yes	Yes	No	No	No
General terminal fee	No	No	Yes	Yes	No	No	No

Notes: [1] Lower for propeller aircraft.
[2] Manchester passenger charge is on arrivals and at Toronto on arrivals and departures. Elsewhere it is only on departing passengers.
[3] New York has several passenger charges imposed by federal agencies and Sydney has a federal government passenger tax. But revenues do not go to the airport authorities.

structure. In practice, detailed recommendations, in the same document, on the charging systems to be adopted meant that a cost-based charging structure was impossible to apply. Among the Council's detailed recommendations were the following:

1 Charging systems should be simple and suitable for general application.
2 Landing charges should be based on the weight formula.
3 No differentiation in rates should be applied for international flights because of the stage length flown.
4 Charges should be non-discriminatory both between foreign and national users and between two or more foreign users.
5 A single charge should be applied for costs of as many as possible of the facilities and services provided.
6 Passenger-service charges are not objectionable in principle but there are practical objections to their being collected direct from the passenger (ICAO 1979a).

Strongly influenced by the ICAO recommendations, nearly all countries adopted the weight-based landing charge as the basis for raising airport revenues. This system was a victory for simplification over the cost principle. Clearly, it must be difficult to ensure that users bear their 'full and fair' share of airport costs if the charging structure is to be simple, with the minimum of separate charges, with no differential charges and with weight as the basis of any landing fees.

In November 1981 the ICAO Council agreed a revised statement on airport charges which incorporated most of the principles adopted in 1967. But there was increased emphasis on cost recovery and a clarification of what costs should be recovered by airport charges (ICAO 1981). The 1981 ICAO statement re-emphasized the general principle that it is desirable that users ultimately bear their full and fair share of the cost of providing the airport. The cost to be shared was the 'full economic cost to the community of providing the airport and its essential ancillary services, including appropriate amounts for interest on capital investment and depreciation of assets . . .' (ICAO 1981). Where they could produce sufficient revenues airports should also provide for retirement of debt and for reserves for future capital projects. Clearly, in ICAO's view airports should try as far as possible to be financially self-sufficient not only in terms of covering their operating costs but also in terms of capital and investment costs.

Once again ICAO, when discussing pricing principles, argued strongly in favour of cost-related charges and against charging on the basis of ability to pay. But when looked at in detail ICAO's proposals on charges seem to bear only a limited relationship to costs imposed by users and are in some cases mutually contradictory (see Table 4.3). For instance, while there may be some correlation between aircraft weight and airport costs, weight is not the only factor determining the costs imposed on an airport by a particular aircraft. Therefore, a weight-based charging structure cannot be expected to reflect the costs of providing facilities for that aircraft. Such a structure involves little

Table 4.3 ICAO and IATA recommendations on airport charges

	ICAO	IATA
1	Should be simple	Agree
2	No discrimination against foreign airlines or between them	Agree
3	Landing fees based on weight	Agree
4	No differentiation for international flights or by stage distance	Agree
5	A single charge where possible	Agree
6	Landing fee to cover lighting and radio aids	Agree
7	Passenger charges acceptable but collected from airline	May be economic necessity but collect from passenger
8	Security charges *only* to cover relevant costs and if non-discriminatory	Not justified; it is government responsibility
9	Noise surcharge *only* to cover noise-alleviation measures	Not justified
10	Fuel throughput charge to be considered as concession fee	Only if covering costs of fuel facilities; not justified as concession fee
11	?	Peak-period surcharges not justified

Source: Compiled from ICAO and IATA sources.

more than averaging out of costs among users. Uniform charges based loosely on average costs in turn contradict the principle of no cross-subsidization if users do not in fact all impose the same costs.

ICAO's policy on airport charges was parallelled in many respects by the airlines, through the International Air Transport Association (IATA). From early on IATA accepted the principle that airports should recover reasonable costs and that aircraft weight should be the basis of the landing fee. IATA subsequently endorsed ICAO's 1981 principles on the assessment and allocation of costs. Many of the detailed IATA recommendations mirror those of ICAO (see Table 4.3). But in one or two respects IATA policies differ. IATA is more hostile to passenger-related charges and argues these should be paid directly by the passenger. It is also opposed to noise surcharges, to higher-peak period charges and to fuel-throughput charges which are in the nature of a concession fee.

From the point of view of airport financial viability it is difficult to conceive of more inappropriate charging policies than those put forward by ICAO and IATA. Pricing based on the weight formula has the merit of simplicity and in that sense conforms closely to the ICAO principles. But a simple pricing policy is no recipe for financial viability; far from it. Weight-related charges may lead to poor utilization of resources, over-investment in facilities and users gaining at the expense of producers. This is particularly the case where users who impose high costs by operating at night or at peak periods or by requiring special facilities are not charged accordingly.

As previously mentioned, many airports around the world have deviated in one important respect from the ICAO and IATA recommendations by introducing discriminatory higher charges for international or long-haul flights. It can indeed be argued that in situations where costs are difficult to identify and apportion, a pricing policy based on ability to pay is as good as any other in terms of airports' ultimate financial performance. But it would seem that many elements of airport costs are identifiable and can be allocated among airport users. In this kind of situation a cost-related pricing policy may well yield a more efficient solution all round than an 'ability to pay' charging policy.

LEVELS OF AIRPORT CHARGES

As a result of ICAO and IATA recommendations considerable uniformity has arisen world-wide in the *structure* of airport charges (see Table 4.2). Yet at the same time the *level* of charges varies enormously from one airport to the other.

Although the complexities of airport charging structures can make any attempt to compare the levels of charges extremely complicated and hazardous, broad comparisons can be drawn by examining the representative airport charges for one or more aircraft types. The representative airport charges early in 1991, including passenger-related charges for a landing and take-off by a Boeing 747-300 with 280 passengers (i.e. a 70 per cent factor), are shown in Table 4.4. Charges imposed by government agencies other than the airport are excluded.

An examination of Table 4.4 highlights certain features of airport charges world-wide. First, the table underlines the wide range in the level of charges with the total charges for Tokyo, Oslo or Manchester (summer) being about three to four times as high as those of Buenos Aires. It is also evident that charges at European airports tend to be among the highest while charges at many Third World airports are generally low as are those at United States airports. Second, it is also noticeable that while passenger charges in Europe are levied directly on the airlines, as recommended by ICAO, and included in the ticket price, elsewhere the practice is generally to charge the passengers direct on departure. This means that from the airline's point of view the perceived cost of landing at European airports is much higher than that of landing at other airports since the airlines are unconcerned with payments made by the departing passengers direct to the airport. Third, it is evident that at many airports the passenger-related charge has now become much more important than the aircraft-related landing fee based on weight. For about half the airports surveyed the passenger charge generated over 50 per cent of the total aeronautical charges (excluding parking fees, lighting fees, etc.) for a

Table 4.4 Representative airport charges February 1991 for Boeing 747–300 (with 280 passengers)[1]

| | Aircraft fee | Passenger charges paid by | | Terminal or airbridge Fee | Total |
| | | Airline | Passenger | | |
	(US$)	(US$)	(US$)	(US$)	(US$)
Tokyo	7,202		4,446		11,648
Manchester					
(summer)	5,519	4,366			9,885
Oslo	5,529	4,230			9,759
Heathrow					
(peak)	1,672	7,341			9,013
Stockholm	5,717	2,846			8,563
Vienna	4,859	3,673			8,532
Manchester					
(winter)	5,519	2,893			8,412
Gatwick					
(peak)	1,602	6,200			7,802
Frankfurt	5,174	2,244			7,418
Dublin	3,740	3,583		32	7,355
Toronto	1,393	4,539		746	6,678
Caracas	1,134		5,167		6,301
Amsterdam	3,598	2,564			6,162
Paris	3,423	2,329			5,752
Hong Kong					
(peak)	1,140		3,588		4,728
(off-peak)	1,076		3,588		4,664
Delhi	2,980		1,516		4,496
New York JFK	1,468			2,660	4,128
Singapore	2,030		1,965		3,995
Beunos Aires	2,718			77	2,795
Heathrow					
(off-peak)	863	955			1,818
Sydney	1,576				1,576
Los Angeles	494			840	1,334

Source: Compiled using IATA *Airport and En Route User Charges Manual* (IATA annual).

Notes: [1] Assumes MTOW of 379 tonnes, MAW of 379 tonnes and MLW of 261 tonnes. Flight is scheduled international; charges shown are for a single landing and take-off. Only charges imposed by the airport authority itself are included.

Boeing 747, while at some airports the figure was over 70 per cent (see Table 4.5). However, revenues of airports which generate a disproportionate share of their aeronautical revenue from passenger-related fees are much more suscept-ible to downturns in traffic than revenues more dependent on the aircraft fee. This is because passenger numbers are affected more directly and immediately when traffic falls than are aircraft movements. Finally, a small number of

Table 4.5 Relative importance of aircraft and passenger charges February 1991: passenger charges as a percentage of total aeronautical revenue from Boeing 747[1,2]

Where passenger charge paid by airline	(%)	Where passenger charge paid by passenger	(%)
		Caracas	87
London Heathrow (peak)	81		
London Gatwick (peak)	79		
		Hong Kong (peak)	76
Toronto	68		
London Heathrow (off-peak)	53		
Dublin	49		
		Singapore	49
Manchester (summer)	44		
Oslo	43		
Vienna	43		
Amsterdam	42		
Paris	40		
		Delhi	34
Stockholm	33		
Frankfurt	30		

Source: Compiled using IATA annual.
Notes: [1] Total aeronautical revenue here includes only aircraft landing fee, passenger charges and terminal or airbridge fee.
[2] Boeing 747 charges based on MTOW of 379 tonnes with 280 passengers.

airports have introduced some kind of peak charge. Manchester, Hong Kong and London's two airports at Heathrow and Gatwick are among these (The rationale for such peak charging is discussed on pp.93–8.)

Whatever their level of aeronautical fees most airports will be under growing pressure to increase their charges so as to generate more revenue. They will need to do this in response to rising costs often brought about by new investments, or to compensate for lost duty-free revenue in Europe, or in order to reduce existing losses. In generating increased revenues from aeronautical sources airport managements will need to resolve two key questions: first, what is the optimum or target balance between aeronautical and non-aeronautical revenues that they should aim for; second, what pricing policy should they adopt in order to generate the required level of aeronautical revenue?

Chapter 5

Alternative pricing strategies

AIRPORTS' LEGAL CONSTRAINTS

It is not generally appreciated that airports or governments do not have an entirely free hand in deciding the structure of airport charges, particularly those for international flights. In considering any new pricing strategies it is important to bear in mind the legal constraints (ICAO 1980). These stem initially from the Chicago Convention, the multilateral agreement signed in 1944 and dealing with many aspects of air transport operation. The Convention, as subsequently amended, has been signed by and is legally binding on more than one hundred states. Several of its articles deal with airports. Article 28 requires contracting states to undertake, as far as is practicable, to provide airports, radio services, meteorological services and other navigation facilities which conform to the procedures and rules which may be recommended or established pursuant to the Convention. Under Article 37 the International Civil Aviation Organization (ICAO) is required to produce international standards and recommended practices in a number of areas including those for airports and air traffic control. The detailed recommendations and standards are incorporated in Annexes to the Convention which may be revised from time to time. Annex 14 deals specifically with airport facilities and design standards.

Having ensured the provision of airport facilities to a worldwide standard, Article 15 in the Convention imposes a charging philosophy for these facilities. Airports in contracting states must be open under uniform conditions to the aircraft of all other contracting states (ICAO 1980). Moreover any charges imposed or permitted to be imposed by a contracting state for airport or navigation facilities should not be different for foreign carriers than those imposed on its national airline/s for similar services. In other words, all carriers should be charged on the same uniform basis. Peak charges for instance may be acceptable under Article 15 if all users in the same period pay the same charge, but not if some peak users pay a lower charge. Any pricing structure which levies different charges on particular airport users would contravene Article 15. The requirement is that all users should be treated equally rather than fairly. This leaves the way open for them to be treated equally unfairly (Philipson 1991). As mentioned earlier, the Council of the ICAO subsequently defined the pricing principles on which airport charges should be based (see pp.71–5). But whatever the basis of the charges, the Chicago Convention required them to be non-discriminatory as between users.

In many countries and certainly in the major aviation powers, the Chicago Convention has been given the force of law by being incorporated into their domestic legislation or regulations. In the United Kingdom this has been done through a succession of Acts of Parliament which have given the Secretary of State for Transport statutory powers to make regulations or orders giving effect to the provisions of the Chicago Convention. The most recent Act to do this was the Civil Aviation Act 1982, and in particular Section 60 of that Act. The Secretary of State is empowered to make the appropriate provisions through the Air Navigation Order (HMSO 1988). The Order lays down the various rules and regulations governing the operation of aircraft, airports and air traffic control facilities in the United Kingdom. It embodies many of the principles and recommendations of the Chicago Convention. Thus Section 78 stipulates that airports for public use are licensed by the Civil Aviation Authority (CAA) on condition that they shall at all times when available for the take-off or landing of aircraft be so available to all persons on equal terms and conditions (HMSO 1988). In this way, the provisions of the Chicago Convention have been given effect in British law and are binding on the British government. The same is true in many other countries.

There may in addition be other specific laws or government regulations in particular countries limiting airports' pricing freedom. These controls may be of a general nature requiring airports to seek government approval before increasing or changing their charging structure. Or there may be a general requirement that all charges at all airports or at all major airports in a country should be uniform, thereby preventing any individual airport from deviating from the general structure of charges. Alternatively the controls may be very specific and detailed, as in the case of the London airports or of Manchester airport. Following the decision to privatize the British Airports Authority (BAA) in 1986, the UK Department of Transport imposed an annual limit to increases in its airport charges. They could only increase by an amount equal to 1 per cent less than the rate of inflation. Manchester airport was also constrained in a similar way by the CAA (see pp.30–1). These limits are reviewed and adjusted every five years by the Monopolies and Mergers Commission and the CAA. They were last revised in 1991.

Finally, some bilateral air services agreements between states may also in practice impose limitations on airport authorities' freedom of action. A good example is the 1977 bilateral between the United States and the United Kingdom (HMSO 1977). Under Article 8 (2) each state agreed to use its best efforts to ensure that the other country's airlines have the widest possible choice of ground-handling arrangements at their airports including the ability to do their own ground handling. On the question of airport charges Article 10 of the bilateral is very specific. The two contracting parties are enjoined to use their best efforts to ensure that user charges imposed or permitted to be imposed by its competent charging authorities . . . are just and reasonable (HMSO 1977). To be just and reasonable they must be equitably apportioned among categories of users (ibid.), and they must not be higher for the foreign airlines than for a state's own carriers (this is similar to Article 15 of the Chicago Convention). They are to be considered just and reasonable if they meet these conditions and reflect but do not exceed the full cost of providing the appropriate facilities and services. Charges may provide for a reasonable rate of return on assets after depreciation, and should be based on sound economic principles and on the generally accepted accounting practices within each country.

A key issue which arises is whether airport authorities, particularly if they are independent of government control or are private companies, are constrained by bilateral air services agreements even though they are not parties to such agreements. The BAA had suggested in the past that it was not bound by the 1977 bilateral with the United States for this very reason. In strict law this is correct, but in allowing for the setting up of BAA Plc in the 1986 Airports Act (section 30(3)), the UK government gave the Secretary of State for Transport additional powers to give directions to any airport in order to discharge international obligations of the United Kindom. Other governments which allow the privatization of airports may need to take similar powers.

It is clear from the above that airports, whether government owned or privatized, may be constrained in their charging policies both by domestic regulations and international air law. At the very least, if their country is a signatory of the Chicago Convention, they will be unable to discriminate between their own national airlines and foreign carriers and they will be required to treat all prospective airport users equally. This is critically important when discussing new and alternative pricing policies.

SHORTCOMINGS OF TRADITIONAL CHARGING STRUCTURES

The public-utility and social-service considerations which underpinned early airport development led, as was outlined earlier, to the implementation of an ill-defined pricing strategy of cost recovery and non-discrimination. In practice this meant average-cost pricing which was tempered in many cases by ability-to-pay considerations.

During the last decade many airports have been asked by their governments to become much more commercial in their approach. This trend will undoubtedly accelerate during the 1990s. As commercial criteria replace or at least modify earlier social-service criteria, the crucial question is whether the traditional structure of airport charges lends itself to this fundamental change in philosophy or should be abandoned altogether.

To answer this one must first consider the degree to which the present airport charges attain the objectives of a commercially orientated pricing policy. These objectives may be summarized as follows:

1 ensure efficiency in allocation and use of airport rescources;
2 generate revenue sufficient to cover costs and, hopefully, to generate profits;
3 provide a sound guide for future investments.

An efficient allocation of airport resources requires that the price paid by any user reflects the costs which they impose on the airport. If prices reflect costs then two things follow. First, no one will purchase a particular airport service unless they value it at least as highly as the cost of producing it. Second, the risk of misinvestment or over-investment in particular airport facilities is reduced or eliminated. This is so because if prices reflect cost then demand levels will represent the true demand for that facility and will thus provide an indication of whether additional units of that facility are needed at that price. Conversely, prices below cost may stimulate extra demand and induce investment in facilities which do not cover their full costs.

A key question, therefore, in assessing the suitability of traditional airport pricing structures in a more commercially oriented environment is the degree to which they reflect costs.

The provision and maintenance of runways, taxiways and aprons is one of the two major costs items in airport operations. Airport charges based on aircraft weight reflect the cost of providing these facilities but do so only indirectly and rather inaccurately. The required strength of a runway, which determines its cost per square metre, is dependent not only on the weight of the aircraft but also on the configuration and number of their undercarriages. These factors also determine wear and tear on the runway and therefore maintenance costs. A large aircraft such as the Boeing 747 has landing gear which produces lower pressure on the runway than some aircraft which are smaller and lighter. Thus the Boeing 747 requires runways of lower strength and imposes lower maintenance costs than some smaller aircraft yet on a weight-scale basis must pay substantially higher landing fees.

Runway length, the other determinant of runway costs, is only indirectly a function of aircraft weight since aircraft of the same weight may need different runway lengths for take-off. The width and layout of taxiways, aprons and ramps is dependent on the size and, in particular, on the span and length of aircraft and on the configuration of their undercarriages. Manoeuvrable aircraft may require less apron pavement than other aircraft of the same weight. Clearly there are parameters other than weight which are significant in determining the costs imposed on an airport by particular aircraft types.

The second major airport cost item is the *airport terminal and its associated facilities*. The costs imposed by particular aircraft on the terminal facilities are less a function of aircraft weight than of the type of service being operated and the terminal facilities required. A Boeing 747 may require a gate lounge and

twin airbridges from the terminal while a fifty-seater aircraft may need no lounge and just stairs to the apron. At London Heathrow it has been estimated that the terminal costs of handling inter-continental passengers may be two to three times as great as the costs for domestic or short-haul passengers. Traditionally, neither aircraft nor passenger charges have fully reflected such cost differences. For instance passengers changing aircraft and using the transit lounge are not charged a passenger fee by most airports yet they may require much additional terminal space.

The disadvantage of the traditional charging system, which aims to recover costs by a combination of average-cost pricing and ability to pay and which fails to charge differentially on the basis of real allocation of costs to different types of users or to different time periods, can be summarized as follows:

1 There is no inducement to aircraft manufacturers and airlines to develop and use aircraft which require short runways or runways of lower load-bearing strength or aircraft which need smaller apron and parking areas. Aircraft with any of these characteristics would impose lower costs on the airport yet they would still be charged on a weight basis and would not themselves benefit from any reduction in airport costs as a result of these improvements.

Since many of the technical improvements which would stabilize airport costs would tend to increase airline operating costs, airlines naturally choose to keep their own costs down rather than to reduce airport costs.

Put another way, when new aircraft types require capital investment by the airports to provide longer runways or to modify terminal buildings, these increased costs are met not by the new users but they are averaged out among all users. There is therefore little inducement for airlines introducing new aircraft or operating techniques to ensure that they minimize the costs they impose on the airport. The present charging structure does little to stop the airlines making more and more demands for new and improved facilities at airports.

2 Airlines will try to schedule as many flights into the peak periods of the days as possible since there is no cost penalty to them for using the costly facilities which are needed to meet these peak period demands. An average-cost charging structure must inevitably, within the constraints of the overall pattern of demand, stimulate the demand for airport facilities at the peak periods and hold back the demand for off-peak facilities. In turn this puts pressure on airports to provide additional runways or terminals as congestion builds up at peak periods. There is no inducement for high-density operators to move flights from peak to off-peak periods or to use fewer, larger aircraft during busy periods.

3 Where an airport is operating at full capacity for certain periods of the day, there is no way under the present charging system to ensure that the airport facilities at peak periods are used by those who value them most highly.

Peak-period runway, terminal and apron slots are allocated by airport scheduling committees to airlines previously using them on the basis of so-called grandfather rights. Ideally when demand for scarce facilities exceeds the supply, a system of differential charging would ensure that those who value the facilities most highly are allowed to use them. But under the current charging system this clearly does not happen except at a handful of airports and then only to a limited extent.

4 The present charging structure fails to discourage general-aviation aircraft or relatively small air-transport aircraft during busy periods. Such aircraft tend to land and take-off at lower speeds than larger jet aircraft and consequently they occupy the approach and runway facilities for a longer period of time. At the same time small aircraft require greater horizontal separation from larger aircraft because of both turbulence problems and their own slower speed. Therefore they reduce the effective runway capacity and add to delays. Yet these smaller aircraft pay much lower landing charges even though they use the airport's landing facilities for a longer time and reduce its effective capacity. A few airports have started to penalize such aircraft by charging them a fee which is disproportionately high for their weight or by having a single runway movement charge for all aircraft irrespective of weight.

5 The principles of average-cost pricing and non-discrimination often bring about a situation where landing and other fees tend to be the same, or very similar, at all the major airports within one country or region. It is unlikely that the costs of handling aircraft and passengers at different airports would be the same or that all airports would be equally efficient or inefficient in their operations. But unless differences in costs and efficiency are reflected in the level of charges, there is no inducement to airline operators to use the lower-cost facilities.

Overall, the failure to relate prices more closely to costs inevitably means that traffic peaks, which are costly to handle and to provide for, gradually build up, while at other times of the day or at other airports the facilities are grossly under-utilized even though the costs of providing them are relatively low.

The present airport charges cannot possibly provide a guide to further investment. First because, as previously noted, the weight-scale landing fees and the passenger service charge do not reflect the runway and terminal costs imposed by different users nor are they differentiated to take account of the variation in costs at different times of the day. Prices are based on an averaging out of costs among all users.

Second, such average-cost charges are particularly ineffective as investment guides because airport landing fees and other charges are deliberately kept low by a policy of maximizing revenue from rents and concessions. Many airports, especially the larger ones with a relatively high income from rents and concessions in the terminal area, cross-subsidize their traffic operations from their commercial revenues. In this way, their landing and other fees may often represent even less than an average cost. This will also be the case at airports which do not try to cover their full costs.

The effect of these shortcomings must be to distort the patterns of demand for airport services and ultimately to distort the pattern of investment. The demand for facilities at certain airports and at peak periods at many airports is artificially high because the airport charges are lower than the costs of providing these facilities. The airport authorities, in an effort to satisfy this demand, become involved in a costly and ever-growing cycle of investments aimed at satisfying projected peak demands or specialized demands from long-haul operators or others requiring new types of facilities. Yet if the costs of runway extensions or terminal improvements were met entirely by the few long-haul flights which require them, then the long-haul operators might reconsider their re-equipment decisions. In this way airport costs would be kept down and investments undertaken only when really justified.

In brief the existing aeronautical charging policies appear to ensure neither an efficient use and allocation of airport resources nor a sound guide to future investment. Do they at least succeed in meeting the third objective of pricing policy, namely the generation of sufficient revenues to cover costs including a margin for profit? They appear to do so given that many airports do produce substantial annual profits (see Chapter 1). However, the position is not clear cut because few airports separate out their aeronautical or traffic-related costs and revenues from their commercial activities. Since in practice most larger airports expect to use commercial revenues to cross-subsidize traffic areas, it is not clear whether aeronautical revenues in themselves generate enough revenue fully to cover all aircraft, passenger and traffic-related costs.

Finally one needs to consider the question of equity. The traditional charging philosophies were based on the concept of users paying their 'full and fair' share of costs. In practice this has meant an attempt to average out costs so that all users pay on the same basis for using airport facilities. This implies taking all the costs which an airport expects to incur in a year and dividing them equally between the expected number of users, namely the total tonnage of aircraft using the runways and the total number of passengers processed through the terminal. The principle is to calculate for each user an equal share of a large total cost. Some airports have modified this by charging more for larger aircraft or for passengers on certain types of flights. But essentially the charges are assumed to be 'fair' because they are equal or at least similar for all users. But, as one has seen earlier, if different users impose very different costs then the system of charges is far from fair. Certain low-cost users are being charged much more than the costs they impose in order to cross-subsidize others, some of whom may in any case be able to pay their own higher costs.

TOWARDS COST-RELATED PRICING

The preceding analysis pushes one inevitably towards cost-related pricing. Economists have long argued that the pricing policy which was most likely to lead to an efficient allocation of resources would be one where the price of a good or service was set equal to the marginal cost of providing that good or service. The marginal cost is the cost that would be incurred in producing an additional unit of output. Alternatively it can be thought of as the cost that would be saved if that additional unit were not produced.

In the case of airports, the economic rationale for marginal-cost pricing is that it leads to an efficient allocation of resources between airport users. It does this because, if the price of an airport facility or service is set at its marginal cost, then it will only be used by those potential users who value it at least as much as the cost of producing it. Those who value the service less than the cost of producing it will be inhibited from using it. If marginal-cost pricing prevails, resources will be allocated by airport managers to providing additional facilities or services in the knowledge that potential users are prepared to pay the marginal or additional costs of the extra units provided.

Conversely, if airport charges are set below marginal cost some users will demand services for which they would not be prepared to pay the marginal cost. Responding to such demand, airports may invest resources in providing additional services or facilities for users not prepared to cover the additional costs that such provision would create. If on the other hand charges were raised to marginal cost, then demand would fall off and some resources would be released for use elsewhere. If alternatively charges for a facility were to be set above marginal cost then demand would be choked off and no additional resources would be invested in that facility even though users would be prepared fully to cover the additional costs they would impose to meet an increase in demand. In both situations there is a loss of efficiency in the allocation of resources.

Marginal-cost pricing is concerned with current and future costs not with past costs. The original historical cost of a terminal or runway is a sunk cost which remains unaffected by an additional user. So it has no part to play in marginal-cost pricing.

A distinction has to be made however between short-run and long-run marginal costs. Short-run marginal costs include only those that can be varied in the short term to meet changes in demand such as any additional costs of lighting, cleaning or extra staff. In a wider sense, they may also include external marginal costs, such as congestion and delay costs imposed by aircraft users on other airport users or noise costs imposed on the surrounding community. Investment costs in additional facilities are excluded since new projects cannot be undertaken in the short term. Long-run marginal costs are those costs, including investment costs, that can be varied over time to satisfy additional demand. The investment costs are not the historical capital cost of existing facilities but the future costs of the new facilities needed to meet this additional or marginal demand.

Setting airport charges on the basis of long-run marginal cost (LRMC) should be an important input in the management of an airport's investment programme. If prices paid by current users reflect the costs of adding the extra capacity needed to meet any projected demand, airport managers can gauge from the current demand generated at those prices whether users are prepared to meet the costs of any new facilities. It is for this reason that LRMC pricing has long been advocated for capital-intensive industries traditionally within the public sector such as electricity supply. LRMC pricing is calculated by estimating the future capital and operating costs of a new invesment and then selecting a set of charges that would give a present value of zero for the investment after discounting at the prevailing discount rate.

In industries, however, where investments are very large and lumpy, such as airports, pure LRMC pricing poses difficulties. This is because an additional runway for a single-runway airport is not truly marginal since it doubles the airport's capacity at a stroke. The same might be true of a new terminal. Thus various different sets of charges might be used to produce a present value of zero. The fact that airports produce a multiplicity of services – runway slots, taxiways, parking stands, airbridges, passenger lounges, etc. – further complicates LRMC pricing. Finally, there is the problem that demand for airport facilities varies by time of day, week or season thus creating further pricing problems.

Thus in adopting the principle of cost-related pricing, airports are forced to use a combination of short-run and long-run costs as the basis for such pricing.

THE APPLICATION OF COST-BASED PRICING

Identifying marginal costs

In order to apply cost-related pricing one needs to identify the components of marginal cost that are to be used as the basis of pricing.

At an airport with a single runway and one terminal operating well below capacity with traffic evenly spread throughout the day, the marginal cost of handling additional flights or passengers is close to zero. An extra passenger flight will really have little cost impact beyond some very marginal wear and tear on the runway and possibly some increase in terminal cleaning costs. Further flights can be handled with again little increase in operating costs especially if evenly spread through the day. Aircraft or passenger charges can be based on these short-run marginal costs and will inevitably be low. These low charges will encourage further use of the airport. This is as it should be. Since the facility is there anyone prepared to pay their marginal costs should have access to it. In this way one maximizes the potential use of the airport. This is also why the capital costs invested in the runway and terminal are

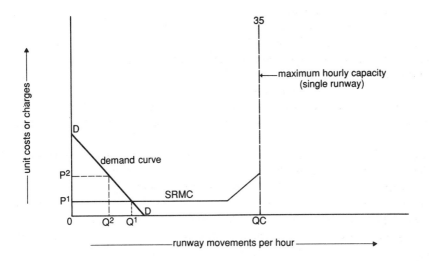

Figure 5.1 Short-run marginal-cost price pricing with no peak congestion

ignored in short-run marginal cost (SRMC) pricing. These facilities and the resources invested in them cannot in the short term be converted to alternative uses. Once built the more people who use the facilities, after covering their marginal costs, the greater is the consumer benefit derived from the original investment. Charging marginal users for the sunken investment costs would merely reduce demand and thereby consumer benefit.

As traffic at the airport grows peak periods will begin to build up as traffic becomes more concentrated and dense at certain times of the day. Airport operating costs during these peak periods may rise as more staff are needed for security, cleaning, information desks and so on. Such staff will be under-utilized in the off-peak hours. Lighting and air-conditioning or heating costs may also rise. Thus the SRMC of handling peak traffic begins to rise above the SRMC of off-peak traffic. If and when the differential between peak and off-peak operating costs becomes substantial then one may introduce separate charges for the two periods but both based on short-run marginal cost.

In time, peak demand will grow to the point where additional capacity is required. This may be in terms of an additional runway, new parking stands, an expansion of an existing terminal or an entirely new terminal. The marginal cost of handling additional peak traffic now becomes very high. Can such new investments be justified? If peak users are charged a fee which covers both their operating costs and the costs of the additional facility required, one will have a clear indication from the resultant levels of demand whether the facility is required. If peak demand continues to exceed available capacity at these higher LRMC prices then further investment is clearly justified.

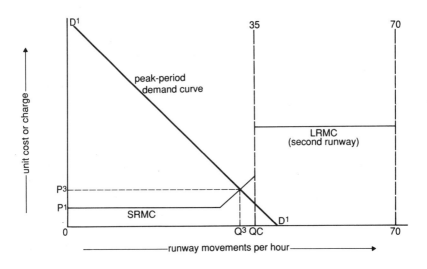

Figure 5.2 Short-run marginal-cost pricing in peak period

These three stages of marginal-cost pricing can also be shown diagrammatically. (The analysis is in terms of runways but it applies equally to any major airport infrastructure.) The first stage is that of airports with plenty of runway capacity at all times of the day (Figure 5.1). The runway charge per air-transport movement on the runway is shown on the vertical scale and the average number of movements per hour is shown on the horizontal scale. The point QC represents the maximum of thirty-five movements per hour at the existing capacity. In order to handle more than QC movements one would need to build a second runway. This is not necessary at this stage. Demand shown by the diagonal line (D–D) is well within capacity. The SRMC is very low, and if one charged on this basis traffic would be Q^1. If one tried to recoup all costs including sunken capital costs the charges based on some kind of average total cost would be much higher, say at P^2. The effect of this would be to cut traffic to Q^2. The runway would become even further under-utilized and average-cost charges the following year might have to go up further. But since the runway has been built it would be better to have it used as much as possible since in the short run it has no alternative use. A SRMC charging structure would maximize usage and consumer benefit.

The second stage is when traffic builds up to such a level in one or more peak hours that marginal costs begin to rise (Figure 5.2). This may be because extra marshalling staff and ground equipment are needed for the peak hours but will not be used in the rest of day. The SRMC for the peak hour/s is higher than for the off-peak and therefore charges during the peak period will be set at P^3. Demand would then be close to full capacity levels at Q^3. Off-peak charges will remain at P^1.

As traffic congestion builds up at peak periods there may also be an increase in congestion costs (that is in delays imposed on other aircraft using the airport at peak times as well as other airport users) and in external costs as well through increased noise and environmental pollution. Some economists would argue that short-run marginal cost pricing at peak periods should reflect both the airport's internal costs and these external costs. Such an approach would be likely significantly to increase peak charges and further dampen demand. Calculating such external costs, however, does pose serious methodological problems.

Year by year traffic will grow. In other words the peak demand curve D^1–D^1 will shift bodily to the left to D^2–D^2 in Figure 5.3. When peak demand is at or near the single runway's capacity the peak users should be charged on the basis of the long-run marginal cost of building and operating the second runway which would be needed to increase runway capacity to seventy movements per hour in order to satisfy that demand. Provided a new runway can be built this unit charge should be at P^4 at least until the second runway is completed. Peak demand will at first be cut back along the D^2–D^2 demand curve because of the increase in charges. If the charge is P^4 peak demand will be Q^4. Over time demand builds up and the demand curve moves bodily to the right to D^3–D^3. If, at the P^4 price, demand eventually exceeds QC or thirty-five runway movements an hour, which is the capacity of the single runway, then this is a clear indication that a second runway is needed. But demand is less at this price level than it would be if all peak users were charged at P^5 which is the short-run marginal cost at peak periods. (see p.98 below for further reference to Figure 5.3.).

Currently it is the role of the airport scheduling committees to allocate the available runway slots on the basis of agreed guidelines. In this way effective demand is cut back to QC. But if peak-hour users are prepared to pay the LRMC and demand continues to exceed single runway capacity, then this is a clear indication that an additional runway should be built.

How does one identify the 'marginal' user at the peak who is to be charged the higher LRMC? It would be invidious if not impossible to pick an individual user. The need for extra capacity arises because at certain peak periods demand as a whole already exceeds supply or is expected to in the near future. To avoid undue complexity all these peak-period users are charged the LRMC. Extra traffic during peak hours can only be met by constructing a new runway, a terminal or parking stands depending on the nature of the capacity constraint. Conversely, if one or more peak-period flights were cancelled or if there were no future growth in traffic one could escape any additional investment. Since one cannot differentiate between individual peak users or flights they must all be charged the LRMC. This is done by calculating the capital cost of the new facility and converting it to an annual cost by discounting it to present-day values at the appropriate discount rate. This would produce a figure to be recovered each year from those users identified as being in the peak period;

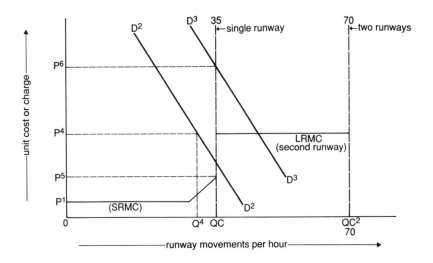

Figure 5.3 Short-run marginal-cost pricing when peak demand exceeds run-way capacity

this figure would be averaged out among them, and to it should be added any operating costs associated with the new facility.

The process of establishing long-run marginal costs starts by distinguishing that element of traffic which is responsible for the cost of providing additional capacity such as terminal and apron capacity, from that element which can continue to be accommodated within existing capacity. Thus before building the fourth terminal at Heathrow the then British Airports Authority had to forecast the hours at which passenger throughput would exceed current capacity – excluding the fourth terminal. Traffic at these peak hours could then be identified as that contributing to the need for additional capacity. The next step of the process was the cost analysis. The capital costs of the terminal were derived from cost plans and contract information. These could then be converted to an annual charge by amortizing them at an appropriate discount rate. Projections of operating costs for the fourth terminal were obtained from the specialist staff responsible for running and maintaining terminals, and with the aid of current and budget cost data for the operation of existing facilities.

BAA Plc, which as the British Airport Authority pioneered marginal cost pricing for airports, identified four categories of costs to be used for long-run marginal-cost calculations (Toms 1991):

1 *Capacity Costs* are incurred in the provision of the terminal facilities themselves. They include construction costs plus rates (property taxes) and a proportion of maintenance costs. Since these costs are not necessary for

the accommodation of the growth in off-peak traffic which can be fitted within existing terminals, they are attributed to peak traffic only.

2 The same applies to *Fixed Costs* which are costs incurred once the new facilities are brought into use; thereafter they do not vary. Examples include terminal management staff, and a proportion of cleaning costs.

3 *Throughput Costs* arise as a result of traffic passing through the terminal. They include a proportion of staff cleaning and maintenance costs, and are allocated to both peak and off-peak traffic.

4 Finally *Time Costs* relate to the length of time during which the terminal is operational – for instance lighting costs during night hours and shiftworking costs. These are again divided between peak and off-peak traffic.

(Toms 1991)

After making detailed adjustments the unit passenger charges could then be calculated by dividing the costs allocated to peak and off-peak periods to the Terminal Four traffic projected for each period.

The resulting charges would then be applied to all traffic at the airport, since traffic remaining in the existing terminals is as equally responsible for the need for additions to capacity as that traffic which is physically accommodated in the new terminal.

The prices which result from such an analysis represent the stable floor price below which investment in new terminals would not be justified financially. They assume stability in the level and structure of charges over the life of the investment, and in practice they may be subject to some variation depending upon the build-up of traffic.

(Toms 1991)

The same costing approach could be adopted for other discrete airport facilities such as the runway or the aircraft parking stands, where these can be expanded to meet growth in demand.

Covering total costs

Airports, particularly if given the freedom to operate on a fully commercial basis, will expect to at least cover their full costs including depreciation and interest charges. They may even go further and expect to produce a return on investment commensurate with that in other, similar industries. But by its very nature marginal-cost pricing will not necessarily produce sufficient revenue to do this.

Where charges are based on SRMC they will be relatively low and will in any case not cover the capital or the depreciation costs of the facilities already built unless demand has built up to a high level. If the long-run marginal cost is falling over time then here too charges based on LRMC will fail to recoup total costs since they will be below average long-run costs. Only if long-run marginal costs are rising and above average costs will revenue normally exceed total current costs. But this will only be so for those facilities being charged for on this basis.

The above cost analysis could be carried out separately for discrete elements of an airport's infrastructure such as runways, taxiways, aircraft parking stands, airbridges, gate lounges, baggage-handling areas or the terminal as a whole. In practice, it is likely that differential peak and off-peak charges will only be applied to three or four of these facilities. One is most likely to find marked peak and off-peak differentials in the following charges:

1 aircraft landing fees (for runway use)
2 aircraft parking fees (if there is a shortage of stands at certain times)
3 passenger charges (for terminal facilities)
4 airbridges charges (if there is a shortage of airbridges).

If more than one of these facilities has higher peak-period charges, then it may well be the case that the timing of the peak periods are different. For instance the peak runway period may not coincide exactly with the peak demand for terminal space.

Where an airport has two or more terminals with discrete users, for instance a terminal exclusively for domestic passengers or one for general aviation, then passenger charges may vary by terminal. This will be so if one terminal has spare capacity and the other does not and if this spare capacity cannot be used for the type of traffic being handled by the other congested terminal or if the unit costs of adding to capacity are different (for instance where domestic capacity is less expensive per passenger than international).

One would also expect charges to vary between airports in the same country or region. They should be very low at airports with plenty of spare capacity even at peak periods and much higher where one or more of the key facilities are congested.

Strict application of marginal-cost pricing will lead to accounting losses at many airports, even though there may be improved efficiency in resource allocation. This is clearly unacceptable if airports are to be commercially oriented. Therefore, one needs to find ways of recouping total accounting costs without distorting too much the allocative efficiency of marginal-cost pricing.

The pricing policy which can be adopted to do this is that called 'Ramsey pricing' after the English economist who developed it (Ramsey 1928). This suggests that where marginal-cost pricing is unable to generate revenues to cover some required revenue target, then it is economically most efficient to raise the extra revenue required from different users in inverse relation to their elasticity of demand for airport services, in other words by charging 'on the basis of ability to pay'. Such a policy will have the least impact on the pattern of demand and output which would have prevailed under pure marginal-cost pricing. In this way the allocative efficiency is least distorted.

In combining marginal-cost pricing and the concept of 'ability to pay', airport authorities have three potential sources of revenue to close the gap between their income from marginal-cost charges and their targeted total revenue.

First, they can use the revenues generated from their commercial or non-aeronautical activities, where these are over and above the fully allocated costs of providing for such activities.

Second, they can charge aeronautical users on the basis of their ability to pay. When demand is very price sensitive and there is ample capacity the charges will be no more than the low SRMC. When and where demand is inelastic to price levels then charges could be raised above both short-run and long-run marginal cost in order to generate additional revenues to cover an airport's total accounting costs.

PEAK CHARGING IN PRACTICE

The BAA Plc approach

The British Airports Authority pioneered the application of cost-based pricing in the early 1970s (Little and McLeod 1972). Starting at that time from a fairly simple peak-charging structure it has progressively developed more complex and sophisticated charges for its London airports. The aim has been to move towards long-run marginal cost pricing using the arguments and the costing methodology outlined about (see pp.86–91).

BAA Plc, as it now is, has estimated the passenger-related costs for peak-period traffic and for total traffic at both London Heathrow and London Gatwick airports, where terminal capacity is inadequate at certain times to meet the forecast growth in demand. These passenger costs are differentiated between traffic categories – domestic, European, North American and other, each of which has different seasonal and daily peaks – and between arriving and departing passengers. If one fully adopted the logic of cost-related pricing there should be different passenger charges for each of these categories of passengers. In practice, the cost differences between the three types of international passengers are too small to justify differential charges. Thus, for reasons of simplicity, BAA Plc has a domestic and an international charge on departing passengers only (see Table 5.1). At London Heathrow in 1991–2 charges were the same for passengers departing in off-peak times but the international charge was almost double the domestic charge at peak periods reflecting the higher costs of handling international traffic. The peak to off-peak differential for both groups was very marked. Domestic passengers were charged nearly four times as much in the peak as in the off-peak and international passengers nearly seven times as much. The peak periods differed between domestic and international traffic and for the former there was a secondary winter peak (November to March) when charges were lower than the full summer peak. The justification for charging structures which differentiate between peak and off-peak is that they reflect the fact that it is

Table 5.1 Passenger charges at London Heathrow April 1991–March 1992

	Charge payable per terminal departing passenger[1]	
	Domestic (£)	International (£)
Peak periods[2]		
1 April to 31 October	8.41	15.32
1 November to 31 March	5.51	–
Off-peak periods[3]	2.28	2.28

Source: BAA 1991b
Notes:
[1] A rebate of 30p per passenger applies to flights departing from stands requiring the coaching of passengers to aircraft or from stands which are pier served but do not have an air jetty.
[2] Peak periods are defined as:
Domestic: 0700–0829 GMT and 1830–1959 GMT, 1 April to 31 October (Monday to Friday only) and 0800–0929 GMT and 1930–2059 GMT, 1 November to 31 March (Monday to Friday only);
International: 0900–1529 GMT, 1 April to 31 October.
[3] Off-peak: all other times

the peak demand which causes the requirement to build new terminals. The domestic to international differential reflects the higher costs of handling the international passengers. There was also a £0.30 rebate per passenger on aircraft not using a pier and requiring buses or using a pier without an air jetty. This was supposed to reflect the costs incurred by airlines in coaching their passengers between the terminals and their aircraft.

When it comes to aircraft landing fees, Heathrow and Gatwick airports have abandoned the weight-related charge in peak periods and moved to a fixed runway movement or occupancy charge unrelated to aircraft size or weight (see Table 5.2). As with the passenger charge there was, in 1991–2, a higher landing fee at peak periods than in the off-peak to reflect the higher marginal cost of using scarce runway resources at peak periods. Though the peak landing fee for aircraft of 16 to 50 tonnes was almost two-and-a-half times the off-peak fee, the peak-to-off-peak differential was much less marked for the landing charge than for the passenger charge. It should be noted that the peak times for runway demand and for terminal use in Tables 5.1 and 5.2 do not correspond. Quieter aircraft paid slightly lower landing fees while the noisiest aircraft not meeting ICAO *Annex 16* (Chapter 2) noise levels (ICAO 1971) were surcharged 25 per cent. There was no distinction between domestic and international flights since they use the same runways and impose the same costs. The runway pricing philosophy adopted was not based on long-run marginal costing as described in the previous section since additional runways cannot be built, either at Heathrow or Gatwick. It was more akin to a rationing approach as outlined on pp.98–9 below.

Table 5.2 Charge on landing at London Heathrow April 1991–March 1992

| | Peak[1] | | Off-Peak | |
	Standard[2] (£)	Rebated[3] (£)	Standard[2] (£)	Rebated[3] (£)
Aircraft up to 16 tonnes	–	414.90	–	50
Aircraft 16 to 50 tonnes	461	414.90	192.50	173.25
Aircraft over 50 tonnes	461	414.90	335.40	301.86

Source: BAA 1991b.
Notes:
[1] Peak period: 0700–0959 GMT and 1700–1859 GMT, 1 April to 31 October.
[2] There will be a surcharge of 25 per cent on the standard charge for jet aircraft not meeting ICAO *Annex 16* (Chapter 2) (ICAO 1971).
[3] Rebated charges apply to ICAO *Annex* 16 Chapter 3 and non-jet aircraft, and to all aircraft under 16 MT.

Table 5.3 Aircraft parking charges[1] at London Heathrow April 1991–March 1992

Per quarter hour or part thereof	£3.90 plus 5p per tonne
Peak parking period	Each minute counts as 3 minutes at a stand served by a pier between 0700 to 1229 GMT 1 April to 31 October.

Source: BAA 1991b.
Note: [1]Based on weight of aircraft in tonnes and charged per quarter hour.

In trying to relate the costs of providing aircraft parking stands more closely to the parking charges, both Heathrow (see Table 5.3) and Gatwick have abandoned the traditional two to six-hour free-parking period. The argument is that, if aircraft stands are in short supply, airlines should be encouraged through the pricing mechanism to vacate them quickly so that another airline may use them. But while aircraft pay for parking in quarter-hour units from the moment they occupy a stand, the fee is still based on aircraft weight. This is only indirectly cost related. It would be better to charge on the basis of the area occupied, that is the aircraft's length times its wing span. On the other hand, for parking stands served by a pier the parking charge in 1991–2 was trebled during periods of peak demand. This was to reflect the long-run cost of building new parking stands adjacent to piers.

At London's Heathrow airport the adoption of LRMC pricing principles has created a complex charging structure with the three fee elements, the aircraft landing fee, the passenger charge and the parking charge, each having its own peak and off-peak periods with different charges for each. At Gatwick the charging structure in 1991–2 was similar to Heathrow's but the level of charges was somewhat lower and the peak periods differed. At the BAA's third London airport, Stansted, the charges were much lower and the peak to off-

Table 5.4 Airport charges[1] at London-Heathrow for Airbus A320[2] on international flight by time of day

Month/time of landing[3] in 1990	Aircraft landing charge (£)	Passenger charge (£)	Aircraft parking charge (£)	Total (£)
April-October 0730 hrs	Peak 414.90	Off-peak 241.68	Peak 57.90	714.48
April-October 0830 hrs	Peak 414.90	Peak 1,623.92	Peak 57.90	2,096.72
April-October 1030 hrs	Off-peak 301.86	Peak 1,623.92	Peak 57.90	1,983.68
April-October 1300 hrs	Off-peak 301.86	Peak 1,623.92	Peak 19.30	1,945.08
April-October 1600 hrs	Off-peak 301.86	Off-peak 241.68	Off-peak 19.30	562.84
November-March any time	Off-peak 301.86	Off-peak 241.68	Off-peak 19.30	562.84

Notes:
[1] These charges exclude a navigation services charge of £133 paid to the Civil Aviation Authority.
[2] A320 with maximum take-off weight of 73.5 tonnes and 70 per cent seat factor (i.e. 106 passengers) on departure.
[3] Departure assumed fifty-five minutes after landing.

peak differentials were less marked reflecting the fact that both terminal and runway capacity were more adequate even at peak periods.

The complexity of Heathrow's charging structure can be gauged from looking at the charges that an Airbus A320 aircraft on an international service would have paid in 1991-2 for a single landing and departure at different times of the day and of the year (Table 5.4). Because the designated peak times for the passenger, landing and parking charges are all different, the total aeronautical fees to be paid by the airline change hour by hour during the day from a maximum figure of £2,097 if all charges are at their peak level to a low of £563 in off-peak periods. For the five winter months when there are no peak charges the A320 would pay £563 irrespective of the time of landing. Charges at all times would be slightly lower and further complicated if the A320 were parked on a stand providing a £0.30 per passenger rebate. In peak hours using such a stand would also avoid the peak parking charge. The ratio of the highest to lowest charge in Table 5.4 is 3.7:1.0. The charges for domestic flights would be significantly lower and more complex with variations between summer peak, winter peak and off-peak.

It has been suggested earlier (see pp.80–4) that a commercially oriented pricing policy should ensure efficiency in the allocation of resources, should generate sufficient revenue to cover its costs and should provide a guide to investment. To what extent has the BAA's peak pricing strategy achieved this?

It is difficult to judge whether it has led to greater efficiency in the use of resources without more detailed inside information. However, there is some evidence to suggest that the peak charges have induced a few airlines to reschedule their flights slightly earlier or later to reduce their total airport charges (Doganis, Dennis and Graham 1990). On the question of cost recovery, the BAA themselves have argued over the years that aeronautical charges do not cover the full current costs associated with the aeronautical or traffic activities at Heathrow and Gatwick (see Table 3.3, p.60). Since, as we have seen earlier, long-run marginal costs are in most cases likely to be below average accounting costs, accounting losses are inevitable if one moves towards long-run marginal cost pricing (see pp.91–2). At London's airports such losses have been covered by surpluses generated from commercial activities.

But has this pricing policy provided a real guide for future investments? It could be argued that the complexity of charges and the very low off-peak charges have confused the issue. Airlines paying the high charges for peak-period flights in the summer months know that they will pay less than a third of these charges per landing and departure during the five months November to March. Averaging these out over the year, they end up paying less at London's airports than at other European airports (see Table 4.4, p.76). Thus there is little inducement for them to curtail demand for runways or terminal space at peak periods. Nor is peak-period passenger demand affected since the peak passenger charges are not passed on to the peak passengers but are averaged out among all passengers. BAA Plc would counter this argument by saying that if an airline had switched a daily international Airbus A320 flight at Heathrow in 1991 from a departure time of 0905 hours to 0855 it would have saved a total of £290,000 or about US$0.05 million during the April to October season. If it had switched a Boeing 747 aircraft with an average 70 per cent passenger load the saving would have been around £766,000 or US$1.3 million. BAA Plc economists would argue that airlines' failure to shift their flight timings marginally to make such savings coupled with the fact that demand for runway slots at peak periods exceeds the slots available provides a clear indication of the value airlines place on obtaining additional capacity at peak periods.

Peak charges at other airports

A small number of airports around the world have also introduced peak charges. Such charges, however, have not been based on any marginal-cost pricing philosophy as is the case with London airports. Rather the peak charges seem to be based on ability to pay. Demand at peak periods is less responsive to increases in airport charges than off-peak demand. While higher peak charges are justified on the grounds that peak traffic is more expensive to handle than off-peak, there is no serious attempt to defend the peak charges through any detailed costings. On the contrary, the increase in total airport charges arising from the peak surcharge, at airports where is it is imposed, is rather small. It is unlikely fully to reflect the cost differential between peak and off-peak traffic. Thus at Manchester early in 1990 a Boeing 747 with 280 passengers would have paid only about 17 per cent more in the peak summer period than in the off-peak winter season. At Hong Kong the increase would have been only 1.3 per cent (see Table 4.4 p.76).

A number of UK regional airports impose seasonal peak charges by increasing the passenger charge for the summer months irrespective of time of day. This is done by Manchester, Luton and East Midlands airports. Outside the UK the trend is toward imposing a peak surcharge on the aircraft landing fee rather than on the passenger fee. Both Athens and Hong Kong have aircraft-related peak charges. Such landing peak charges are likely to be imposed during certain times of the day rather than just on a seasonal basis. Thus at Athens there is a 25 per cent surcharge on the basic landing fee for aircraft landing between 1100 and 1700 hours from June to September. Interestingly in 1990-1 Frankfurt, Toronto and Sydney airports all introduced minimum landing fees at peak periods to discourage small general-aviation aircraft. New York had done this earlier.

A RATIONING STRATEGY

It may well be that some of the non-BAA airports that have introduced peak surcharges are using them as the way of rationing the limited airport facilities when demand for them exceeds supply. The use of airport charges to ration scarce facilities might be a sensible pricing strategy, especially in situations of excess demand where new facilities just cannot be provided because of the absence of suitable land or space or because of government controls. This is most likely to occur where an airport is in or near a built-up area or when there are physical barriers to expansion. When capacity cannot be extended and demand exceeds the available capacity then one might introduce progressively higher peak charges to reduce demand to the level of capacity available. This is a form of rationing by price. It can be justified on the grounds that it should ensure that those who most value the facility are the ones given access to it.

In congested airports the application of this principle means having a unique runway charge irrespective of the size of aircraft. A very small business aircraft has to pay at least as much as a jumbo Boeing 747 would pay for using a congested runway at peak times. The small aircraft denies a landing to the larger one and must pay a charge equivalent to the benefit the latter would have gained from using the runway. This is known as the 'opportunity cost'. In the case analysed earlier in Figures 5.1 to 5.3, the runway charge to clear the market and reduce demand at peak periods to the runway's capacity of thirty-five movements an hour when demand is D^3–D^3 would be P^6 (see Figure 5.3, p.90). This would be the market-clearing price but it is only cost based in the sense that it relates to opportunity cost.

Because most congested airports are in a monopolistic or quasi-monopolistic situation peak-period demand is likely to be relatively inelastic to price changes. Therefore, the market-clearing prices that would need to be charged would be very high. Such airport charges are likely to be well above the average accounting cost of providing the airport facilities concerned, with the result that airports adopting a rationing strategy may well generate large and excess profits. The airports would be generating scarcity rents as distinct from monopoly rents. Very high peak charges may be counterbalanced by very low off-peak charges but profits are still likely to be excessive at many airports where peak demand is high. Normal profits may be achieved by having zero or negative off-peak charges. In the latter case airlines might receive payments for landing in periods of low demand.

While this might be close to a profit-maximizing strategy, huge airport profits are unlikely to be acceptable either to the public or to the relevent governments especially if they are not re-invested in enlarged airport facilities. Another disadvantage is that allocating slots purely on the basis of ability to pay might well squeeze out services which are considered socially or politically desirable such as air services to distant or isolated communities. Moreover, such a pricing strategy might well violate Article 15 of the Chicago Convention (ICAO 1980) which requires that airports should be open to all on an equal basis at least as far as international flights are concerned. In practice, in most countries governments can still effectively control airport charges or regulations to prevent airport authorities from generating excessive profits. Therefore a true rationing strategy, with the very high landing charges this would require, is unlikely to be adopted.

GRANDFATHER RIGHTS OR SLOT AUCTIONS

If, as is likely to be the case for the vast majority of airports, simply rationing by price is unacceptable, how should scarce airport facilities be allocated to potential users when demand exceeds supply?

Air traffic world-wide is expected to grow during the 1990s at an average rate of about 6 per cent per annum despite the dramatic downturn in 1990–1 as a result of the Gulf crisis. As a result and in the absence of new airport projects, there will be growing pressure on runway and, to a lesser extent, terminal capacity at many airports around the world. At most congested airports extra terminals can be built relatively easily and quickly on existing airport land. For runways this is more difficult because of inadequate land at existing airports or because noise constraints prevent building. Solutions must be longer-term and slower especially if requiring new sites. Therefore runway shortages, as were discussed earlier (see pp.33–40), will become increasingly acute at many European and several United States and Asian airports.

Two related problems will arise. First, if demand for runway or terminal use exceeds supply how does one allocate or ration it? Second, in an increasingly liberalized/deregulated environment how does one ensure that the benefits of greater airline competition are not undermined by monopolistic or oligopolistic control of runway slots by one or two airlines at each of the major national airports?

There are three possible approaches to the problem of allocating scarce runway resources. One could continue to rely as at present on what is essentially airline self-regulation. One could hand over the problem to governments or some independent regulatory authority. Or, finally, one might try to introduce an economic approach based on use of the pricing mechanism.

Airline self-regulation

Airline self-regulation is the traditional and widespread approach used outside the United States to allocate runway and terminal slots (that is arrival or departures times) between airlines. This involves two stages: overall and world-wide schedule co-ordination at twice-yearly IATA meetings, and local co-ordination at individual airports usually through their own scheduling committees.

At the twice-yearly IATA timetable co-ordination meetings, airlines from all over the world come together to discuss initial assignment of schedules submitted by airlines in advance. Where there is a conflict between airlines, priorities are given to historical precedence (that is, you can keep a slot previously allocated if you have operated it) and to the financial impact of not obtaining a contested slot (that is, the airline which has most to lose in economic terms is given preference over another). These meetings are particularly useful in ensuring the availability of inter-linked slot times at several airports which are essential for multi-stop services.

When runway congestion begins to build up at airports outside the United States, slots are normally allocated through the airport scheduling committees. All airlines operating to an airport are normally members of its scheduling committee. The base airline, or if there are several the largest base airline, provides the administrative support and the committee's chairman. In some countries such as Germany, there may be a government-appointed co-ordinator who administers and controls the workings of the committee. This is to ensure impartiality. The committees follow agreed IATA procedures. Airlines apply to the committee twice yearly for runway and terminal slots for their winter and summer schedules. The committee or co-ordinator allocates the slots on the basis of the following rules:

1 airlines are entitled to keep slots granted to them in the previous corresponding summer or winter season provided they have used them; these are the so-called 'grandfather rights';
2 services of longer duration get preference over those that are of shorter duration (i,e, a year-round service would have priority over a summer-only service);

3 services operated on more days of the week have priority; for instance a daily service at a particular time would have priority over a service offered at the same time but operated only five days a week.

Once the airport scheduling committee has allocated slots on the basis of these priorities, airlines can exchange slots among themselves provided they have broadly similar operating characteristics. An individual airline can also change the use of its own slots, for instance, by switching a slot from a domestic to an international service or even from scheduled to charter. At London's Heathrow and Gatwick airports it is estimated that up to 10 per cent of slots change hands every year as a result of decisions of the scheduling committee and subsequent exchanges between airlines.

The advantages of the current system based on airport scheduling committees can be summarized as follows:

1 The system works and is internationally integrated. It is virtually world-wide and is accepted by the vast majority of airlines.
2 It is not disruptive. There are no sudden and large changes from year to year.
3 Airlines' past investments in developing new routes and schedules are rewarded with grandfather rights.
4 Where slots are available new entrants can obtain them at no cost.
5 Some market flexibility is provided through 'one for one' trading or swopping of slots.

While the scheduling-committee system has worked well for many years and has certain advantages, there is little doubt that such a system becomes increasingly anti-competitive as slots at peak periods are used up. It entrenches existing carriers who have grandfather rights to a large proportion of the slots at a particular airport. Where, as in much of Europe, the national-flag carrier controls 30 to 50 per cent of the total slots at the major airport/s they exert more or less monopoly power over those airports. New entrant airlines have difficulty obtaining a range of slots to mount effective competition except possibly on one or two routes. In the latter case, the incumbent base carrier can flood those routes with extra frequencies by switching to them some of its existing slots thereby making it very difficult for the new entrant to flourish. Thus British Airways exerts a stranglehold over Heathrow, where in 1989 it operated 38 per cent of all slots, making it virtually impossible for other British carriers to become effective competitors except on a limited number of routes and then only if they already have grandfather rights to a sufficient number of slots. In contrast to British Airways, the much smaller British Midland operated only 116 slots a day in 1989 or 12 per cent of the total while other British carriers had only six to twelve slots each per day. Entirely new entrants would have little chance except as marginal carriers. Even new charter airlines may find it impossible to set up operations at a slot-limited airport since they may be unable to obtain sufficient slots spread through the day to ensure that they can operate three return trips daily with each aircraft. This is an essential feature of charter economics in Europe (Doganis 1991). Thus in recent years is has become virtually impossible for a new charter airline to set up operations from London's Gatwick airport.

The potentially anti-competitive features of the scheduling-committee system have long been recognized by governments and regulatory bodies. Thus in 1969–70 when the first scheduling committees were set up in the United States at four airports, Chicago O'Hare, New York's Kennedy and La Guardia airports and Washington National, they had to be given explicit immunity from anti-trust legislation. This continued until slot trading was introduced at these airports in 1986. In the United Kingdom the Civil Aviation Authority expressed its own views clearly in 1986:

> the Authority believes the scheduling system has worked to good effect for many years and has served the industry well. It is, in the Authority's view an asset not to be discarded lightly. On the other hand, it is likely necessarily to have more and more anti-competitive effects as the pressure at Heathrow and Gatwick becomes intolerable.
>
> (CAA 1986)

The European Commission has manifest its concern about slot dominance in two ways. Early in 1988 in allowing British Airways to take over British Caledonian, which was based at Gatwick, it pushed British Airways to agree that it would use no more than 25 per cent of the Gatwick slots in the 1989–92 summer seasons. Subsequently, the Commission put forward its own proposals for slot-allocation rules at airports within the European Community. These are discussed later (see pp.105–6).

Apart from the risk of becoming anti-competitive the current system has further shortcomings. It does not allocate slots to the airlines or users who would value them most. It is an inequitable method of distributing scarce resources. Thus a small domestic flight with thirty passengers or an international stopping service with thirty to forty disembarking passengers may keep out a business flight with 250 passengers at peak time because the former have grandfather rights. Yet the latter airline or its passengers might be prepared to pay a great deal more to gain access to that peak-hour slot. Nor does the present system provide a guide to the need for future investment in new or improved runway facilities. In other words, normal market-price mechanisms do not apply. There is no indication how much airlines would be prepared to pay to obtain an additional slot.

Whatever the strengths and weaknesses of self-regulation, the system will become increasingly unworkable as demand for limited capacity grows. It will also appear increasingly anti-competitive as deregulation spreads and new entrants and newly established airlines find it very difficult or impossible to obtain the number and range of slots necessary to mount effective competition against the airlines with established grandfather rights. Two alternatives are likely to be considered: administrative regulation of runway capacity, or the introduction of some form of pricing mechanism.

Administrative regulation of slot allocation

In order to ensure a more competitive airline environment and/or in the pursuit of wider aviation or social and political objectives, governments or regulatory authorities may decide to intervene in the slot-allocation process. They are unlikely to take over and control the scheduling system entirely. It is much more likely that governments will impose certain restrictions, priorities or codes of conduct and then leave it to airport scheduling committees or schedule co-ordinators to work out the detailed allocation of slots to particular airlines. This then becomes a form of mixed regulation.

A frequent form of government restriction is by *type of traffic*. In pursuit of social or economic objectives a government may decide to give priority to commercial flights, that is to restrict business or general aviation or air taxis. Or it may favour international over domestic services or scheduled over charter flights. It may decide to limit or exclude all-cargo flights. In several countries, this principle has already been adopted and used in one form or other. In 1977, for example, the United Kingdom government adopted a number of so-called traffic-distribution rules as a way of regulating access to runway capacity at the two major London airports, Heathrow and Gatwick. The first rule was that no international airline that did not already operate scheduled services to Heathrow would be able to start services from that airport. Airlines operating into London for the first time would have to use Gatwick or another airport. Second, no series charters could be operated at Heathrow. This made it effectively an exclusively scheduled airport. The third rule was that no new domestic services could be flown into Heathrow by any airline unless specifically approved by the relevant government minister. Such approval could be given only on the grounds that the user benefits overrode the economic and efficient use of Heathrow as an international gateway. The fourth and final rule was that all-cargo, general-aviation and business aircraft could only operate at peak periods at Heathrow and Gatwick after prior authorization. Effectively this meant that they could be excluded from both airports at peak times.

These traffic-distribution rules were re-examined in a number of studies by the Civil Aviation Authority (CAA 1986; CAA 1989a; CAA 1989b) but remained unchanged until early 1991. In March 1991, the UK government, following recommendations put forward by the Civil Aviation Authority (CAA 1991), formally abandoned the first three rules outlined above. This was done partly under pressure from the United States which wanted the rules changed so that United and American Airlines, not previously serving Heathrow, could take over Pan American's and TWA's services respectively.

While in theory the abolition of the traffic-distribution rules allowed new schedule, charter and domestic operators into Heathrow, in practice the number of available slots was very limited. Nineteen new airlines applied for slots in March 1991 and about a dozen were successful. But the slots they were granted were widely scattered and few in number making in difficult to mount commercially attractive schedules. However, Virgin Atlantic, Cathay Pacific and All Nippon Airways were able in the summer of 1991 to mount their first scheduled operations from Heathrow. The basis on which the scheduling committee chose between competing claims was not made public. Nor was it clear on what grounds the allocation of more than 200 Pan Am slots to United Airlines, who had purchased some of the former's transatlantic routes, could be justified given that under the rules then existing UK airport slots could not be traded for cash.

Another form of government intervention might be to ensure that slots are allocated on the basis of some *'quality of service'* variable. One or more criteria might be used. For instance preference might be given to services with the largest number of passengers per flight or those with larger aircraft. Such a priority has several advantages. It promotes efficient use of slots, it reflects passenger preferences and it encourages airline competition. But it favours high-density routes against those with lower traffic levels. To safeguard the latter and to ensure that passengers have the benefit of a wide range of services, preference might be given to increasing the number of destinations served. This would mean that a service adding a new destination would be given preference over an existing service which wanted to increase its frequencies. This would involve some form of *frequency capping*. The government or other regulatory agency would decide that when a certain maximum stipulated frequency was reached on a route no more flights on that route would be allowed, or they might only be allowed at off-peak times when slots were readily available. In the UK after 1986 the government had a deferred traffic-distribution rule which allowed the Secretary of State to introduce frequency capping. But this power, which was never used, was set aside at the end of 1989 on advice from the Civil Aviation Authority (CAA 1989b).

Another method of slot allocation which might favour new entrants would be to impose a random selection process such as a lottery. This requires decisions as to who can enter the lottery and as to whether one allows more entries or higher probability to existing slot users to minimize disruption. Alternatively one might bias the lottery in favour of new entrants to encourage competition. Overall, the introduction of randomness does not seem to add much except that it helps new entrants but at the expense of greater uncertainty.

Whatever the administrative rules or methods adopted one can have safeguards built into them to protect certain types of services. For instance the rules might allocate a minimum number of peak-hour slots for domestic flights or a maximum number for any new entrants.

It is clear that the European Commission has adopted a mixed regulatory approach whereby governments or government agencies lay down certain guidelines or rules on slot allocation but leave it to scheduling committees or co-ordinators to carry out the detailed implementation of the rules. In January 1991 the Commission, following responses it had received to an earlier discussion paper, put forward a proposal for a Council regulation on slot-allocation rules. This was discussed at the June 1991 Council of Ministers meeting but was unlikely to be adopted until early in 1992 following further discussions and possibly amendment. But once adopted a regulation becomes binding on all member states of the European Community. Thus the key provisions of the 1991 proposed regulation are important especially as they may in future be adopted by countries outside the European Community. In essence, the Commission proposed that the existing scheduling procedures should continue to be used as the basis of slot allocation but that conditions should be enforced to ensure that in certain cases the priority of grandfather rights should be superseded in order to promote competition of routes where there was a monopoly or a duopoly (CEC 1991). This would be achieved through implementation of the following proposed rules:

1 member states would be required to appoint an airport co-ordinator at congested airports who would be independent of the airlines and would be responsible for the allocation of slots;
2 scheduling committees might assist the airport co-ordinator in a consultative capacity; the co-ordinator might also attend the IATA scheduling meetings in their own right;
3 the co-ordinator would make all data openly available (i.e. transparency);
4 the existing priority rules would in general continue to apply; but
5 newly created slots, unused slots, abandoned slots and those used for less than 65 per cent of the allocated period would be put into a 'slot pool';
6 at least 50 per cent of the slots in the pool would be allocated to 'new entrants', that is airlines with either (a) less than three slots a day, or (b) less than 30 per cent of slots a day but wanting to enter a route where there were only one or two operators;
7 where slots for new entrants were not available they could be reclaimed from airlines operating more than six slots on the routes which new entrants wish to enter; slots would be reclaimed on a priority basis from those services which were operated with aircraft of less than 200 seats.

The proposed regulation was radical in the sense that it would allow airport co-ordinators to take away grandfather rights from existing carriers in order to help new entrants and to stimulate competition. It could involve capping frequencies on routes at no more than six per airline. It would also put pressure on airlines to increase aircraft size to more than 200 seats in order to avoid losing the slots thereby ensuring better utilization of airport-runway capacity.

While it was uncertain by mid-1991 whether the regulation eventually adopted would have all the above features, there was little doubt that administrative rules of some kind for the allocation of slots at congested airports would be introduced for airports within the European Community and possibly elsewhere in Europe. This is likely to mark a trend, which will spread to other continents, towards increased administrative intervention in slot allocation and away from reliance purely on scheduling committees and grandfather rights.

The value of an administrative approach to slot allocation as opposed to self-regulation is that some policy objective can be pursued. This might be the safeguarding of domestic services or the encouragement of larger aircraft. On the other hand, the weaknesses of such a system are similar to those inherent in self-regulation. Namely, that administrative regulation may still be anti-competitive if it is based on grandfather rights unless, as in the case of the European Commission's proposals, specific rules are introduced to encourage inter-airline competition. Furthermore, an administratively regulated system is unlikely either to ensure that scarce runway slots are used by those who value them most or to provide a sound guide to future investment since it would not use any form of economic or pricing criteria in the allocation of slots.

An economic approach

In a situation where demand for runway slots, especially at peak periods, is greatly in excess of supply then an economic or pricing approach to slot allocation would have two key aims. First, to ensure that those who get most benefit from the scarce resource, that is those who value it most, gain access to it. Second, to use the pricing mechanism as a guide to the need for future investment or disinvestment.

One approach would be to use *peak pricing*. Currently, however, peak charges as used by BAA Plc at Heathrow and Gatwick and by one or two other airports only meet the second of the above objectives. In the case of BAA Plc its peak charges, as discussed earlier, are, in theory, related to long-run marginal costs and should provide a guide to investment. But the peak charges are not used either to allocate peak slots between users, or to clear the market until demand falls to the level of capacity or supply available which would be rationing by price. In other words, current peak charging does not ensure that those who value slots most acquire them, because the scheduling committees are still at work at airports with peak charges allocating peak-period slots to airlines on the basis of grandfather rights and other traditional criteria. Peak charges have had only a limited effect on shifting demand out of the peak period and no effect on passenger demand since they are not passed on to the passengers.

A more effective approach would be to introduce some form of *auction system* whereby airlines could bid for each slot or bundle of slots at particularly congested airports and highest bidders would be granted the slots they had bid for. The economic rationale for such a system is strong since it ensures that those airlines (and presumably their customers) who would get most benefit and value from the slots would actually use them. The bid prices would also establish the true market price or value attached to a marginal slot and would thereby provide a guide to future investment. But while simple in theory an auctioning system poses many problems in its application:

1 To avoid countless bids or bid rounds it would be better to auction slots falling in hourly blocks, especially as airlines are likely to be indifferent to timings within a few minutes.

   So an airline would bid for any number of slots in individual peak hours at different prices. For instance, it might bid $500,000 for five daily year-round slots between 0900 and 1000 hours, $425,000 for a further four slots, for two at £350,000 and for one at $118,000 all during the same hourly period.

2 Clearly the value of slots obtained in one peak hour depends on how many bids were successful in the preceding hour. Thus if an airline were awarded all its bids in the first peak-hour auction it might not want more in the next hour. If, conversely, it achieved none of its first bids, the value of slots in the second hour being bid for would be enhanced. So ideally bidding should be in rounds not all at once.

3 Once the bid price had been accepted that should be the only charge the airline would pay for using that runway slot for a year (or for the bid period) irrespective of the type of aircraft actually used. No further landing charge would need to be levied.

4 Bids would have to be for pairs of landings and take-offs (say an hour later).

5 Some way would have to be found to co-ordinate bids at different airports since the value of a slot at one airport depends on having access to a slot at the corresponding airport to which a service is planned. Does this mean one must allow simultaneous rounds of bidding at airports with similar peak/capacity problems and with high frequency of services between them?

6 If auctions were annual it would be difficult for airlines to plan their schedules and fleets in advance. To provide some security for planning and investment, bids should give access to slots for a specified period of time such as five or six years.

7 There may be a need to allocate quotas or to group slots by administrative decision into particular categories and then to auction each group separately. Thus there may be a number of slots reserved for domestic services, or for particular routes, or even for smaller aircraft. The purpose of such quotas would be to achieve specific social, economic or political objectives.

8 A decision would also have to be made as to who could bid for slots. Should it be only airlines or even corsortia of airlines? Or could they be bid for by aircraft manufacturers, towns wanting to establish a link with that airport,

other airport authorities, or even banks or financial institutions? The more open the bidding the more likely are the bid prices to correspond to the true value of the slots.

Slot auctions might be the preferred approach in economic terms. But moving away from a system based essentially on historical precedence, that is grandfather rights, might not be possible or acceptable even if the above practical difficulties could be overcome. In the first place, it would be very disruptive if existing users were to lose slots overnight, especially if the number of slots lost were high. Routes and services which had existed for years might disappear altogether. Airlines would have to cut back both on their operations and on their staff numbers, and their profits would be adversely affected. This would create enormous turmoil and confusion in the airline industry as well as public and political disquiet. Disruption could be reduced by a slow, phased introduction of an auction system. Second, slot auctions are in essence no different from rationing by price and would have the same advantages as the latter. These were discussed earlier (see pp. 98–9). In particular, slot auctions could generate excessive profits at airports short of runway capacity. Airport authorities would be accused of abusing their monopoly position especially if physical, noise or other constraints prevented them from building new runways with a view to reducing both the slot and bid prices and the profits. High monopoly profits would be politically unaccep-table in most countries. This problem might be alleviated if the money raised by slot auctions, or most of it, went to the government especially in situations where there was little scope in investing it in additional capacity at the airport where the slots were auctioned. In the third place, if foreign airlines were priced out of a particular airport by the auction system it might conflict with the bilateral air-services agreements and the Chicago Convention's non-discriminating clauses (see pp. 78–9). The airlines pushed out might well start legal proceedings to regain their slots or they might ask their own govern-ments to retaliate in kind. This would create further confusion and uncertainty especially for those airlines that had won their bids. Finally, if the prices paid for slots were not reflected in what the passengers pay because of averaging out of airline costs and because of airlines' internal cross-subsidies, can one be sure that those who value the scarce slots were actually using them?

Given these disadvantages of a straightforward auctioning system, an intermediate approach might be to introduce some form of *slot trading*. Under a slot-trading system airlines would still enjoy grandfather rights and would be able to obtain access to available slots through the scheduling committees or other existing procedures. There would be a market in slots only where demand for slots at particular times exceeded supply. However, to ensure that such a market was free any trading would need to be through an independent slot broker. If airlines traded directly with each other there would be a risk of anti-competitive practices by slot owners to keep out particular competitors.

To ensure political or social objectives, quotas of slots might be reserved for particular types of services, such as domestic flights. Thus a domestic slot might only be sold to another carrier wishing to operate a domestic service.

A slot-trading system was introduced in April 1986 at four United States airports, Washington National, Chicago O'Hare and New York's La Guardia and Kennedy airports, because the scheduling committees had been unable to reach agreement in previous years under the growing pressure of demand for slots and had effectively given up. That pressure had become more acute as a result of deregulation and intense inter-airline competition. The trading system introduced in 1986 allocated 95 per cent of slots to existing users in four categories: essential air services, commuter, domestic and international. The remaining 5 per cent were allocated by lottery with preference given to new entrants. The allocated domestic and commuter slots were each given at random a withdrawal sequence number. If a new slot is needed for international or essential air services the domestic or commuter slot with the highest withdrawal sequence number is repossessed by the airport. Slots which are not used at least 65 per cent of the time are also forfeited (Starkie 1991). Trading, that is buying and selling, short-term leasing or swapping of domestic or commuter slots, has been allowed but slots cannot be changed from one category to another. Slots are designated by the hour (e.g. 0800 to 0900), and their value depends on their time and on their withdrawal sequence number. Clearly a slot with a withdrawal number suggesting a high probability of being repossessed by the airport is of diminished value. Slots are traded through a clearing house, the Airline Reservation and Reporting Center, operated by the airlines' trade body the Air Transport Association. The Federal Aviation Administration is notified of slot transfers but the financial terms of the transfer are not generally made public. Early in 1991 the going rate for the more sought-after slots was around $1.5 million. Airlines would have to pay landing fees on top of that. When Eastern Airlines collapsed in 1991 its slots at these four airports were sold off by a more or less public auction. Prior to that only a small percentage of slots were traded each year. Many more changed hands as a result of airline mergers and takeovers.

Within the constraints imposed by the four-fold categorization of slots, the US system allows free trading of slots so that those who value them most should, in theory, be able to buy them. Thus slot trading would seem to ensure that the maximum benefit is achieved from use of scarce runway resources. Everyone would appear to benefit. If an airline owning a slot values it at say $700,000 in terms of the financial benefits it can obtain from using it but can find a buyer who is prepared to pay $800,000 for it, the seller clearly benefits from the sale. The buyer is also better off in that they value the slot at at least $800,000 and possibly much more. Even if the buyer fails in operating a profitable service with this slot they can resell it and recoup much if not all their original investment. As a result the high initial slot price may not be such a barrier to entry. Slot trading achieves increased efficiency in the allocation of runway space without the direct involvement of the airport or the airport's own charging system.

The limited US system shows clearly that slot trading can be made to work but it also has drawbacks. While making some allowance for new entrants, a system such as that set up by the Federal Aviation Administration is still potentially anti-competitive. Existing large airlines with many slots can abuse their position to keep out newcomers or potential competitors. For instance, the 65 per cent 'use it or lose it' rule means that airlines can retain five slots while only using four by swapping flights between them. There is also a practice known as 'babysitting' whereby an airline temporarily allows another to use its slot so as not to lose it. Thus incumbents can protect unused slots to prevent new entrants using them. If new entrants do get slots, existing airlines can switch their own slots around so as to flood the new entrants' markets with frequencies. A further potential drawback is that existing slot holders may make substantial windfall profits as a result of a government decision to introduce a trading system. This may be politically unacceptable. Many would argue that any profits from selling runway resources should accrue to the airport authorities that built them and ultimately own them. Furthermore, if airlines are to trade freely in their slots, then should ownership of slots be a taxable asset? As in the case of slot auctions, slot trading may favour long-haul services by having a quota of slots for particular categories of flights. Finally, trading of slots for international services clearly contravenes the Chicago Convention (ICAO 1980) which requires airports to be available to all on an equal basis. It also contravenes those bilateral air-services agreements which stipulate that airport charges should be cost related. The Federal Aviation Administration having foreseen these legal obstacles excluded international slots from the trading process at the four US airports. Unless international law is modified it seems difficult to envisage the widespread adoption of slot trading at major congested airports outside the United States.

Growing governmental concern over the whole issue of allocating scarce runway capacity can be seen in the October 1990 decision of the UK Department of Transport and the Civil Aviation Authority jointly to commission a study on alternative systems of slot allocation. A year later, in October 1991, the consultant's report put forward for public consultation two alternative and contrasting allocation methods (DTp 1991). The first, described as a *regulatory system*, involves least disruption to current arrangements while introducing some flexibility. Grandfather rights are retained but 5 to 10 per cent of slots would be surrendered every two or three years to a slot pool. Slots from this pool would be allocated to new entrants if and when the need arises. This system is similar in some respects to the regulation being prepared in 1991 by the European Commission (CEC 1991). The alternative might be described as a *market hybrid system*. If this were adopted all slots would be divided into categories in pursuit of particular policy objectives. For example, they might be divided into domestic, intra-Community and international groups with a specific number of slots allocated to each. Slots within some or all of the categories might then be auctioned off on seven-year leases. In order to provide such slots, airlines currently enjoying grandfather rights would offer 20 per cent of their grandfather slots for auction each year but they would be able to keep some of these if they were willing to match the highest price bid for them. Revenue raised from the auctions would be treated as a tax and go to the government and not to the airport. This market-orientated approach has several features found in the United States' slot-trading system discussed earlier.

In parallel with the public consultation process mentioned above, the United Kingdom took another important step in the autumn of 1991. Schedule co-ordination at London's Heathrow airport previously in the hands of the secretary of the airport's scheduling committee was transferred to an independent company, Airport Co-ordination Ltd.

In conclusion, it seems that in terms of economic efficiency and ensuring maximum benefit from the use of scarce runway resources, slot auctions or slot trading would appear to be preferable to grandfather rights. Both slot auction and trading, however, appear to contravene existing international and in some cases national laws while auctions in addition pose many practical difficulties as well. It seems, therefore, that in the near future the most widely acceptable and feasible system of slot allocation that encourages competition is likely to be one based on administrative intervention along the lines of the 1991 European Commission's proposed regulation (CEC 1991).

The creation of the single European market in January 1993 and the transformation of intra-Community air services from international to domestic could provide an opportunity for introducing limited slot trading along the lines of the United States system. This could be limited to a proportion of slots, at half a dozen or so congested European airports, that would be used exclusively for 'domestic' (i.e. intra-Community) services. This might overcome the legal obstacles previously mentioned.

Chapter 6

Developing a commercial strategy

STRATEGIC OPTIONS

As in recent years airports have become more commercially oriented they have tried to generate an increasing share of their revenues and of their profits from their commercial or non-aeronautical activities. They were in many cases forced to do this either because of growing airline opposition, often orchestrated through the International Air Transport Association, to further increases in aeronautical charges or because their own governments held back or limited such increases. At the same time, in many countries the loosening of administrative links between airports and their governments together with pressure from governments on their airports to be more financially self-sufficient and less reliant on government support meant that airport managers had both the freedom and the incentive to become more commercially oriented. The growing emphasis on generating more commercial revenues were discussed earlier, in Chapter 3 (see pp. 58–61). At many airports round the world commercial income has been rising more rapidly than their traffic, particularly at the larger international airports. Thus in the period 1976–87 passenger traffic at Frankfurt airport rose by 63 per cent but concession and rental income rose by 284 per cent. For all airports, even the smaller ones which are more heavily dependent on aeronautical charges, generating more commercial revenues is attractive because it is much easier generally than trying to increase aeronautical revenues. To do the latter one must either stimulate traffic growth, which is relatively difficult for an airport to do on its own though it must try to do so, or increase aircraft or passenger charges, which may be difficult or impossible because of airline or government opposition. In the circumstances maximizing commercial revenues would seem to be a sensible policy for airports setting out to be more business-like and financially self-sufficient.

In pursuing commercial strategies airport owners and operators have to make a choice between two alternative strategies. They can follow the *traditional airport model* which is one where airports see their primary task as being to meet the basic and essential needs of passengers, airlines, freight forwarders and other direct airport customers or users. This is the strategy traditionally followed by government-owned airports particularly if operated and managed by a government department such as the Ministry of Transport or the Department of Civil Aviation. Many state- or city-owned American airports still follow this approach. Such a strategy has critically important implications for airport planning and design. In particular, it means that the airport is oriented primarily to facilitating and speeding up passenger handling and throughput, and all extraneous or unnecessary activities are kept to a minimum with relatively little space being allocated to them. Nevertheless, within the design and space constraints imposed, airports following this traditional strategy can still try to maximize commercial revenues. But clearly they are likely to be severely constrained in what they can do, particularly within the terminal, both by the lack of space and the priority given to meeting passengers' primary needs.

The alternative strategic option is that of the *commercial airport model*. The aim here is to maximize income from any appropriate activity at the airport. This in turn means that one regards the airport as a business opportunity which not only serves its direct and traditional customers – airlines, passengers, cargo shippers and so on – but also a wider range of potential customers including airport and airline employees, visitors, people meeting passengers, local residents in the surrounding communities as well as local businesses and industries. The design implications of such a strategy are that while every effort is made to facilitate the movement of passengers and cargo through the airport every effort is also made to maximize the opportunities for generating additional commercial income even from activities which may not be directly related to air traffic such as light industry or leisure complexes. To be most effective such a strategy requires abundant and flexible space both within and outside the various airport terminals and buildings. If sufficient space is not currently available some airports may have no choice but to adopt the traditional airport model.

In Europe, Athens airport (run by a government department) and Frankfurt (operated by an airport authority) epitomize the two models. Athens is very traditional in its approach. At its two terminals in 1991 it provided the minimum of passenger shopping and catering facilities. On the landside, that is before passport control, the two terminals between them provided only three small bookshops, which also sold confectionery and some souvenirs, three stand-up cafes and two restaurants, one of which was outside the terminal building. There were in addition two newspaper kiosks, several bank exchange offices, car-hire desks and two post offices. But the numerous bank offices only provided currency-exchange facilities and did not undertake any other banking activities. On the airside, that is the departure area after immigration control, the two Athens terminals between them had one restaurant, one cafe, one stand-up bar and two newspaper kiosks; they also had a duty-free shop each. Yet in 1989 Athens airport handled 10.5 million passengers. One can contrast that with Frankfurt which within its one terminal had ninety-four shops which included six duty-free shops, a supermarket, antique shops, fur shops, a dry cleaners, a shop selling traditional German costumes and several up-market fashion and shoe shops. There were, in addition thirty-three restaurants and bars catering to a variety of gastronomic tastes, two amusement salons, four cinemas including the only English-language cinema in Frankfurt, a bowling alley and the largest discotheque in Germany the Dorian Gray. Next to the terminal there was a very large hotel and an office complex providing $47,000m^2$ of high-class office space. The contrast with Athens is very stark yet Frankfurt in 1989 was handling only two-and-a-half times as many passengers as Athens or about twenty-six million.

Frankfurt represents an extreme example of the commercial airport model. The airport is very fortunate in that, when it was opened in 1972, the terminal building was provided with more than adequate space on three levels. In subsequent years the airport set about utilizing more and more of this space, much of which was unused in the early days, as well as land around the terminal. Unlike Athens airport which has only attempted to cater for very basic passenger needs, Frankfurt identified several target groups, in addition to passengers or cargo forwarders, for whom the airport could provide facilities and services and from whom it could generate commercial revenues.

Circumstances will vary from airport to airport but, in principle, airport planners and commercial managers could target eight groups of potential customers all of whom require a variety of facilities and services within or close to the terminal areas. Each of these represents a different market segment with its own needs and requirements which must be clearly understood if airports are to maximize their revenue-generating potential. There are, moreover, smaller discrete sub-markets within some of the larger groups.

1 By far the most important market group in terms of spending power is the *passengers* who will tend to buy certain travel necessities such as newspapers, books or toiletries but who are also very susceptible to impulse or spontaneous buying provided they are stimulated to do so by the availability and display of the appropriate merchandise. Departing, arriving and transfer passengers are likely to have different requirements and spending patterns. Airports must be responsive to these in planning their commercial facilities. Passengers are critically important as a source of revenue in passenger terminals but cargo shippers and forwarders may be an important source of revenue in cargo areas and terminals.

2 The *airlines* themselves clearly have very specific needs not only in terms of office space, check-in-desks, discrete first-class or business-class lounges and so on in the passenger terminal but also in terms of space for cargo handling and storage, maintenance facilities, flight kitchens, staff facilities, etc. Airlines whose home base is at an airport will be particularly demanding

in terms of space and facilities. Passengers, freight forwarders and airlines are between them an airport's main customers. The passengers generate the bulk of the concession revenue and the airlines would normally generate most of the rental or lease income. But other market groups should not be neglected.

3 Potentially the second most important group in terms of concession revenue are *airport employees*, that is all those working at the airport for airlines, the airport authority, the concessionaires and so on. They can represent a very sizeable captive market but their motivation is quite different from that of passengers. It is primarily convenience, the ability to undertake normal everyday shopping during working breaks without having to travel to distant town centres. They need above all foodstores, but also most of the other types of shops and services found in high streets. Because Frankfurt airport caters for this target group it has found that employees working at the airport spend approximately 15 per cent of their net household income at the airport's shops and service facilities (Heinzelmann 1991).

4 At larger airports a distinct group of employees may be the *airline crews*. They have their own particular needs arising directly out of their work. They are particularly interested in dry cleaning, shoe repairs, hair-dressing salons and tailors as well as the facilities required by other airport employees.

5 *Meeters and greeters*, that is people accompanying passengers to or from the airport, do not go to the airport with the aim of making purchases. However, if they spend time waiting at the airport they can be induced to spend money on both catering and shopping outlets if these are made accessible and attractive.

6 Another distinct group are the *visitors* to the airport who come primarily for sight-seeing and are interested in souvenirs, especially those that are airport or airline related, and in catering outlets.

7 A group frequently neglected by airports are the *local residents*. They can be attracted to use the airport by the convenience of doing so if the range of shops and services available is wide. Road or even rail access to larger airports is frequently easy for those living nearby, and parking near or in the terminal is frequently much simpler than finding parking spaces in town-centre shopping areas. Moreover, airport shops will normally have much longer opening hours. The needs of local residents are fairly similar to those of the airport employees but the range of shops needs to be much wider to make airport shopping attractive, and could include furniture, electrical goods, hardware and so on.

8 Finally there is the local *business community*. Rather than shops they are likely to require office space, conference and meeting facilities which can enable them to take advantage of the airport's air links. Alternatively they may need space for the manufacture or warehousing of goods likely to be moving in or out by air. Most of the business community's needs do not

necessarily require space within the terminal but close to the terminal area. They need land, warehouses, hangars or office buildings from which the airport can generate substantial rental income.

Frankfurt airport has had both the space and the commercial acumen to try to meet the needs of all these target groups in and around its main terminal. An analysis of concession revenues earned by the airport authority has shown that 76 per cent comes from passengers, 13 per cent from airport employees and the remaining 11 per cent from visitors of various kinds including meeters and greeters and local residents (Heinzelmann 1991). This excludes rents from office space, land, etc. As a result of its strategy, Frankfurt had developed the extensive and very wide-ranging shopping, leisure, business and service facilities which were summarized earlier. Athens in contrast targets only two groups at its two terminals, the airlines and the passengers, and provides only the very minimum of facilities for both.

Airports world-wide fall somewhere in the range represented by the two extremes of Athens and Frankfurt. Whether they have followed the traditional model or the commercial model will depend partly on the strategic options adopted by the management and in particular on which of the above customer groups they have decided to target. But the model adopted will also be dependent on the volume and composition of the traffic handled by each airport, by the terminal space and land available and the degree to which the management has been given the freedom to adopt commercially oriented policies.

There is no doubt that for the reasons discussed earlier airports are increasingly making strategic decisions which are pushing them towards adopting the commercial airport model. If airports are to be run as businesses and to be financially self-sufficient, as governments increasingly want them to be, then this is the correct strategy. Given the constraints which exist on raising more revenues from aeronautical charges, then airport managements should try to maximize revenues from commercial sources. At the very least they should generate sufficient revenue to meet their financial targets. To do this they need to decide which customer groups or market segments they should target, and they need to understand the range of facilities which can be provided to meet the needs of different target groups (see pp. 117–121). But a large number of factors will influence an airports's ability to maximize its commercial revenues. There are first of all certain external factors, which are crucially important in affecting revenue generation or strategic options but which are largely outside the control of individual airport managements. These include the airport's traffic levels and its proportion of international traffic, exchange rates and the level of taxes or duties imposed on alcohol or tobacco. Then there are a variety of factors which can be influenced directly by management. These are the area and the location of terminal space allocated to commercial activities, the nature of the contracts negotiated with the concessionaires and the quality of the concessionaires themselves. In order to understand how commercial revenues might be maximized, all these factors are discussed in the next chapter.

POTENTIAL SOURCES OF COMMERCIAL REVENUES

As a starting point it is useful to appreciate the nature and range of facilities and services that airports might provide in order to increase their total income from all commercial sources, that is both rents and concession fees. The distinction between the two is not always clear cut. Rental income arises primarily from the renting or leasing of space either to direct airport users such as airlines, freight forwarders and handling agents, or to indirect users such as hotels, catering firms, manufacturing companies and so on. Such rental income is based essentially on the amount of space occupied by the tenant or the number of specific facilities such as check-in desks that they use. Concession fees arise essentially from payments made to the airport authority by the providers of various services for the right to offer their services on airport land. The nature of concession fees are detailed later (see pp. 152–4), but they are generally based in some way on the concessionaires' volume of business rather than on the space occupied though some concession agreements may include a straightforward ground–rent element.

Rental or lease income can be generated from the following activities:

1 provision of space and facilities to direct airport users, that is companies that need to be in or on the airport. These include airlines, handling agents, freight forwarders, tour and travel agents, warehouses, public-transport operators and so on. Their space needs may vary from office space and hangars, to vehicle parking spaces, exclusive passenger lounges or land for building maintenance facilities. They may also pay rents for check-in facilities, or the use of baggage conveyors or other airport-owned equipment such as buses. Government agencies, such as immigration or health services, might also fall into this category if they can be induced to pay for some of the space they occupy;
2 provision of enclosed space, whole buildings or land for companies for whom an airport location is advantageous but not essential. These are likely to include providers of in-flight catering, light manufacturing or assembly industries and other businesses which might benefit from easy access to air services.

In addition to generating rental income airports may provide some or most of a very wide range of shopping and service facilities to meet the needs of different targeted market segments. These will normally produce concession fees though there may also be a rent element in the concession agreement. But among some smaller airports, particularly if run by a government department, the limited number of shops provided may be let on the basis of flat rents with no additional concession fee as such. Commercial activities or services which may generate concession income generally fall into one of the following categories.

Duty-and tax-free shops. For airports with international air services duty and tax-free shops are potentially the most important source of concession revenues. The reasons for this are two-fold. First, since the savings in such shops compared to city-centre street prices are very substantial, spending by passengers is very high compared to what is spent in other shops. Second, because the profit margins earned by the concessionaires are also high the airports, if they have the right sort of concession contract, can take a large share of the profits earned. Thus in 1987 thirty French airports took only 8.5 per cent of the concessionaires' turnover from the landside duty-paid shops as a concession fee but 27.3 per cent of the turnover generated by concessions in the tax-free transit areas of these airports (Carré 1990). The two key product ranges are likely to be spirits and tobacco products. Traditionally these have been by far the most important sources of duty-free sales and hence of airport concession revenues. But the range of products on offer should, if possible, also include perfumes, electrical and photographic goods, watches, fashion goods and other products which may be highly taxed in that country. At the larger airports the share of duty-free sales generated by alcohol and tobacco products though still very high is declining as these other products increase their sales.

Duty-and tax-paid shopping. Since duty-free shopping is only available to passengers who have entered the departure or transit lounges a wide range of duty-and tax-paid shopping needs to be provided in the public landside areas of terminals. Such shops will be of three kinds. First, those that are selling products essential for passengers such as newspapers, books, tobacco, sweets, travel goods and certain basic drugs and toiletries. Second, there will be shops selling goods which may be bought by passengers on impulse and if attracted to do so but which are not essentials. One might place speciality food and flower shops, fashion goods and clothing, souvenirs, glassware, records and videos in this category. Finally, there are those shopping outlets which are geared to meet the needs of airport employees, local residents and possibly visitors who might decide to shop at the airport. All of them will certainly use the shops in the first two groups which are more passenger oriented but in addition they will need supermarkets, hardware stores, furniture shops, electrical goods stores, betting and other shops normally found in a town shopping centre.

Catering facilities, both for eating and drinking, are another potentially important source of concession revenue for the airport. They should be both on the landside and in the transit area. The number and type of restaurants, cafes, snack bars and bars that are needed will depend on which of the different market segments previously outlined the airport is targeting in its commercial policy. Clearly if an airport is planning to provide only for passengers then its catering outlets will be more limited than if it is also trying to meet the needs of the airport employees, visitors and local residents or businessmen.

Services. Passengers and many others using the airport also need access to a range of services. The most important are banks, the post office, travel agents, car hire and hotel reservations. Of these the banks are the most widely needed and used but it is the car-rental companies that produce the most concession revenue. Thus at Frankfurt airport studies have shown that 12 to 13 per cent of all departing passengers used a bank and only 4 per cent needed access to car hire. Yet about 7 per cent of the airport's total concession fee income came from car-rental companies and only 1 to 2 per cent from banks (Heinzelmann 1991). At many United States airports car-rental concessions are the most important single source of concession income for the airport especially if it has few international passengers. Another passenger requirement may be for accommodation and associated services. Facilities such as showers and short-stay beds may be provided within the terminal, as at Singapore, or in an adjoining hotel. The above services may also be used by non-passengers but the latter may need additional services which are likely to be of little interest to passengers. These include laundry and dry cleaning, hairdressing, beauty salon, medical services, tailoring and possibly conference or meeting facilities. Transport services providing access to an airport may be used by anyone. At many airports particularly in the United States buses, coaches and taxis may be required to pay a fee to the airport for gaining access to its passengers.

Leisure facilities. Non-passengers at the airport may also value a range of leisure facilities such as cinemas, discotheques, night clubs, billiard rooms, a gym or health centre and even a swimming pool. They might even want a golf course between the runways as at Bangkok's Don Muang airport. Some of these facilities may be used by passengers especially if they are provided within the airport hotel. But they are not primarily targeted at passengers. One exception might be video games which some airports make available in public and passenger areas to keep people and children amused while waiting. In 1989 the fifty video games machines at Gatwick airport generated nearly half a million pounds in revenue.

Car parks are another major revenue earner for airports especially those which have poor or no public transport access. They may be operated by the airport directly or by a concessionaire and are geared primarily to meet the needs of passengers, greeters and meeters, and visitors of all kinds. Airport employees may have their own reserved car parks which may not generate revenue for the airport authority. Petrol and car service stations may also be provided as a concession.

Advertising. Provision of advertising outlets is another discrete activity which may take place at airports and can be used to generate concession revenue.

Table 6.1 Sources of concession-fee income at London Gatwick and Frankfurt airports (excluding rents)

	Gatwick 1987–8 (%)	Frankfurt 1989–90 (%)
Duty and tax free:		
Liquor and tobacco	37.8	
Other tax free	29.1	
Total duty-free shops	66.9	37.0
Skyshops (papers, books, sweets, etc.)	8.8	
Other shops		15.2
Car rental	3.0[1]	7.2
Catering	7.6	8.0[2]
Advertising	1.4[1]	4.0
Other	12.3[3]	28.6
Total	100.0	100.0

[1] Estimated figures.
[2] Includes hotel.
[3] Includes car parks, banks, hotel desks.

The above are the concessions oriented towards passengers, airport employees and others using the terminal facilities. Their relative importance as sources of concession income will vary from between airports but Table 6.1 shows the position at London Gatwick before the opening of the second terminal and at Frankfurt airport in the late 1980s. In both cases the dominant role of duty-free shopping is clear. At Gatwick it generated two-thirds of concession revenue. But this was partly because landside space and shopping facilities were very limited before the second (North) terminal was opened in March 1988. With the development of that terminal a large landside shopping area was opened and this will have pushed down the share of duty-free revenue at Gatwick.

Airports may also generate concession income from services which are geared to meet the needs of airlines.

Aircraft-related services. These include aircraft marshalling, aircraft cleaning and provision of in-flight catering by flight kitchens. Where such services are provided by airlines for their own aircraft no concession fee would normally be charged. If, however, they are provided by specialist aircraft-handling companies or catering companies the airport may be able to charge them a concession fee for providing such services. In a few cases, airlines providing any of these services for other airlines may also be charged. In addition aviation-fuel suppliers may have to pay the airport a concession fee per litre or gallon of fuel uplifted by their customers.

Passenger, baggage or freight handling. Finally concession revenue may also be generated from specialist companies or airlines providing passenger, baggage or freight handling for others. In return for such fees the airport authority may well agree to limit the number of companies that may be permitted to provide these services. Of course, if the airport authority itself provides some or all of these services, the revenue earned is no longer a concession fee since the airport has to meet the cost of supplying such services out of the revenue generated.

THE RIGHT ORGANIZATIONAL STRUCTURE

If an airport authority decides to follow a strategy of developing along the lines of the commercial airport model then the first priority is to ensure that it has the right organizational structure to do this. Traditionally, airport management structures have reflected a functional approach in dividing up responsibilities and lines of authority. The airport's activities have tended to be split into a number of functional areas. Usually these include operations, administration, engineering, finance and possibly also personnel or safety. Each of these is headed by a senior manager directly responsible to the airport director. The organizational structure is fairly flat with several directors and sometimes several managers each heading an activity and each reporting directly to the managing director. An example of this type of organization drawn from a European airport is shown in Figure 6.1.

In airports, run on traditional lines such as the one illustrated, one can immediately discern that there is very little prominence or authority given to commercial activities. This is because compared to the other activities being undertaken by the airport they are not considered functionally important. In fact, at this and other similar airports it is actually quite difficult to identify from the organization chart who has responsibility for commercial policy in general and for concessions, advertising or car parking in particular. Frequently commercial responsibilities are widely scattered. The operations or engineering department may be responsible for allocating space for shops, catering outlets or other commercial activities. Contracts may be negotiated either by the properties section, by the legal department or even by staff in finance. Car parking may on the other hand be let out as a concession by the operations departments. Confusion abounds. There is no clear centre of responsibility, for developing and co-ordinating the airports' total commercial potential. It may still be the case that the airport is generating substantial revenues but it is unlikely that it is grasping all the commercial opportunities open to it or that it is maximizing its commercial revenues.

In order to achieve the latter an airport must be organized in such a way that commercial activities are given the importance they deserve, since they may be generating 25 to 60 per cent of an airport's total revenues. This means there needs to be a clearly identified focus of responsibility for commercial activities.

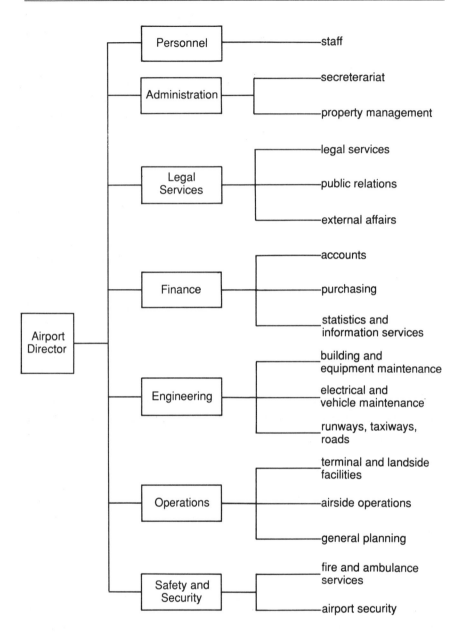

Figure 6.1 Traditional airport organization

The airport must be organized into different business areas with a senior manager responsible for each rather than along functional divisions. An airport following the commercial airport model is a business as well as a provider of services. Each of the business directors then either retains the functional skills which they require within their own department or draws upon the skills as necessary from separate service departments or from outside the airport organization.

A good example of an airport whose organization is focused on maximizing commercial revenues is London's Gatwick airport. Its 1990 organization chart is shown in Figure 6.2. It is immediately apparent that commercial activities are given high prominence and authority within the overall management of the airport. The director of commercial services is one of only three directors who sit on the Board of Gatwick Airport Ltd, and operates at an equal level to the director of operations. This is how one would expect a commercially oriented company to divide its responsibilities, especially in view of the fact that in 1989 Gatwicks's commercial director was responsible for 59 per cent of the airport's income and all of its profits while the operations side generated 41 per cent of income and was unprofitable (see Table 3.3, p. 60). Since one of the prime objectives of the airport business is to increase revenue and remain profitable then a clear focusing of responsibilities for commercial activities on a senior manager or director seems highly appropriate.

In 1990 the Gatwick commercial director had three senior managers working to him (see Figure 6.3). One was the commercial manager whose department, with only twenty staff of different disciplines, was responsible for generating the maximum possible revenue by providing the best service to the airport's customers in terms of choice and value for money. The department had six sections, of which three were each responsible for operational areas (catering, retail shopping and retail services) while the other three provided services or facilities to the three operations managers. The property manager was responsible for the renting out of office space, cargo sheds and warehouses, airline lounges and check-in desks. He also dealt with the handling concessions. Finally, the marketing manager was concerned with promoting and marketing the airport as a whole to airlines and other potential clients. The only important commercial activities not under the aegis of the commercial director were car parks and taxi, coach or bus services. These were controlled by the Onward Travel Manager who reported to the Operations Director.

Local circumstances will determine the best organization structure for each airport. They do not need to copy London's Gatwick. But they must like Gatwick have an organization in which responsibility for commercial activities is clearly centred and is given the importance that it merits as a major source of revenue generation. This is a prerequisite for maximizing commercial revenues. The traditional airport approach of functional divisions in which commercial activities are split and scattered among several departments is no longer adequate.

Another key aspect of organizational structure is the degree to which an airport authority becomes directly involved in operating the various

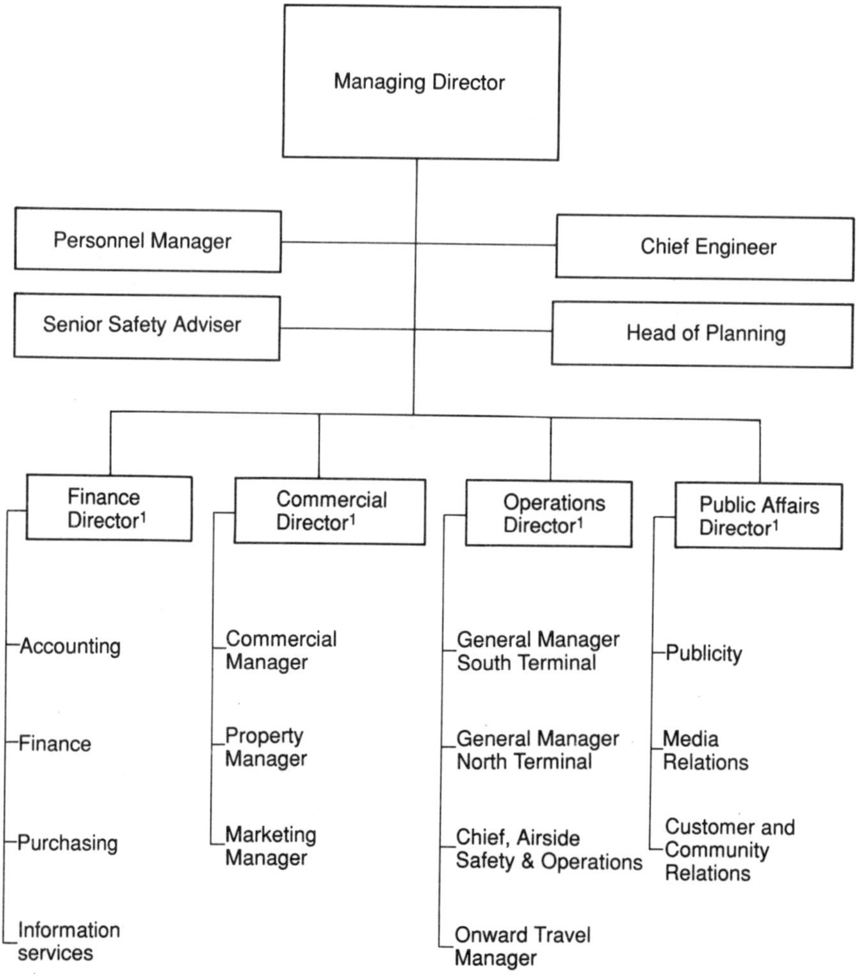

```
                        ┌─────────────────────────┐
                        │    Managing Director     │
                        └────────────┬────────────┘
                                     │
   ┌──────────────────────┐         │         ┌──────────────────────┐
   │  Personnel Manager   │─────────┼─────────│   Chief Engineer     │
   └──────────────────────┘         │         └──────────────────────┘
   ┌──────────────────────┐         │         ┌──────────────────────┐
   │ Senior Safety Adviser│─────────┼─────────│   Head of Planning   │
   └──────────────────────┘         │         └──────────────────────┘
                                     │
       ┌───────────────┬─────────────┴──────────┬───────────────┐
 ┌──────────┐   ┌──────────────┐        ┌──────────────┐   ┌──────────────┐
 │ Finance  │   │ Commercial   │        │ Operations   │   │ Public Affairs│
 │Director¹ │   │ Director¹    │        │ Director¹    │   │ Director¹     │
 └──────────┘   └──────────────┘        └──────────────┘   └──────────────┘
```

Finance Director[1]	Commercial Director[1]	Operations Director[1]	Public Affairs Director[1]
─Accounting	─Commercial Manager	─General Manager South Terminal	─Publicity
─Finance	─Property Manager	─General Manager North Terminal	─Media Relations
─Purchasing	─Marketing Manager	─Chief, Airside Safety & Operations	─Customer and Community Relations
─Information services		─Onward Travel Manager	

Figure 6.2 Commercially oriented airport organization: Gatwick Airport Ltd in 1990
Note: [1]On Board of Directors of Gatwick Airport Ltd.

concessions available within its airport. One of four choices can be made in regard to each concession. It can be provided by:

1 the airport authority;
2 a wholly owned subsidiary of the airport authority;
3 a joint venture company with airport participation; or
4 an independent concessionaire,

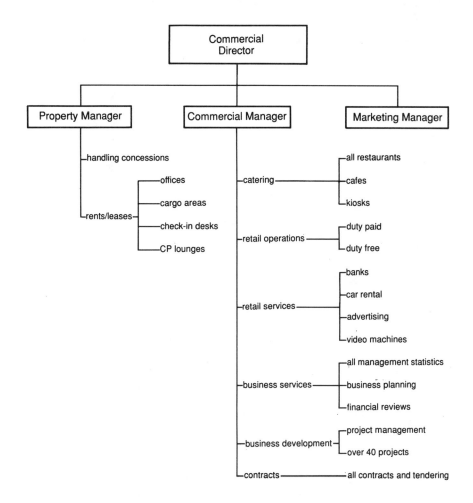

Figure 6.3 The commercial department of Gatwick Airport Ltd in 1990

The advantages and disadvantages of each of these approaches are summarized in Table 6.2. There appear to be several disadvantages in airports becoming directly involved in operating commercial outlets, the most critical being their lack of expertise in so many different areas particularly those involved with retailing. They are most likely to operate a concession themselves if the activity requires limited commercial skills, if it involves a level of investment which a concessionaire may be hesitant to undertake or if the commercial risk is relatively low. The two best examples are car parking

Table 6.2 Impact of alternative approaches to operation of airport concessions

Approach to concessions	Advantages for airport authority	Disadvantages for airport authority
(a) *Airport operates* e.g. duty free (Dublin) car parks (Manchester) handling (Paris)	It has full control Maximum flexibility Retains all profit	Incurs all investment Incurs all operating costs May lack expertise Staffing problems Profits may be less Carries all risks
(b) *Wholly owned airport subsidiary* e.g. advertising (Frankfurt) hotels (BAA)	As above: plus Easier to attract expertise Greater staff/wage flexibility Possibly tax benefits	As above; plus May be too small for effective marketing
(c) *Joint venture* e.g. catering (Amsterdam) Duty free (Milan)	Retains share of profits Easier to control than (d) Investment cost shared	Responsibility confused Cannot change concessionaire Revenue may not be maximized
(d) *Concessionaire*	Maximizes concession income Ensures best expertise Limits management problems Can change concessionaires	Less flexible once contracted Airport needs contractual expertise Requires close monitoring

and passenger, baggage or freight handling. A large number of European airports do run their own car parks though in some cases they may bring in a specialist company to manage the facility for them and to whom they pay a management fee. Several airports are quite heavily involved in providing a range of handling services, But as we shall see later (Chapter 8), provision of such services does not appear to increase profitability: costs as well as revenues are much higher since this is a very labour-intensive area. Unlike parking, airport handling services are rarely a monopoly, since usually one or more airlines will also be providing such services. One or two airports in Europe do operate other facilities but they are the exception. For instance, the Irish Airports Authority operates the duty-free shops at all its airports.

In a few instances the airport may set up a wholly owned subsidiary to operate a particular concession. The purpose of breaking off this activity from the airport authority is to create a separate corporate identity and thereby to attract more experienced staff and managers. The risk is that the subsidiary company will never be large enough to compete effectively with the large-scale retailers or providers of the services in its own field. An example is BAA Hotels Ltd set up to build and operate on- and off-airport hotels. It is difficult to believe that a small hotel chain with a handful of hotels can serve the interests of the London airports better than a major international chain. Another example was BAA Plc's decision to set up a fully owned company selling teddy bears (soft toys) through its own airport shops. This was not a success and the operation was sold off after a couple of years.

If an airport authority wishes to encourage external investment in certain facilities while maintaining some direct influence and control, it may set up a joint venture company as Amsterdam airport did with KLM and others to operate Schiphol's catering outlets. The major disadvantage of joint-venture concession companies is that an airport authority effectively loses its freedom to appoint different concessionaires in the future who may offer it better terms. It becomes tied in to using the joint venture company in which it has a share.

The airport authority is most likely to use concessionaires for activities which require specialist retailing or commercial expertise, where the level of investment needed by the concessionaire is limited and where revenue generation may involve some risk depending on performance. Most retailing and shopping concessions are of this kind. Most airports believe that they should themselves concentrate on those activities in which they have expertise, namely the provision of facilities for the efficient and safe handling of aircraft, baggage and freight and for the easy and comfortable processing of passengers. Airports are not retailers, hoteliers or shopkeepers, and should leave such services to the relevant experts.

Yet, one cannot emphasize too strongly that commercially oriented airport operators must approach the development of commercial activities at their airports in the same way as would a successful retailer. They must use the same tools and skills in marketing as are used by retailers, to explore the needs of the different market segments which their airports can serve in order to determine what goods and services can be profitably provided. Such a market-oriented approach requires a proactive and determined effort to market the airport and to find potential concessionaires. It is the antithesis of the passive airport landlord inviting bids for concessions through the press.

RENTAL POLICIES AND RECHARGES TO TENANTS

Rents are the second most important source of commercial revenues after concession fee income. Among European airports, rents generate on average between 8 per cent and 10 per cent of total airport income which is close to about half the income produced by concessions. An additional 4 to 5 per cent of

revenue comes from recharges to tenants. Among the larger United States airports rents and lease charges produce on average nearly a quarter of their total revenue.

As airports grow in size and traffic throughput, we have earlier noted a tendency for two things to happen. First, non-aeronautical or commercial revenue grows as a proportion of total revenue. Second, concession revenue grows as a proportion of non-aeronautical revenue. As a consequence rents and other non-concessionary income such as recharges to tenants are especially important for smaller airports where concession revenue is more limited, and for those airports where concession fees are low or are on a fixed flat-rate basis.

Rents will be paid for office and other floor space, which may be covered (e.g. hangars) or in the open, for the use of specialized equipment such as check-in desks or conveyor belts, for land and possibly for whole buildings. A key question is what pricing strategy should be adopted in fixing the level of rents to be charged.

In the normal situation the price of office floor space or the rental charge for specialist equipment is a function of the costs of supply and the interplay of supply and demand for that space and equipment. For many wishing to rent space or facilities at an airport, a free-market situation does not exist since they have no choice but to be at the airport. The airport for them is a monopoly supplier. But it must be careful not to abuse this monopoly power, particularly as some of its captive customers notably the airlines will be providing it with considerably higher revenue through the aeronautical charges they pay. On the contrary it may wish to increase its aeronautical revenues by offering airlines cheap rents as an inducement to start serving that airport.

Some airports have felt that the preferred option is to fix rents at levels which are comparable to those charged for similar types of properties or land in the neighbouring areas. In practice, this is very unsatisfactory, because it is often far from easy to fix or establish the rental required and also because it is difficult to adjust such rents upwards as an airport's facilities improve or as its traffic increases. There is the added problem that rents fixed in this way may be below the cost of providing the space or facility rented if rentals in neighbouring towns or districts are particularly low.

So airports may turn to the third alternative which is to fix rents on the basis of cost recovery. In other words, using conventional costing methods they work out an annual rent per square metre based on the fully allocated costs of building and maintaining each particular floor area within each terminal, office building or freight warehouse. Such rents must also cover the costs of financing the construction unless the finance has been provided by the future tenants through advance rentals. The latter is most likely to be done when an airport builds a facility for the exclusive use of a single airline or other tenant. While the working out of cost-based rents in the ordinary business world is fairly straightforward, the application of cost recovery for airport-terminal rents poses several problems. The most difficult to resolve is what proportion of a terminal's costs should be recovered from the floor rents. Some of the terminal costs are in theory allocated and recovered through the passenger charges. Fees from concessionaires should also generate a significant amount of revenue. Should rents then only be used to meet those remaining costs not covered by the passenger charge and the concession fee income? In that case they would be well below the cost of providing the floor space being rented. In practice many airports will try to fix their rents, if cost based, on the full costs ignoring the effect of these other revenues on the grounds that they will be used to cover the costs of common floor space which cannot be rented out, such as that at check-in areas, departure lounges and so on.

While some airports may use only one or other of the above methods for fixing rents, many airports use two or more of these methods in combination. Most frequently they may start on the basis of the actual cost of the facilities but may negotiate around this figure in response to the assessed market value of the space being provided. A 1979 study by the International Civil Aviation Organization (ICAO 1979) of over one hundred airports in sixty-one countries around the world showed that 25 per cent based rents on costs while another 34 per cent used a combination of costs plus some other factors which most frequently included market values (Table 6.3). The use of market values as an input in calculating rents is likely to have increased since the late 1970s. Clearly as airports become more commercially oriented, then basing rents on market values which are dependent on the interplay of demand and supply makes financial sense. Market-related rents should generate higher rental income than if cost based. But airports must be careful not to abuse their monopoly power.

Most airports provide one or more of the essential services to their tenants for which they must charge the tenants. These are known as 'recharges' to tenants. Such services usually include heating or air conditioning, water, electricity, cleaning and waste disposal and sometimes telephone services as well. A key question which the airport needs to resolve is whether it should supply these services at cost (i.e. only charge the actual costs to the tenants) or whether it should make a small profit from recharges to tenants. Amsterdam, for example, has in the past charged cost plus 10 per cent.

As far as charging is concerned three basic alternatives are available. First, the cost of certain services may be incorporated in the basic floor/space rental with no separate charge being levied. This may be done with heating, air conditioning or cleaning. Second, individual lessees may have meters on their premises monitoring consumption of electricity, water or telephone time. They then pay on the basis of their actual consumption. Finally, certain services may be charged separately from rents but on the basis of a flat charge per square metre. This is likely if the rents themselves are agreed by tender or are negotiable rather than being based on costs and therefore fixed.

It was argued earlier in Chapter 3 that while rents and recharges to tenants

Table 6.3 Bases used by airports for establishing rental charges

	% of airports
Basis used exclusively	
(a) Maintenance, administration and capital cost	25
(b) Assessed market value of space	19
(c) Rentals in airport vicinity	2
(d) Other exclusive basis	9
Bases used in combination	
(a) and (b) and possibly (c) or (d)	31
(a) plus (c) or (d)	3
(b) plus (c)	10
(c) plus (d)	1
	100

Source: ICAO 1979.

are important sources of commercial revenue, the improved financial performance of larger airports, especially those outside the United States, is closely linked with the generation of increased concession income. It is the concession revenues which can be most readily and directly stimulated by more commercially oriented airport managements (see Figure 3.6, p.56). It is therefore worth examining in greater detail the factors that influence airport concession revenues and the degree to which airport authorities can themselves influence those factors to their advantage.

Chapter 7

Maximizing concession revenue

In order for an airport to maximize its revenue from concession fees, the turnover of the various concessions must be maximized and the airport's 'take' or share of that revenue must be as high as is reasonably possible and commercially sound. Total sales by concessionaires depend on three factors. First, the total traffic handled by an airport and, in so far as passengers are the single largest source of sales by concessionaires, the characteristics of its passenger traffic. Second, the total amount of space allocated to those concessionaires operating shops, catering outlets, services and so on and the location of that space within the terminal building. Third, the skill of the concessionaires themselves in generating sales.

To what extent can an airport authority influence any of these factors? Through its marketing efforts and its expenditure on runways, terminals and other facilities an airport may have some influence on its total traffic levels or the composition of that traffic. However, in most cases its influence is likely to be indirect and fairly marginal since traffic generation is a function of both underlying demand, which is itself dependent on various exogenous economic variables, and supply features, which are determined by the airlines. Airports must try to push up their traffic by encouraging the opening of new routes, but their ability to do so is likely to be limited.

When it comes to space allocated to concessionary activities, airport authorities can have a much greater impact in the medium or long term if allowed to do so. In other words, a commercially oriented airport will make adequate and sensible provision, in its master plans and development programmes, to meet the future needs of the different market segments it hopes to target with its concessions. In the short term, an airport authority may be limited by the space and airport layout that was planned some years previously and this may be inadequate for current commercial activities. Skill and the creative redesign of space is then needed in the short term to try to improve the allocation of space available for such activities until investment in new buildings or facilities can be financially justified. Finally, airport authorities cannot directly influence the skill of their concessionaires. However, they can place a high priority on concessionaires' skills and experience when choosing them. Airports can also help concessionaires to market their goods or services by providing them with information of traffic trends and passenger profiles and by careful monitoring of all the commercial developments within the airport.

When it comes to the fee revenue that the airport takes from the concessionaires, this is an area over which the airport management has much more direct control through the contractual arrangements that it enters into for its concessions. But great skill is needed to ensure that the airport's concession fees are not so high as to demotivate or even undermine the concessionaires.

IMPACT OF TRAFFIC CHARACTERISTICS

In order to maximize concession revenues airport operators need to target all their potential customer groups. Yet despite their efforts it is inevitable that passengers will remain by far the most important source of concession revenue. Even at Frankfurt airport, which as we have seen earlier targets airport employees, local residents and others, it is still the passengers who generate around three-quarters of the airport's concession fees. At airports which, either because of lack of space or as a matter of policy, target primarily passengers then the latter's share of the concession income will rise to 90 per cent or more. This is the case with the Athens airport which basically caters only for passengers. Therefore at all airports the characteristics of their passenger traffic and the buying behaviour of those passengers together have a major impact on sales achieved by concessionaires. Since the airport's concession fees will normally be related to concessionaires's total turnover, passenger volume and mix are major determinants of the concession-fee income generated by airport authorities.

The total volume of passenger traffic handled has a major impact on concession income since it affects the range of shops and facilities that can be profitably operated. If total traffic levels are low then they may only be able to support shops and services meeting essential passenger requirements such as newspaper/book shops, banks, car-hire desks or ordinary bars and restaurants. As an airport's total passenger throughput expands then the possibility of introducing less essential concessions which are used by only a small percentage of passengers increases. Such non-essential outlets may include a high-quality restaurant or shops selling antiques, expensive food products or fashion goods. The impact of airport size, in terms of passenger traffic, on concession revenue was clearly illustrated diagrammatically in Chapter 3 (see Figure 3.6, p.56).

While the overall volume of passengers handled clearly affects the range of commercial opportunities that can be exploited, it is the various characteristics of that passenger traffic that ultimately influence the concession revenue generated per passenger. The most important aspect of the passenger mix is the proportion of passengers on international as opposed to domestic flights. It is only international passengers who can enjoy access to tax- and duty-free shops which are by far the most significant source of concession revenue. In addition international passengers in most countries tend to spend longer at the airport than domestic passengers and are therefore likely to spend more than the latter on catering outlets and in duty-paid shops. Finally, international passengers also attract more greeters and meeters when travelling through an airport. This impacts on catering turnover and duty-paid sales on the landside of the airport.

For all these reasons airports with a high percentage of international passengers are likely to have significantly higher concession income, if properly managed and designed, than airports with a high domestic content.

In most countries, outside the United States, the impact of overall traffic volume and international passengers is frequently reinforced in that the larger airports tend to be the ones with the highest proportion of international passengers. This is because historically in many countries international traffic has grown significantly faster than domestic. At London's Heathrow airport which in 1989 handled 39.6 million passengers, 82 per cent of the traffic was international. In contrast to this at many European regional airports this proportion of international passengers may fall to well below 25 per cent. However, some of the smaller airports in Europe may have a very high international component in their traffic despite their small size if they are used by charter airlines, since charter traffic in Europe is almost exclusively international. Thus, East Midlands airport, a small regional airport in central England, in 1989 handled only 1.5 million passengers yet 73 per cent of these were international mostly on charter flights. Small airports in such a situation may be well placed to exploit the potential advantages of handling a high proportion of international passengers.

International traffic, unless it is purely outgoing charter traffic, will invariably involve passengers of various nationalities. These are likely to have very different spending patterns both in terms of their total expenditure per person at the airport and in terms of the types of products and services that they prefer to spend money on. As a general rule a non-resident will spend more in a particular airport than residents of that country especially when travelling on international flights. The reason for this is that non-residents will normally be using that airport on their return flight when more duty-free purchases are made while residents will be going through on the outward journey. Thus Frankfurt airport finds that its German passengers tend to spend less per head at the airport than do most foreign passengers. But buying patterns may also vary between different nationalities. For instance at many western European airports Japanese passengers tend to spend most whereas North Americans, despite their reputation as big spenders, tend to spend relatively little money in airport shops. The buying pattern of different nationalities is influenced by three factors. First, the relative strength of their currency vis-à-vis the currency of the airports they are travelling through affects passengers' expenditure. Second, the level of duties and taxes in their home countries on key items such as spirits, wines, tobacco products or perfumes has an influence. The higher the taxation in any country the greater will be the savings enjoyed by its citizens in buying duty-free goods and therefore the greater is likely to be their expenditure. This explains why Norwegians or Swedes tend to spend more heavily than other nationalities on spirits and wines both on their outward and return trips. Finally, social and religious customs impact on spending patterns. In some countries such as Italy it is the custom for travellers to bring back gifts for close family and other relatives. Such travellers are likely to be big spenders at airports, particularly on their return journey, but they may need to be offered a wide range of potential purchases. On the other hand, passengers from Moslem countries are unlikely to be big spenders on spirits or wines.

In brief, an airport's concession revenue will be strongly influenced by the proportion of international passengers in its total traffic and the split of those passengers between different nationalities including its own. But other characteristics of its traffic may also be important. One of these is the degree of peakiness in the traffic. When traffic is very high at particular times or seasons, congestion in the terminal tends to reduce the proportion of passengers who actually make a purchase by nearly half. Also important is the length of time spent at the airport, since a longer time provides both an opportunity and a need to spend money in shops or catering outlets. As mentioned earlier international passengers spend more time at the airport than do those on domestic flights. Charter passengers also tend to arrive much earlier because the charter airlines frequently ask them to do so as they use fewer check-in desks and queues build up. Passengers transferring between flights, especially if it is a domestic-to-international or international-to-international transfer, are likely to spend long periods in the transit lounge and may spend money in order to relieve the tedium of waiting. This does not apply at United States hub airports where flights are organized to minimize transfer times. Where, as in Singapore, Bangkok or Dubai, transit passengers on long-haul flights are allowed off their aircraft they tend to be keen to spend money on low-priced duty- or tax-free goods.

Another significant traffic characteristic is the business:leisure split. While business passengers are likely to have greater spending power they may actually spend less than leisure passengers on shopping and duty-free goods. This is because they spend less time at the airport and also because as frequent travellers they are less likely to buy, say, duty-free goods on every trip. However, they are likely to be more frequent users of banking services, of airport hotels and especially of car-hire firms than leisure passengers. The duration of the trip is also important. Passengers who are going to be away for only a day or two are likely to spend considerably less than those staying away for two weeks or more. Frankfurt airport found that while only 25 per cent of its passengers going away for one day used its terminal shopping facilities, the proportion rose to about 50 per cent for those going away for two weeks or longer (Heinzelmann 1991). A very high proportion of the very short trips, those returning on the same day or the next day, is likely to be for business purposes.

An example that highlights the difference between business and leisure passengers is that of London City Airport. Built in the old docklands of East London and opened in 1988 for short-take-off aircraft flying to the nearer European destinations, it boasted of having a ten-minute minimum check-in time before departure. It could do this because of its small size and the short distance to the aircraft. As a result average time spent at the airport was very low and this, combined with the fact that the majority of passengers were frequent business travellers on relatively short trips, meant that duty-free sales and concession revenues were well below expectation. This despite the fact that virtually all the traffic was international.

The traffic levels and characteristics of an airport are crucially important in determining an airport's concession revenue. But unfortunately an airport authority or its managers have relatively little influence over volume and type of traffic handled. Through their marketing efforts they may attract one or two new airlines or induce existing airlines to open new services but such efforts in most cases will have only a marginal impact on traffic patterns. It is the airlines who determine the latter and they in turn respond to perceived passenger demand.

Furthermore, both traffic levels and passenger spending patterns can change suddenly and for reasons totally beyond an airport's control. Airlines may cut routes or open new ones at short notice. Exchange-rate changes may suddenly make an airport's shop prices much cheaper or more expensive for an important group of customers. Imposition of higher duties on alcohol or tobacco may boost sales of such products without any action on the part of the airport.

An airport management can do relatively little to influence its traffic levels, other than ensuring an adequate and efficient provision of facilities and services for the handling of aircraft, passengers and freight. It can do nothing to affect external factors such as exchange-rate or taxation changes. But it can do a great deal to increase the use of its concessions and the volume of sales generated within its given traffic levels and characteristics through detailed knowledge of the buying behaviour and requirements of the different passenger groups that it handles. Such knowledge is decisive in ensuring that the correct range of products and services is provided to meet the needs of specific market segments in order to maximize concessionaires' sales. This knowledge can only be acquired through regular and frequent surveys of passengers aimed at ascertaining the facilities they use, their expenditure patterns and the needs of different and discrete segments of the passenger market. Similar surveys should also cover airport employees and the various categories of visitors to the airport if the airport aims to target such groups as well.

SIZE AND LOCATION OF SPACES AVAILABLE

The *total amount* of enclosed or open space available for rent or leasing both within the terminal and elsewhere on airport land clearly affects the total income an airport can generate from rents and concessions. Unlike overall traffic levels, which in most cases can only be influenced marginally by an airport authority, the total amount of space for concessions, office rental or hangars or to meet other specialist requirements is very much under the control of the airport. However, that control may not be total or unconstrained. In the case of airport land outside the terminal which may be leased for the building of maintenance facilities, hotels, offices, warehouses or factories there may be planning or zoning controls on what can be built. There will also be height and locational limits imposed by the need to comply with regulations relating to runway safety clearances. In some countries there may be some legal constraints on the uses to which airport land may be put. Frequently only airport-related activities may be permitted. When it comes to the terminal buildings themselves, an airport is limited in the short term by the size and configuration of the rentable spaces currently available. Through careful planning of existing facilities and some reallocation and reconfiguration of spaces within the terminals it may be possible to increase the areas of rentable space. In the longer term, of course, the terminal/s may be extended in some way or an entirely new terminal may be built. When planning extensions or new terminals airport planners can build into the designs as much additional space as their commercial colleagues require provided the extra revenue generated covers the additional cost of providing such space.

Some existing terminals may have been originally designed and built with so much spare capacity that they can readily accommodate the increased space needs which a more commercially oriented strategy demands. An example of this in 1991 was Madrid's Barajas airport. Its international terminal had vast interior spaces and only a limited range of shopping facilities. The latter could easily be expanded within the existing space. Elsewhere additional space for expanding concessions may be limited and airport managers may have to be creative in their use of space to try to maximize commercial opportunities. In particular, they will need to decide how to divide space between that needed for basic passenger or baggage handling and processing and for essential amenities such as lounges, rest rooms or catering, and that which can be used to generate concession revenues. In other words, they must decide on the desired balance between facilitating an easy and speedy flow of passengers through the terminal and ensuring that passengers are offered a wide range of shopping opportunities.

Most non-aeronautical or commercial income is likely to be generated from passenger-related concessions. The concession revenue generated per passenger is influenced partly by the total amount of space allocated for retailing and other commercial activities and partly by the *location and layout* of such spaces.

The first locational factor, the position of shops in relation to passenger flows is of prime importance. This determines the level of passenger penetration, that is the percentage of passengers that makes a purchase in a shop. The best locations for shops are in the direct line of passenger flow and, in the departure lounge, as close as possible to the departure gates or gate lounges. The latter is important because many passengers only feel comfortable shopping if they know they are near to or can actually see their departure gates. The impact of location on passenger penetration is shown in two different departure-lounge layouts as in Figure 7.1 (Brendel 1991). It is clear that requiring passenger flow to go through a shopping area significantly increases sales penetration. A good example is found in the North Terminal at Gatwick airport. The large duty- and tax-free shopping area has been placed directly and immediately across the path of passengers entering the departure lounge from immigration control. The natural flow is to walk through this area set up in an open department-store style. The paper in which Figure 7.1 was first published also suggested that to achieve 40 per cent penetration even in the best locations one should be no more than 80m from the gates or the departure-lounge exit. It is important to bear in mind that the better the location for a shop the greater is the amount of space it needs since it will attract more customers.

The second locational factor is the floor level on which shops or services are provided in relation to the passenger flows. Because of space constraints many airports must, of necessity, locate certain commercial outlets on floors to which passengers do not have to go to in the normal course of departure. For example, restaurants at many airports, such as Athens are on a floor above the departure-lounge level. Having to go up or down a floor level to shop is clearly a disincentive, made worse if passengers have to use stairs rather than escalators. Frankfurt airport, which has shop and catering facilities on three floor levels, estimates that the need for passengers to move up or down a floor reduces the potential turnover of shops by about 40 per cent (Heinzelmann 1991).

The third locational factor is the split of available space between landside and airside facilities. In some cases this may be predetermined by the design of the building, in others flexibility in the use and configuration of the internal space may give airport managers some discretion. But it is also a matter of commercial strategy and the number of market segments that are to be targeted. Surprisingly, Amsterdam's Schiphol airport has virtually no commercial activity in the check-in area or prior to passport control. In contrast to this the North Terminal at London's Gatwick airport has a middle floor between the departure and arrival floor with an extensive shopping area in which several well-known British retailing companies have their own shops. This area is open to all, though for passengers the location is not very suitable

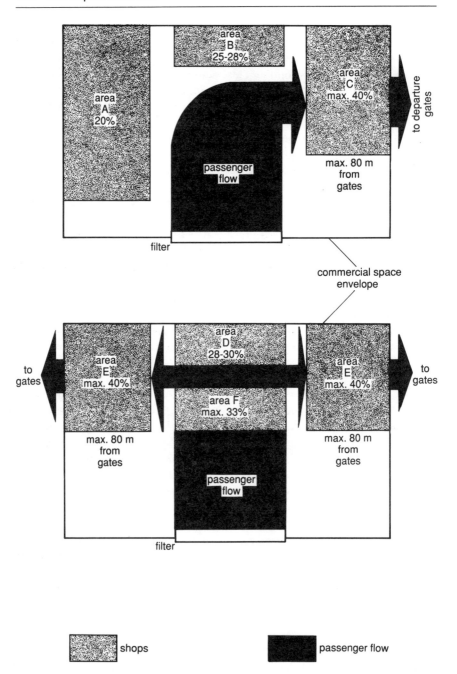

Figure 7.1 Impact of shop location on percentage of passengers making a purchase
Source: Brendel 1991.

since it involves moving down one level after check-in.

A related locational question is how much to offer in the arrival area. On the airside, that is before customs control, the best commercial opportunity is the provision of duty-free shopping. A few airports now have arrivals duty-free shops including Singapore, Kuala Lumpur, Bangkok, Buenos Aires, Rio de Janeiro and Reykjavik. The more successful of these arrivals shops generate about 10 per cent of their airports's total duty-free sales though in certain circumstances they rise much higher. For instance, at Cairo airport returning Egyptian workers push up sales in the arrivals duty-free shops to 50 per cent of the total. In most of Europe, however, the tax authorities are unlikely for the time being to allow duty-free shopping on arrival, especially as the duty-free facility for intra- European Community travellers is to be withdrawn. At European as at most other airports commercial opportunities on arrival will be largely in the landside area after customs. Traditionally arrival areas have had banks and car-hire and hotel desks for arriving passengers and sweetshops, bookshops and catering outlets geared largely for greeters and meeters. But there is an increasing awareness that a wider range of retail outlets might also be offered for both passengers and other groups. These might include flower shops, food shops or chemists. There is a real constraint though in that many terminals have been designed with a limited amount of free space in the arrivals area. Adding more shops may be difficult.

In simple terms passengers, or for that matter greeters and meeters, must come into contact with the commercial activities in order to be in a position to buy anything. The greater the number of opportunities offered to them the more likely it is that purchases will be made. This is where a conflict arises between the traditional airport model and the commercial airport model.

In the traditional model the terminal is organized to move passengers through to a boarding gate or lounge with simple and direct flows with little conflict or interruption. Shops and catering, if any, on the landside require a detour and an effort by the passenger to leave the normal flow routes. Even the duty-free shops and catering in international departures may require a similar detour and an effort to leave the flow routes from immigration through to the gates. It is quite possible to walk from the entry doors of some terminals to the aircraft without directly passing by a shop, a service counter or a catering outlet.

The traditional approach is shown in Figure 7.2(a). While this approach can be seen in the design and layout of many older airports it is surprisingly also found in some newer airports. The second and newest terminal at Paris Charles de Gaulle airport is an excellent modern example of the traditional approach. In Terminal 2B there are minimal landside shopping or catering facilities on the departure level. Reversing the sequence passengers are encouraged to go immediately through passport control with their luggage into a departure area. Check-in desks are along one side of this elongated departure area while a few rather small duty-free shops are along the other side. Passengers are diverted from shopping by the need to check in first. After checking in passengers tend to go directly through into the gate lounges which are conveniently located immediately behind each desk. Once there they discover that there are no catering or shopping facilities and that it is difficult to get back into the departure area. Processing of passengers may be relatively quick, but the opportunities of selling to passengers have been minimized and concession revenues per passenger are unnecessarily low.

In contrast to this approach, the commercially oriented airport attempts to direct passengers through the commercial activity areas as a necessary route through the terminal to the aircraft (see Figure 7.2(b)). The principle is to avoid the psychological and physical separation between airport processing time and shopping/refreshment time. Passengers (and companions) must be routed directly past or through the commercial areas and encouraged to linger and spend time there. The most interesting opportunity in the commercial model is to avoid the cocooned waiting time at the departure gate. Removing this 'processing' time could add more than another 50 per cent on to the 'free' time available to use for shopping and refreshment. There are ways to reduce if not eliminate this time. The principal design feature is to avoid having enclosed lounges at departure gates. The pier should be open and permit passengers to come and go from the immediate area of the departure gate. Buying refreshments or something from a shop should be made as easy as possible *after* the passenger has registered at the gate. Small kiosks and cafes within the pier should be considered.

It is not too far fetched to think of the passenger terminal as two distinct shopping centres. The first is a landside shopping centre with check-in desk attached but one which is normally open to all, that is passengers, airport employees, visitors and greeters and meeters. The second shopping centre has departure gates attached to it and only passengers can shop and eat or drink there. There are many examples of this shopping-centre approach at international airports other than Frankfurt airport. London's Heathrow Terminal 1 has a departure hall which is a thorough mix of check-in desks, shops, services and catering outlets. They all co-exist sharing the same common space. Physical boundaries between functions are minimized. The most physical of the boundaries is the staircase access to mezzanine-level catering outlets. Some of the departing party can be looking at shops whilst the leader of the party checks in. Companions can remain around and have something to do without any additional psychological effort to identify and to find the facilities on offer. Those who are shopping can, in many cases, still maintain sight of their party leader who is queueing to check in. The whole environment is one of a mixed-use, populated, thriving and welcoming place.

Concession revenue is generated not only from shops and catering outlets but also from service concessions such as banks, hotel desks, insurance and car hire. Of these the car-hire concessions are likely to be the greatest generators of concession fees because the sales or turnover of car-rental companies at

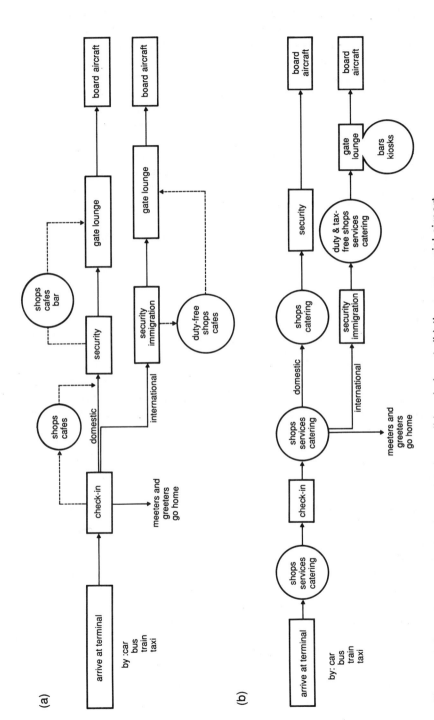

Figure 7.2 Departing passenger flows: (a) the traditional airport; (b) the commercial airport

airports can be enormous, especially at airports with poor public-transport access and those which are tourist destinations. Thus at France's Nice airport in 1987 the car-hire companies generated 46 per cent of the total sales turnover of all the airport concessionaires taken together, including the duty-free shops (Carré 1990). At many United States airports the car-rental concessions are the largest single source of concession-fee income. Thus in allocating space airports must ensure that the service concessions are adequately provided for both because of their importance to passengers and as a source of concession revenue.

As far as passenger terminals are concerned it is crucially important to approach their design and layout with the intention of facilitating the maximization of concession revenues. In practice, and within the constraints of the terminal site and existing buildings, this means trying to provide the maximum amount of space for both landside and airside commercial activities. It means locating that space directly in the line of passenger flows and ideally on the same floor levels as the passengers.

There are some additional commercial activities apart from shops and services in the terminal area which can generate concession revenues. The two most important are hotels and advertising. As a rough guide it has been estimated that in Europe a throughput of a million largely scheduled passengers can support a one-hundred-bed hotel. Thus once traffic gets above this level airport hotels start to become financially viable. An airport with ten million passengers should be able to support up to 1,000 hotel beds, that is 500 hotel rooms, in its immediate vicinity. Airports have a clear interest in ensuring that such hotels are built on airport land both to ensure closer and easier access for passengers and in order to generate some concession income. Any hotel concession is likely to generate both rent for leasing airport land and a concession fee based on the hotel's turnover. Thus it is important for airports to try to earmark suitable land close to their terminals for hotel development. They may also need land for other related concessions such as a conference centre or leisure complex. Land must be kept to meet not only immediate hotel needs but also to accommodate any future growth in the number of hotel rooms required.

Airports provide first-class advertising sites because they have important and clearly identifiable groups of people moving through them who can be directly targeted. Prime advertising sites at large airports can be rented for very substantial amounts of money. Some airports have set up their own small departments to act as advertising agencies. The larger airports, however, realizing that this is a highly specialized field, give all their advertising outlets to specialist advertising agencies who then pay a concession fee. The airport authority in return ensures that all the necessary advertising sites and outlets which the agency can sell are made available as far as this is possible.

SKILL OF CONCESSIONAIRES

Through the amount of space it allocates to concessions and through the locations chosen the airport authority attempts to convert passengers and others into potential customers. The concessionaire's role is to induce potential customers to become actual customers and to spend as much as possible. They do this through the ways they display and offer their goods or services, through the range of goods on offer, through their pricing strategy and ultimately through their skill and professionalism as retailers or providers of services.

The layout of airport shops, as with all retailing, has a major impact on the value of sales achieved per customer. Key decisions have to be made by the concessionaires. How should they display their goods to attract customers? Should they offer goods on open shelves so that customers help themselves or should they only have goods available at counters manned by sales staff? Current retailing practice favours the former but the more expensive the goods offered the more customers expect service from high-quality sales staff. Thus if a shop is selling expensive perfumes or high-fashion goods experienced assistants will help push up sales rather than leaving customers to pick out goods for themselves from accessible displays. The layout of shops is also important particularly for those selling a wide range of products such as duty-free shops. Customers must be encouraged to browse and to see as many goods on offer as possible. In the simple traditional layout shown in Figure 7.3(a) passengers can walk through quickly without seeing all the goods on display unless they make a deliberate effort to do so. Sales are likely to be restricted. Two other approaches, either the directed or the open-flow layout, appear to be more successful. In the more complex layout in Figure 7.3(b) passengers are forced to walk past most of the display shelves by using counters and shelves in the shop to direct the flow of passengers. Examples of this type of layout are the duty-free shops at Milan and Brussels. The alternative is to have entirely open shopping areas with scattered displays and counters where passengers can move in and out at any point as if in an open market. This is the approach adopted at London Heathrow, in the Harrods airside shop in Terminal 3 and the airside shop in Terminal 4 (Figure 7.3(c)). Note that this layout requires individual cash registers on many counters. Both the directed and open-flow layouts have been shown to increase the sales per passenger compared to more traditional layouts.

The range of goods on offer at both landside and airside shops clearly must impact on the total turnover of concessionaires and therefore on the airport's concession revenue. The number of shops and the size of shops available, which are both dependent on the airport authority, limit what can be offered. But within these physical constraints at any airport, the concessionaires and the airport's commercial managers must together consider what types of shops, and for that matter catering outlets, should be offered and what range

(a)

(b)

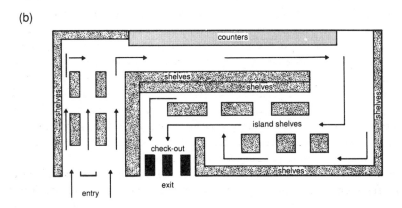

(c)

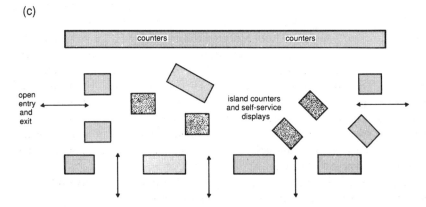

Figure 7.3 Alternative layouts for duty- or tax-free shops or other shopping concessions: (a) non-directed flow; (b) directed flow; (c) open flow

and quality of goods each should sell. The goods on offer must be matched to the target markets be they passengers or airport employees or visitors. Passenger profiles and needs will vary from airport to airport depending on the nationality of the passengers, purpose of travel, average age, local circumstances and so on. Airport retailers must be finely tuned to the needs of their markets if they are to maximize sales. Two examples illustrate this. The landside chemist's shop at Geneva airport is one of the few airport shops in the world where one can buy crutches! This chemist caters for skiers with leg injuries on their way home from the Alps. At Sharjah airport in the Middle East the Weitnauer Group, which runs the duty-free shop, ensures that when a China Airlines flight flying to or from Taiwan comes through the gold counter is staffed by twelve sales assistants and the goods on display are 22 carat gold – that is what this market requires. When German charter flights come through the 22 carat goods on display are replaced by 18 carat and only six assistants are needed. This is really fine tuning to individual market requirements.

The pricing of goods and services will also impact on sales. Staffing costs of airport shops or service desks is high because of the long opening hours, sometimes requiring three shifts, and the need to stay open on weekends and public holidays. Despite this, it is important to ensure that in the landside shops and catering outlets prices are no higher than in comparable city-centre shopping areas. In airside shops, it is crucial that the savings from the absence of taxes and duties are passed on to passengers and are not merely converted into high profits by the concessionaires. Airport commercial managers need to monitor prices to ensure passengers get a good deal and that prices are competitive with those of neighbouring airports. While the concessionaire may prefer high prices and larger profit margins even if this means lower sales, the airport is interested in high sales and high turnover, since the concession fee is normally a percentage of the latter. There is a potential conflict of interest here which frequently requires airport intervention in and control of concessionaires' pricing policies. In the United Kingdom the BAA Plc board of directors has laid down the minimum saving against high-street prices that must be offered on each particular product range at its airports' duty- and tax-free outlets. For instance, in 1990–1 on blended whiskies, rye whisky, gin, vodka and rum the saving had to be at least 40 per cent; on cognacs and brandies 35 per cent; on aged whiskies, wine, champagne, port and sherries 20 per cent; on cigarettes, tobacco and cigars (other than British or Dutch) 40 per cent; and 35 per cent on British and 25 per cent on Dutch cigars. While not all airports may be as detailed in their price controls, they clearly have an interest in ensuring prices are low enough to stimulate demand and sales. Some airport authorities ensure that their concession contracts give them some powers in relation to prices charged while the majority rely on friendly persuasion and having co-operative concessionaires.

The quality of the personnel employed by concessionaires also helps in generating sales. Passengers, in particular, are demanding and have high expectations. Concessionaires must make sure that they have highly motivated and efficient staff. This is easier to do if the concession contracts let out by the airport are rather longer than three years or less. Employers may also have to offer bonuses or commissions of various kinds to motivate their staff in view of the fact that they are required to work unsocial hours and that staff facilities at airports are often relatively poor because of the shortage of space.

To maximize sales the marketing skills of the concessionaires must be combined with the airport authority's more detailed and longer-term knowledge of the characteristics of the different market segments being targeted at the airport. The airport will also have a better understanding of future traffic and market trends. Since a great deal depends on the professionalism of the concessionaires, choosing the right concessionaires is one of the most critical functions of the airport commercial manager. The final choice will depend partly on the overall commercial strategy being adopted with regard to the number and range of concessions and partly on the methods used in the selection process.

THE PORTFOLIO APPROACH

Before selecting concessionaires airports should decide their overall concession policies. Airports wishing to be commercially oriented need to embrace an approach to commercial activities which parallels that adopted by the best retail managers in normal shopping environments. Like the retail manager of a new shopping centre in a new town, the airport commercial manager needs to adopt a portfolio concept. The portfolio should vary between airports and even terminals in the same airport in response to different passenger characteristics. This means that airport commercial managers should be proactive. They should seek out and develop the type of concession which they feel best meets the needs of their particular target groups rather than sit back and wait for offers.

An example can be found in the redesign of Terminal 3 at Heathrow in 1990. Here a deliberate choice was made for up-market outlets to form a portfolio of shops both landside and airside which the commercial management believed would be of greater interest to the international, long-haul departing passenger and would thereby produce greater sales per passenger. This passenger segment is one which is spending more than the average on the cost of the flight. It is also composed predominantely of non-UK nationals and hence is attracted to the best UK brand names, such as Harrods, which it will not find available at its destination.

A contrasting portfolio approach in 1990 was that seen in the selection of shops in the two terminals at London's Gatwick airport. In this case the passenger mix was just under 50 per cent charter, principally to European destinations. The schedule traffic is a mixture of both European and long-haul. The mix of shops chosen includes several which by market surveys have been shown to appeal across the spectrum of potential customers from the higher-income groups to the lower-income groups. These included the familiar specialist retailers of Body Shop, Tie Rack, Knickerbox and Alto (videos and recordings) together with mainstream but lower-priced clothing brand names of Dorothy Perkins (ladieswear) and Burtons (menswear). There was also a childrens clothing shop and a soft toys shop to interest parents and children passing through the airport on holiday. The portfolio approach at Gatwick extends to entertainment activities for those who tend to wait longer for their flights, particularly those on charter flights who are required to check-in early. These entertainment activities at Gatwick include gambling machines, games machines, children's rides and an area showing satellite T.V.

The portfolio approach is also reflected in the catering concessions. Again using the example of the Gatwick terminals, the catering mix reflected what the commercial management believed the demand to be. Thus there were no waitress-service restaurants in either terminal. There was a general self-service restaurant in each terminal and a pub-bar with food available. In addition each terminal had a large and separate hamburger concession which gained custom from all income groups and especially appealed to the leisure and lower-income segment of the traffic. The mix was futher extended by the addition of small cafes, juice stands and coffee shops which widened the range of food and drink on offer. The portfolio thus caters to those at either end of the spectrum, allowing the purchasing of a cup of coffee or of a full meal.

A portfolio approach requires careful planning of the range of concessions and their position within the landside and airside areas. Some airports have decided to position most of their concessions in a single area central to the main line of passenger flow. An alternative strategy is to establish 'shopping centres' in different parts of the airport each of which provides the same broad range of shops together with some catering facilities, but only one or two of which have the full range of outlets and services. The aim is to ensure that passengers can always shop within easy access of immigration control, if they are landside, or of their departure gates if airside. Passengers are more at ease if they are aware of where they have to go to next and sales tend to increase. Frankfurt airport, for instance, has six distinct shopping centres. While they broadly duplicate each other in terms of the range of shops, customers' interest can be stimulated if the concessionaires are different. At Changi's Terminal 1 in Singapore there is a main shopping centre at either end of the main departure lounge but passengers who make the effort to visit both find they are virtually identical. Greater variety would surely push up sales at airports with two or more shopping centres.

The portfolio has to differentiate between arrival and departure areas and between landside and airside locations since requirements differ considerably. Clearly many of the services, such as car hire or hotel desks, are only needed landside. Equally some types of shops do better landside and others can do better if in the tax- or duty-free area. An example of different sales patterns can be seen in Figure 7.4 which shows the average share of different product groups in total landside and airside facilities at French airports in 1987. Tobacco and alcohol products and perfumes generated 75 per cent of airside sales. But in the landside shops there were negligible sales of alcohol products and perfumes though sales of tobacco products were 17 per cent of the total. The biggest landside sales were from newspaper and bookshops (36 per cent), and sales of fashion goods (16 per cent) and regional or local products.

At a number of the better-performing airports there is an increasing usage of brand names as concessionaires. This policy is to make more use of brand names which are familiar to the people who will use the terminal. There are many examples of brand names at London terminals which are taken straight from the high street. These include Body Shop, Tie Rack, Sock Shop, Knickerbox, Burton, Dorothy Perkins, Aquascutum, Bally, Scotch House, Our Price Records, W. H. Smith Newsagents and others which the UK public and some of the international public will recognize. The same is true at Frankfurt but not for example at Paris Charles de Gaulle. This is a deliberate policy. It is considered that people are more likely to make impulse purchases in stores whose name they know and in which they feel comfortable both with the style and pitch of the products and also with the prices and value for money being offered.

Prior to this the British Airports Authority, for example, had used its own name for certain outlets. These included 'Skyshop' for its newsagents/ bookstores. The policy was followed even though BAA did not operate the Skyshops themselves but contracted W. H. Smith, Trust House Forte and others as concessionaires to operate them. The latter names meant more to the public than did 'Skyshop'. In the late 1980s Skyshops were replaced by the brand name of the concessionaire. This policy was then extended albeit slowly into the catering area. Again we have noted that at Gatwick in 1990 there were two hamburger restaurants. These were McDonalds and Burger King which are both well-known international brand names. The customer knows exactly what to expect in these restaurants and would have no hesitation in using them.

An interesting consequence of this approach is likely to be that those airports which have previously offered the whole of a particular type of activity to one concessionaire will no longer be doing so. For example if one concessionaire has operated all the duty-paid retailing the introduction of brand names will introduce competition within the terminal and bring to an end the exclusive provision of retail shops by single concessionaires. The new approach is already well developed in the London terminals. However, where most of an airport's passengers are not local residents and its national retailing companies are not well known, the use of local brand names may not be effective and the airport may need to create its own brand image.

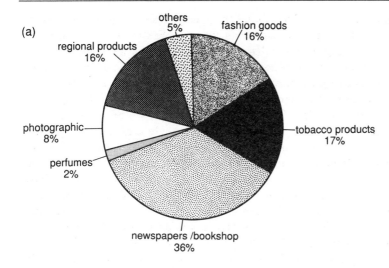

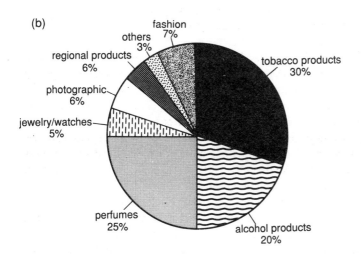

Figure 7.4 Sales of landside and airside shops at French airports in 1987: (a) landside sales (US$51 million); (b) airside sales (US$178 million)
Source: Carré 1990.

CHOICE OF CONCESSIONAIRES AND CONTRACT TERMS

The process used in selecting concessionaires has considerable impact on an airport's commercial revenues because it ultimately determines what proportion of each concessionaire's turnover is paid to the airport in the form of a concession fee. The key factors in the selection process which affect the airport's take from each concession are first of all the degree of competitiveness in the tendering for concession contracts; second, whether government, airline or airport-owned enterprises or joint-venture companies are bidding for contracts; third, the frequency with which contractors are changed; and finally, the number of separate concessions offered.

Competition in tendering for concessions is crucial in ensuring that an airport obtains as much revenue as possible from each of its concessions. However, the concession fee offered is not the only criterion for choosing concessionaires. Airport commercial directors must be proactive in attracting potential concessionaires to tender for a particular contract. Having decided on the basis of a portfolio approach the nature of the facility or shop they are about to contract for, they should go out and actively search for potential bidders. Ideally, these should be companies or retailers with similar outlets or shops elsewhere in order to ensure greater flexibility and skill in labour management and in merchandise selection and procurement. Potential concessionaires should have an established track record and a strong financial base. For major concessions at larger airports they are likely to be companies that are well known either locally or nationally. They should also be willing to adapt to the particular requirements and constraints of airport operations. It is likely that for any single concession there will only be a handul or so of companies that are likely to meet all of the above requirements. But it is crucial that there are at least two or three strong contenders to ensure competitive bidding. This is why airports must go out and encourage suitable companies to bid for concessions. The worse situation for an airport is to be faced with only one bid or only one realistic bid. Tenders must be secret and must be fairly detailed covering not only the bidder's financial proposals but also their marketing strategy, merchandise range and prices as well as their staffing proposals. The successful bid should not be the one necessarily offering the best monetary returns to the airport but the one which overall meets the airport's marketing and commercial requirements. After all a company proposing to pay a high percentage of its turnover to the airport may ultimately generate poorer concession revenues than a company offering a lower percentage because the former may be less successful in its marketing and in pushing up its total turnover.

Another important aspect of concession policy is the frequency with which existing concessionaires are replaced by new ones. Some airports have adopted a policy of encouraging existing concessionaires to renew or extend their contracts, if they have been successful in generating concession revenue and if they have developed close co-operation with the airport management. Amsterdam airport, for example has rarely changed concessionaires. Such a policy could be defended on the grounds that existing concessionaires have built up an understanding of and insight into the market at their own airport which it would be difficult for an entirely new concessionaire to obtain quickly. This approach, however, while ensuring a close working relationship between concessionaires and airports, is unlikely to ensure the same high level of concession-fee income for an airport as would an open and competitive bidding system. It also cuts the airport off from any new and innovative concessionaires. Repeatedly renewing existing concession contracts means that existing concessionaires have a permanent licence to make money, possibly at the airport's expense!

Competitive bidding for concessions becomes difficult if not impossible if the airport, the national airline or the government are involved directly or through a joint-venture company in a particular concession. If the airport authority itself provides for instance, the duty-free shopping concession (as the Irish Airport Authority does at its airports) then no bidding is likely to take place. If the national airline or a government-owned company wish to take over certain concessions, the airport may have little option but to enter into direct negotiations with them without going for competitive bids at all. This is particularly likely where the airport is itself owned and run by a government department or corporation. A good example in 1990 was Athens airport. It was run by the Greek Civil Aviation Department while all catering was provided by Olympic Catering, an Olympic Airways subsidiary, and the duty-free concessionaire was another government-owned company. It is very unlikely that an airport faced with such a situation will be able to maximize its concession revenue. If governments wish their airports to become more financially self-sufficient by generating more concession-fee income they must ensure that airport, airline or government-owned companies are not given preferential treatment in bidding for airport concessions.

Originally, airports tended to grant only one concession for each major activity at the airport. So there would be a single catering concession, a single duty-free concessionaire, only one bank and so on. The justification for this was that since each concessionaire had nominally to invest in equipment and facilities which might be worth very little if they lost the contract when its renewal came up, they should be compensated by having an exclusive concession for the duration of the contract. At smaller airports more than one concessionaire of each type might not be viable anyway. Where little airport-specific investment was required of the concessionaire, then multiple concessions might be offered. It is for this reason one frequently finds several car-hire firms or hotel-booking agencies even at relatively small airports. As an airport's traffic builds up, however, and provided there is space available, a policy of encouraging competition within the airport by having more than one concessionaire for certain retail or service activities might both improve customer service and generate more concession revenue. Having more than one caterer, retailer or agency competing for the same market will not only provide greater choice, it will also reduce criticism that the airport or its sole concessionaire might be exploiting a monopolistic situation. Having competing concessions is easiest if an airport has several terminals. But even in single terminals, competition between concessionaires should be encouraged where possible. But there may be difficulties especially in the catering area. If catering outlets are let as different concessions the problems of ensuring separate kitchens, food-delivery routes and storage areas may become acute since much more space will be needed within the terminal than if there is only one catering concessionaire.

All the above factors will affect the degree of competition in the bidding for concession contracts. The more competitive the bids the more likely it is that the airport's potential revenue from the concession fees can be maximized. How much an airport actually gets out of a concession ultimately depends on the contract terms and the fee arrangement. In the early days, and still today at some small or developing country airports, concessions were granted for a fixed annual fee. Sometimes this was based on the area occupied and was more akin to a rent than a concession fee. During the 1960s and 1970s many airports around the world experienced rapid traffic growth. Where this happened, concessionaires were able significantly to increase their turnover and their profits while the airport authorities continued to receive the same fixed concession fees even though they may have invested heavily in developing the airport. Increasingly it was felt that airport owners should share in the benefits of the increased traffic growth which they were helping to generate. The easiest way of doing this was to move from fixed-fee and long-term concessions to shorter-term contracts with fees expressed as a percentage of each concessionaire's turnover. Where turnover was difficult to measure or where profitability was not directly related to turnover, the fee might be expressed as a fixed amount per transaction or per unit sold. Banks, hotel agencies and fuel concessions are often handled in this way. Bank concessions may involve a rent based on the amount of space occupied plus a concession fee which is expressed as a small fixed amount per foreign-exchange transaction undertaken. Hotel agencies may also be charged a fixed fee per booking made. Where airports impose a fee on fuel suppliers it is normally a very small charge per gallon of fuel sold. The aim in all cases has been to ensure that the airports' 'take' grows as the concessionaires' sales increase with traffic growth. Concessionaires are after all given access to a captive high-income market, and often they may be the sole monopoly supplier of that good or service to that market.

Most concessions at larger airports are now let on the basis of a concession fee that is expressed as percentage of the concessionaires' total annual sales or turnover. There are a number of ways of doing this. The simplest is a single percentage figure based on turnover irrespective of the ultimate level of that turnover. A single figure is most likely to be used where the products or services being sold cannot be differentiated as for instance with the car-hire or the flight-kitchen concessions. The latter provide in-flight catering and may be charged around 6 per cent of their turnover in a concession fee. Where the products are more variegated, then an airport will generate higher concession fees if it stipulates a different percentage for each group of products. Since the concessionaires' profit margins vary by type of product, the airport's take should be higher where profit margins are greater. If there is only a single unique percentage fee, the concessionaire will tend to display and sell only those products with high profit margins and may ignore low-price brand leaders and goods with low profit margins. The concessionaire's profits may increase as a result but their total turnover and the airport's concession fees may be reduced. The British Airports Authority in the mid-1980s split duty-free goods, largely alcohol and tobacco products, into more than twenty separate product categories and charged a different concession fee on each. For instance the percentage fee on deluxe whisky brands was higher than for ordinary blended whiskies. There were up to thirty product categories for tax-free goods. For example, the take on tax-free watch sales was about 10 per cent but on costume jewellery it was 15 per cent or so. In the landside shops, that is for duty- and tax-paid goods, there might be up to ten or more product groups –books, newspapers, sweets, souvenirs, etc. – with different concession fees. Even for car-hire concessions one might have a higher concession fee for chauffeur-driven cars as opposed to self-drive car rentals. Most other airports have tended to have fewer separate product groupings than the BAA. Following privatization the latter began to reduce the number of product groupings to facilitate monitoring and control.

The experience of United Kingdom airports suggests that fixing different percentage concession fees on a large number of separate product groupings increases the concession-fee income per passenger generated by each airport. The simpler the concession-fee structure, the lower is the airport's take from concessions and the higher are likely to be the concessionaires' profits.

Most contracts ensure that the percentage fees increase as certain levels of turnover are reached. This can be justified on the grounds that once the concessionaire's fixed costs have been covered by a certain volume of sales then his own profit margins rise and he can afford to pay a higher concession fee. On the other hand, for entirely new concessions one might encourage the operator to develop the market and push up sales by reducing the percentage fee as turnover rises. Concession contracts should also guarantee a minimum concession fee which concessionaires must pay irrespective of sales actually achieved. A usual guarantee is about 80 per cent of the concessionaire's projected fee based on the forecast sales as shown in the tender document.

A key aspect of any concession is the length of the contract period. Concessionaires' preference for longer periods, particularly where they need to invest heavily in fixtures and fittings, conflicts with the airport's desire to benefit from more frequent tendering for concessions. Ideally the length of contract should reflect the level of investment required of the concessionaire. If the airport itself pays for all the fittings and specialized equipment needed then contract terms can be as short as three years. Where concessionaires are required to invest in their own facilities then the length of the contract should depend on the level of that investment in order to allow concessionaires

Table 7.1 The process for successful letting of concessions

1 Develop portfolio strategy
2 Define market strategy for each concession
3 Determine space and location requirements (and availability)
4 Proactively market the airport to potential concessionaires
5 Prepare design concepts and specifications for contracts
6 Tender/negotiation/selection process
7 Monitor and review concessionaire performance
8 Work with concessionaires on improvements and redevelopment

sufficient time to recoup the capital cost involved. Where little investment is needed, as is the case with tie shops, many souvenir shops, hotel reservations or flight-insurance desks, then contracts should be for not more than three or four years. For larger retail concessions involving more substantial invest-ment by the concessionaire four to six years would be reasonable. Most shops would fall into this category as would smaller duty- and tax-free concessions or simpler catering outlets. Where major investments are needed one might go up to seven years but no longer. This would be for large duty- and tax-free shops, for large catering concessions, and even for car-hire concessions when these involve expenditure on large parking and servicing facilities. Handling concessions and flight kitchens are also likely to be in this category. Whatever the length of the contract period it is important, if an airport aims to maximize concession revenues, that no contracts are renewed automati-cally on expiry. All concessionaires should be obliged to tender against competing bids.

The all-important process of letting concessions for a commercially oriented airport is summarized in Table 7.1. The starting point must be for the airport to decide, as previously mentioned, on its retail strategy and portfolio. Then, once an airport has specified the location and space available for a concession, the nature and type of merchandise or services it wants to be offered, the opening hours, the fixtures and equipment included (if any) and possibly the staffing levels it wishes to see used, it can ask potential concessionaires to put in competitive tenders. These should outline the concessionaire's marketing strategy, their projected turnover for each year of the contract terms and their offer in terms of concession-fee rates for different product groups or services. The projected turnover by product group and the percentage concession fees being offered will together indicate the airport's expected concession revenue from each contract. But while the airport clearly wants to maximize revenue it should not necessarily choose the tender offering the highest concession-fee rates. Assuming that all the tenderers meet the criteria previously stipulated, namely that they should be exper-ienced and well-established companies with a proven track record and a sound financial base, the airport should choose the one which will generate high concession revenues and best meet the airport's marketing and retail strategies.

Once the concessionaires have been appointed the airport commercial manager's role is not finished. He or she must be aware of their responsibility towards the concessionaire and of how they can contribute to maximizing the concessionaire's turnover and thereby the airport's concession revenue. The concession contract may include many detailed specifications on shop or desk design, on product display, on opening hours, on staffing levels and so on, possibly even on pricing. The airport needs to check and monitor that the terms of the concession agreement are being fulfilled. But it needs to do more than this. It must work closely with all its concessionaires to push up sales through advertising campaigns, the introduction of new product lines, the redesign of shop layouts and so on. The airport commercial department is in a unique position to do this because it alone has an overview of what is happening at all concessions and of current and future traffic developments. The airport and the concessionaire should be seen not as landlord and tenant but as partners who work together to improve airport business. The department should continually monitor and survey its different target markets and use such information on the buying behaviour of its customers to help its concessionaires push up sales.

The interplay of the various factors, mentioned above, which affect the choice of concessionaires can have a significant impact on the degree to which an airport maximizes its concession revenues. This is clearly illustrated in Table 7.2 which contrasts the airport concession revenues in three European countries in 1987–8. The larger United Kingdom airports have traditionally had a very competitive bidding system for concessions with a complex concession-fee structure involving different percentages on a large number of product groups. As a result 49 per cent of the turnover of duty- and tax-free shops was paid as a concession fee to the airports. Holland is dominated by Schiphol airport at Amsterdam which handles the major part of Dutch air traffic. What happens at Schiphol largely determines the overall picture. Schiphol has extensive duty-free shopping facilities and has developed a close relationship with its concessionaires who are rarely if ever changed. The result is that overall Dutch airports only take 22 per cent of such concessionaires' turnover as concession fees. The worst case is Greece where the single duty-free operator is a subsidiary company of a government ministry, which is expected to produce large surpluses on its sales. As a result the airport, run by another government department, only takes 5 per cent of the turnover as its concession fee.

THE COMPETITORS

Competition between airports for duty- or tax-free sales is fairly limited. Passengers will generally choose the airports they fly to or from on the basis of other more significant factors than on whether they can save a few dollars by

Table 7.2 Duty-free sales and airport concession income 1987–8

Airports in	Total duty- and tax-free sales (ECU millions)	Airport concession (ECU millions)	Airport concession revenue as % of sales
United Kingdom	359	176	49
Netherlands	150	33	22
Greece	62	3	5

Source: NEI 1990.

buying at one airport rather than another. Passengers undertaking a journey which involves an intermediate stop or connection may prefer, if they have a choice, to transit through airports with a wide range of duty- and tax-free goods at low prices. Airports may find it worthwhile to try to attract such passengers through advertising and promotional campaigns. Amsterdam's Schiphol airport has been successful in doing this in the past. It is not clear, however, which airports may have lost concession revenue as a result of Schiphol's success

Airports do face competition in generating concession revenues, particularly in the duty- and tax-free area, but it is not so much from other airports as from the airlines and possibly city-centre duty-free shops. Most airlines try to offer duty-free sales on board their aircraft except where sectors are too short to allow sufficient time to do this. These sales compete directly with those of the airport shops. The latter clearly have an advantage in that they can display a greater of variety of goods while passengers are more relaxed and have more time. Some airlines, such as Singapore Airlines, try to overcome this disadvantage by offering through mail-order facilities a much wider choice of purchases than can be carried on board.

On-board sales are an essential element in the economics of charter airlines (Doganis 1991). It is these airlines which are therefore most aggressive in promoting sales on board the aircraft. They do this in a number of ways. The process was outlined by the inflight sales manager of the Danish charter airline, Sterling Airways, at the Tax Free World Exhibition in Cannes, France in October 1988. The travel catalogues of the tour companies using Sterling advertise their in-flight sales while the travel agents themselves may have display cases with a sample of products. When passengers receive their tickets, these include an order list for on-board sales. Ten days before departure they would also receive a thirty-six page-catalogue. In 1988 about 250,000 catalogues were mailed out (Brendel 1991). Passengers can order by mail before departure for collection on board or they can go to the airport having already decided what they are going to buy on the flight. In either case the airport's potential sales will have already been adversely affected. One day before their return flights, passengers will receive an order list at their hotel which can be handed in before departure or which can be used as a reminder of what can be bought on board. The whole process of selling to passengers is meticulously planned. As a result in 1988 Sterling's on-board duty-free sales totalled US$53 million or about $32 per passenger which was substantially higher than those of scheduled airlines or most airports.

The other acute form of competition for airports is from town-centre or off-airport duty-free shops. Many countries, especially tourist destinations such as Jugoslavia or the Philippines, have allowed such shops for the use of visitors with valid return tickets. The major advantage they offer to tourists is the time and ability to choose and pack the goods they wish to purchase before departure. Airport shopping may be more hurried and requires passengers to carry the goods purchased. Clearly such shops will reduce airport sales and concession fees. Off-airport competition may arise in other areas as well. For instance, there may be car parks, hotels or car-rental companies just outside or close to the airport boundary competing directly with the airport concession-aires. Such competition may not only affect total turnover but may impact on the concession-fee percentages that an airport authority can negotiate. City-centre competition may also be more generalized in countries where taxes are low and price-cutting is widespread. Thus airport shops at both Hong Kong and Singapore airports have difficulty in competing on price with downtown retail shops.

THE KEY TO SUCCESS

Airline or off-airport competitors will clearly affect concessionaires airport sales. But concession revenues can also rise or decline through factors such as the introduction of new routes, airline failures or exchange-rate fluctuations which are largely beyond the control of individual airport managements. Revenues are also very much influenced by an airport's overall traffic levels and the characteristics of that traffic, factors over which airports have only limited control. But airport commercial managers can directly impact on concession revenues through the location and the total amount of space and land they can allocate for concessions. Within any given space constraints, the degree to which concession revenues are maximized will depend on the choice of concessionaires, the contract terms negotiated and the marketing and selling skills of the concessionaires chosen. The key to success is that the airport and the concessionaires should be seen not as landlord and tenant but as partners who work together to improve the airport's business.

Chapter 8

Monitoring airport performance and efficiency

THE NEED FOR PERFORMANCE INDICATORS

All businesses or organizations, whether in the public or private sector, need to measure and monitor their performance. The use of performance measures in the airport industry is particularly important because of the specific character-istics of airports. In a perfectly competitive environment, market forces will ensure that optimal performance can be equated with profitability. However the conditions under which airports operate are far from competitive. Regulatory, geographical, economic, social and political constraints all hinder direct competition between airports. At the same time, the extent to which airports can attract other airports' traffic with different price or service levels is also very limited. In other words the demand for airport services is likely to be relatively inelastic. Most airports therefore enjoy a quasi-monopolistic position and may abuse such a position by extracting high revenues from their customers. In this instance profit measures may not equate with efficiency. Profit alone may not be able to identify, for example, wasteful consumption of resources, and will not provide an airport with the proper incentive to improve its performance. Additional ratios or indicators measuring the inputs and outputs in both physical and financial terms are essential.

Surprisingly, many airports still assess their performance by using criteria based solely on profit measures or traffic growth. This is in spite of a growing awareness by airport managements of the financial and commercial impli-cations of operating an airport. Too frequently in the past governments have set their airports purely financial objectives such as the need to break even or obtain a specific rate of return on net assets. Only a few airports have developed a systematic approach towards measuring performance and even fewer airports include any performance indicators in their published accounts. In general there is no accepted industry practice for measuring airport performance. This is in marked contrast to many other industries and even the airline industry where standard performance indicators have now been widely adopted. Performance indicators are needed by airport owners and managers for several reasons.

In the first instance performance indicators are required to *measure an airport's economic efficiency*, that is the relationship between its inputs (labour, capital, fuel, etc.) and its output. Output might be measured in terms of total revenue, work-load units, passengers, air-transport movements or some other appropriate measure. The performance indicators should be used to ensure that the airport management is making the best use of the resources at its disposal. One reason for doing this, as mentioned, is that profitability does not necessarily equate with economic efficiency particularly for airports that may be monopolies or in a quasi-monopolistic position. Moreover, overall profitability is totally inadequate as a measure of the economic performance of discrete activity areas within an airport.

Most airport planning and investment decisions change an airport's input-output relationships, that is they affect its economic efficiency. Therefore, in considering *alternative investments or developments* it is important to assess them in terms of the effect they aim to have or are expected to have on the airport's input-output relationships. This can be done, in part, by using performance indicators to help ensure that the best decision is made and that the management is more adequately prepared for changes as they occur.

As airports become more independent of direct government control, governments may well need to use a variety of indicators as a way of *imposing performance targets* on their airports. The United Kingdom government in the late 1970s began introducing precise performance targets for all the nationalized industries in addition to the wider financial targets expressed as rates of return on net assets. Prior to privatization, the government and the British Airports Authority had agreed the following main performance targets for the financial years 1983–84 to 1985–86:

1 To achieve, on average, a minimum annual rate of return on average net assets of 3 per cent plus one-fifth of the annual percentage growth in terminal passengers on a cumulative basis in each successive year. This was coupled with the supplementary objective of achieving break-even at the then loss-making Scottish airports within the three-year period.
2 To reduce costs (at constant prices and excluding depreciation) per terminal passenger by one-half per cent a year plus an additional reduction equivalent to two-fifths of the percentage growth in terminal passengers over the three-year period.
3 To increase the number of terminal passengers per payroll hour by one-half per cent a year plus two-fifths of the percentage growth in terminal passengers over the three-year period. (Payroll hours are the total number of hours worked by employees including overtime and the hours of part-time employees.)

The aim of expressing the targets in such a complex way was to differentiate between improvements in performance which arise purely because of traffic growth and those due to increased efficiency and productivity. In addition to these four targets agreed with the government, the BAA set themselves three targets covering their commercial activities (see p. 60) and two relating to service standards.

In manufacturing industries, the quality of the product can be strictly controlled and measured. This is relatively easy because the product has primarily physical dimensions. Problems do exist at the margin when one tries to measure such aspects of a product as its comfort or its taste. But in service industries quality control becomes much more problematic, both because it is inherently more difficult to measure the quality of a service rendered rather than that of a product and also because it is difficult to be objective rather than subjective. Airport service standards up to now have been seen in purely physical terms or in terms of design standards, for instance, in terms of area per terminal passenger or toilets per passenger. But design standards are not the same as service standards. A passenger is not concerned with how many baggage trolleys there are per passenger but with how long it takes to get one. Thus the final justification for performance indicators is that some are needed to *measure airport service standards.*

Inter-airport comparisons of service standards generally pose insurmountable problems. Therefore the discussion which follows is concerned with exploring indicators relating primarily to economic performance. However, it should be borne in mind that there is a trade-off between service quality and economic performance. An airport may, as a matter of policy, provide a very high level of service despite the knowledge that this will worsen some economic performance indicators. This potential conflict between service standards and goal achievement is inherent in service industries.

TO MONITOR OR TO COMPARE

There are clearly several arguments justifying greater use of performance indicators in the airport business, but their primary purpose must be as management tools for the airports themselves. They should be used to analyse and monitor past and present performance. A wide range of indicators need to be developed to enable airport managers to ensure that the various inputs and resources employed at the airport are used as efficiently and effectively as possible to achieve the desired objectives or targets. If the measures or ratios used identify shortcomings in any activity or function they should generate corrective action. The same measures should also be capable of use by airports as an aid to successful future planning. Managers can decide what levels of performance are needed to meet corporate or other objectives and can actually set budgets or targets specifically incorporating the relevant performance indicators as the British government did in relation to the British Airports Authority in the early 1980's.

Performance indicators generally involve a comparison between some measure of input and output. These inputs and outputs can be quantified in physical or financial terms. The relationship between output and the amount of input required to produce it becomes clearer when the raw data are incorporated into performance ratios. However these measures by themselves, while indicating whether performance has improved or deteriorated, cannot give any indication of the overall quality of that performance. They must have a standard for comparison to be meaningful. The usefulness of the ratios therefore depends on the appropriateness of the standards set. Should an airport judge its performance in different areas purely in terms of its own past achievements and set appropriate targets, or should it compare its performance with that of other comparable airports or with some industry 'best' achievable level? In brief, should performance indicators be used merely for internal monitoring or should they also be used for external comparisons?

There are two ways of assessing performance internally. One can monitor an airport's key indicators over time or compare its actual to planned or forecast performance. In the latter case, success or failure is judged by the degree to which forecasts or targets are actually achieved. If past achievements are used as standards for comparison, an improvement in performance can be measured in terms of more output produced for a given level of input or of the same output being produced with a reduced level of input. This will be of great importance to management as it will show trends over the years and will give indications as to the direction in which the airport is heading. However the inherent weakness of this method is that the one airport in question is considered in complete isolation; all the measurements are related entirely to its own sphere of operation. An airport's own performance indicators in isolation do not tell the management how well they are doing in relation to other similar airports. More especially they give no indication in which areas the airport performs particularly well in relation to the industry average or to other airports. To overcome this problem it is crucial to make inter-airport comparisons.

In making inter-firm or cross-sectional comparisons, three different standards might possibly be adopted. An individual airport's performance might be compared with:

1 the comparative performance of a sample of individual airports; in this case comparison is made with a range of different airports to establish the comparative rankings for all those in the sample;
2 the industry average; this poses problems in selecting a sample of firms to establish an average, which will also be relevant to the firm in question; or
3 the 'best' performance levels achieved in the industry; this will give targets to aim for which are actually obtainable.

As in other industries, performance indicators should be used both to monitor the performance of individual airports over time or in relation to budgets or targets *and* to compare their performance with other airports at a particular point in time. But inter-airport comparisons tend to be more difficult to calculate and interpret because of comparability problems. Many airports are opposed to inter-airport comparisons because they argue that these comparability problems invalidate such comparisons and they fear that their data will be constantly misinterpreted by others. Undoubtedly these problems mean that strictly speaking a 'like with like' comparison can never be made. No two airports are identical but this does not mean that performance comparisons are of no use to airports. Differences in performance may very well be due to some individual airport characteristic rather than to managerial inefficiency, but at least by making inter-airport comparisons an airport will be in a position to investigate such factors further and may consequently find some areas of operation where there appears to be room for improvement through management action.

Most of the indicators currently used by airports aim to monitor their own performance over time. Rarely are indicators used to make inter-airport comparisons, and when such comparisons are made they are usually limited to groups of airports within national boundaries. Thus the formal comparisons made by the UK Chartered Institute of Public Finance and Accounts (CIPFA), the French section of the former International Civil Airports Association and the German Arbeitsgemeinschaft Deutscher Verkehrsflughafen (ADV) were all for airports within their respective countries. Moreover, the opposition many airports have to the principle of inter-airport comparisons has resulted in a shortage of published airport financial data. The International Civil Aviation Organization (ICAO) has been the only international body collecting such data on a comparable basis (ICAO 1991). It produces an annual statistical digest of airport financial statistics but the number of governments providing returns is disappointingly small while the financial information on individual airports is very limited. Both the international airport associations (the ICAA and the Airport Operators Council International which merged early in 1991) have been generally opposed to ICAO's data collection. They are not opposed to airports individually providing financial data, indeed they encourage this, but disagree with any attempts to produce such information on a standard format which can be used for inter-airport comparisons.

In 1984 the European Commission approached all the major European airports with a view to establishing indicators which could be used for both inter-airport and internal comparisons. However, the strong objections voiced by the airports resulted in all proposals for making inter-airport comparisons being dropped. The commission, however, is committed to ensuring transparency in airport accounts and the removal of state aid at least to the larger airports. This inevitably means that European Community airports will need to standardize their reporting procedures thereby making inter-airport comparisons easier.

MEASURING AIRPORT OUTPUTS AND INPUTS

Performance indicators are of two kinds. First, there are straightforward measures of outputs or inputs such as total passengers handled or total profits or numbers of employees. Second, there are input-output ratios, which measure the output generated by a given level of inputs. At an aggregate level one needs to find ways of quantifying an airport's output and its major inputs, which are primarily capital and labour.

An airport's output is not homogeneous. It can be determined in terms of aircraft handled, both those involved in air transport and others such as general-aviation or training flights, but also in terms of passengers or freight handled. The problems of measuring total airport output were discussed in Chapter 1 on pages 14–21. That discussion suggested the use of work-load units (WLU) as an output measure which combined both passengers and freight volumes (1 WLU being equivalent to one passenger or 100kg of freight). The financial measurement of output is much more straightforward. It is simply the total revenue received or the value added which is equivalent to total revenue minus the costs of goods and services brought in. At disaggregate levels, output is easier to identify and usually to measure as well since one is concerned with very discrete levels of activity, for instance the number of passengers served in the catering establishments.

When it comes to measuring *labour inputs* in the provision of airport services there are various different physical measures which can be used. The simplest is the total number of employees. However this is not a very appropriate measure as it could include full-time, part-time and temporary staff, all of whom may make varying contributions to the industry by working for different periods of time. Using a man-hour measurement can overcome this problem. This can take the form of either man-hours paid or man-hours worked. The former includes holidays, training, sick leave and other paid non-working time and so does not give a clear indication of the actual resources used. The latter measure is far more appropriate but may be difficult to measure accurately. In addition to this, labour is not a completely homo-geneous input. The quality of labour is affected by age, education, training and so on. Weights can be attributed to each type of employee according to their different level of wages in a attempt to obtain a more reliable input value. An assumption must be made that there is a strong relationship between employment quality and levels of pay which may not always be totally correct. Irrespective of this the detailed data needed for this process may make the method impractical.

The financial value of the labour input is represented by employee wages and salaries and associated costs. This will automatically take into account the different hours worked by employees and their diverse qualities and thus removes the need for making any adjustments to standardize the data. However, it is important to emphasize that this measure is not equivalent to the physical measure. The financial measure is more complex owing to the fact that within a selection of firms in any one industry the employee wage levels may vary considerably. A comparison of airport staff costs will therefore not only indicate the amount of labour resources being used but will also reflect differences in the relative level of wages paid by the different airports.

The problems associated with determining a reliable measure of the capital input are much greater than those concerned with the labour input. This is partly due to the very diverse nature of capital inputs, for example from small pieces of equipment with a very short life expectancy to major long-term investments in land and buildings, and partly due to the difficulties of measuring airport asset values. In physical terms capital inputs could be measured by the production capability or capacity of the airport system. But the capacity of an airport cannot be assessed by one measure alone. The capacity of the runway, terminals, parking aprons and so on can all vary one from another. Additionally there is no uniform method for measuring these capacities since they depend on the service standards set by the airport, for example, the average amount of space required per passenger or the average queueing time at check-in desks.

Annual capital charges, that is depreciation and interest, or net asset values are frequently adopted as measures of financial capital input. It must be remembered however that these values are determined by accountancy policies and will sometimes bear little relation to the actual value of the economic resources used. If more than one airport is being considered it is likely that different definitions of depreciation, asset lives, replacement costs and so on will exist which will arbitrarily affect any comparative evaluation. Furthermore assets funded by government grants will often not be depreciated and will not appear in the balance sheet. In some cases where an airport is under strict state control a separate balance sheet will not exist. Therefore it can prove very difficult to use financial capital measures with any confidence. A similar problem exists when making inter-airline comparisons, and the industry has long since given up trying to relate comparative performance to net assets.

DATA COMPARABILITY PROBLEMS

While there appear to be substantial advantages in an airport being able to compare its performance in key areas with that of other airports, comparability problems do arise. Such comparability problems are inherent in nearly all inter-firm analyses. These difficulties are abundantly apparent in the airport industry. They can be broadly categorized into six groups. They arise from differences in activities performed; in the level of government involvement; in financial accounting procedures; in the nature of any government subsidies; in the sources of finance; and finally in the design or service standards set by each airport.

Differences in activities performed

A range of different services are combined to produce the overall airport product. These services can usually be categorized into two groups: the essential aeronautical services (air traffic control, meteorological services, communications, police/security, fire and ambulance services, etc.) and the commercial activities (shops, restaurants and bars, car parks, car rental, banks, etc.). Handling of aircraft, passengers, baggage and freight, although an essential function of an airport, is often considered as a commercial activity if a concession fee is paid to the airport.

Comparability problems arise because airport authorities, especially those outside the United States, may be involved to quite different degrees in themselves supplying the above aeronautical and commercial services. At one extreme, airport authorities may be little more than landlords providing the basic infrastructure – terminals, aprons, taxiways and runways – while others provide most of the services associated with that infrastructure. Thus the civil aviation department may provide the air traffic control facilities, airlines or specialist firms may do all the aircraft, passenger, baggage and freight handling, and all the terminal services and shops may be operated by concessionaires. Many United States airports as well as some in France and elsewhere are in this position. In contrast, a few airport authorities provide their own air traffic control services, they operate the terminal car parks, and offer handling services. They may also operate the catering outlets and possibly the duty-free shops as well. In practice, as was shown earlier in Chapter 1 (see pp. 7–10), the range of activities carried out by individual airports can vary widely. The extent of an airport authority's exact involvement in the various airport functions and services will materially affect its cost and revenue structures. It will also influence the overall employee levels just as significantly. Moreover differences will be further complicated if the airport authority is not charged the full cost of any service provided by a third party. This is most likely to occur when separate government departments or agencies provide some of the essential services such as policing, fire and rescue or airport air traffic control.

Level of government involvement

Most airports around the world are still ultimately owned by central or local governments, whatever their precise legal form. Because of this and in pursuit of economic or social objectives many governments become involved in controlling the level and often the structure of airport charges. They may even, as in the case of Manila airport, determine by law the rents and concession fees which may be imposed on concessionaires. In many countries, governments insist that airport landing fees and passenger charges should be identical at all airports or at particular groups of airports. The greater the level of administrative interference the less is the airport's ability to influence its revenue levels. This clearly impacts on its revenue-generating performance.

Accounting practices

Airport costs will also be affected by the accounting standards and procedures used. There are major variations in accounting practices because of the existence of different national accounting policies and regulations. The analysis is further complicated by the public ownership of airports, which often results in the adoption of particular public accounting procedures rather than normal commercial practices. In theory these problems could be overcome when comparing airports by selecting just one such system and converting the data for the other airports to this common basis. But this would require very detailed information which would, in most cases, prove too impractical to collect.

One of the key problems associated with airport operations is that frequently a number of the airport's assets will be excluded from the accounts. At some airports, assets owned directly by the government rather than the airport authority or those which have been financed from government grants do not appear in the balance sheet and are not depreciated, as for instance at Vienna. Alternatively these types of assets may be included in the balance sheet but no depreciation will be charged for them in the annual profit and loss accounts. In contrast to this each Italian airport makes extra depreciation payments so that their shareholders' initial investment will be fully depreciated when the airport's concession agreement expires and the airport is handed back to the state. All these varying policies will have distorting effects on the true asset values and depreciation payments and pose difficulties in making meaningful comparisons.

The adoption of differing depreciation policies intensifies these comparability problems. Both historical cost and current or replacement cost are used as a basis for depreciation. Amsterdam airport has been using current cost accounting. While the majority of airports use historic cost accounting, many revalue their assets periodically, thereby increasing their depreciation costs.

Additionally some airports use the diminishing value method of depreciation (e.g. Copenhagen and Frankfurt) whereas the majority calculate it on a straight-line basis. There are even significant differences within these two groups of airports owing to very varied decisions on the life of the assets concerned. BAA Plc actually lengthened the life of its assets after privatization. Between 1988 and 1990 the lives of runways, taxiways and aprons was extended from between fifteen to twenty-five years to one hundred years while that of terminals, which had been up to sixteen years, was lengthened to fifty years, thereby significantly reducing depreciation costs. These are much longer lives than used elsewhere. The calculation of depreciation will also depend on the definitions of operating expenses (which are not depreciated) and capital expenditure (which is depreciated). At some airports, such as Copenhagen, only major fixed assets such as runways and buildings are depreciated whereas at most others depreciation is applied to much smaller investments such as equipment and vehicles.

Direct and indirect government subsidies

Indirect government subsidies have already been mentioned in that some airport services such as air traffic control or police/security may be provided free of charge or at less than cost. This will obviously mean that airports with this type of indirect subsidy will tend to have lower costs than those who have had to pay for the full cost of the service.

Additionally for some airports there may be a number of central or local government staff who are not based at the airport but are fully or at least partly involved in the running of the airport. For example at the smaller UK local authority airports some of the administrative and accounting duties are done at the local government offices rather than at the airport. Ideally the costs and manpower associated with these practices should be identified and charged to the airports concerned in order to ensure greater comparability. A similar situation exists where airports are run by a centralized civil aviation department or are part of a larger airport authority, as is the case with Lisbon airport which is part of ANA, the Portugese airport authority.

Sources of finance

Governments can subsidize airports in a more direct way by providing them with grants for capital investment. Among European airports Geneva, Milan, Rome and Vienna have all in recent years received funding of this nature while several such as Manchester have received European Community grants. At the French airports it is the responsibility of the local Chambers of Commerce, who manage them, to finance all investments on the landside, but the state in some instances has provided grants to assist in airside investment. Loans can also be granted at preferential rates as has been the case, for example, at Copenhagen and Marseilles. All these airports can be contrasted with others such as the BAA Plc airports, Amsterdam and Frankfurt which fund investments from their own revenues and with normal commercial loans. In the United States on the other hand airport development has often been funded through the Airport Improvement Program (see pp. 193–5).

The differing sources of finance impact on airport costs in two ways. First, they affect the annual level of interest charges and also the annual depreciation costs. Second, they influence the level and timing of investments and thereby affect an airport's operating costs.

Differences in design and service standards

Most of the larger airports have their own physical service standards which are considered desirable to provide an acceptable level of service to passengers.

These will be primarily concerned with speed and comfort. For example decisions will have to be made on the maximum times allowable for each airport function (e.g. baggage delivery time, transfer times), on space requirements, on manning levels, cleaning and lighting standards and so on. The smaller airports are also conscious of the service levels being provided but in general have not established such precise service standards. Clearly any decision on service levels will greatly influence an airport's costs and manning levels and consequently its economic efficiency. There is bound always to be a trade-off between economic and service performance.

Moreover there may be various factors affecting an airport's operation which are beyond the airport authority's specific control. For example airports may be forced to close at night because of environmental reasons or they may require two or more runways, not to meet traffic needs, but because of prevailing winds or some other particular climatic or geographical condition.

In addition to all the above there is a further more general but overriding factor which influences all airports' performance, and that is the financial and corporate objectives being pursued. Many European and US airports are merely required to break even financially while relatively few (Frankfurt or Copenhagen) have to achieve specified rates of return on their net asset values. Other airports may, however, wish to generate substantial profits if they aim to self-finance part or all of their investments. Clearly, the financial targets being pursued will impact on several performance indicators.

Do the above difficulties invalidate any attempts to make inter-firm comparisons in the airport industry? Such comparisons could be an essential management tool in improving airport performance in various areas and should be pursued. Comparability problems can be overcome in some cases in two ways. First, adjustments can be made to data to allow for inconsistencies between airports. For instance, to allow for differences in sources of funding and accounting practices one can compare costs *after* excluding depreciation and interest charges. Or one can exclude employees in the handling area when looking at labour productivity so as not to disadvantage those few airports who themselves operate handling services. Second, one can try to limit inter-firm comparisons to airports that are broadly similar in their key operational and financial characteristics. Though ultimately no two airports are the same this is not necessarily a handicap to comparative analysis. Inter-airport comparisons can highlight the impact of any differences on efficiency and performance.

There is one further difficulty that needs to be resolved before comparing airports in different countries and that is how to convert different currencies into a common unit. The use of exchange rates can produce some very misleading results. For example by comparing salaries (converted using exchange rates) of German or Swiss workers with English or Italian workers it appears that the former salaries are much higher. However this may purely reflect the fact that the cost of goods and services in Germany or Switzerland is higher and not that workers can afford to make more purchases than their

English or Italian counterparts. Similarly if the comparative value of one currency suddenly rises it appears that the workers' salary has increased as well. However the purchasing power of their salaries will not have changed.

It is much better therefore to make conversions based on the relative costs of living in each country. In this way currencies are converted in terms of what they can actually purchase and therefore are a much better indication of their real value. These conversion rates are called purchasing power parities (PPPs). In the tables which follow all airport costs and revenues have been converted to pounds sterling using PPPs which have been obtained from the Organization for Economic Co-operation and Development (OECD).

In many instances the problems of currency conversion can be side-stepped by using measures based on indices or percentages.

AGGREGATE AND DISAGGREGATE INDICATORS

Whether monitoring an airport's own performance over time or in relation to some budget forecast or making inter-airport comparisons, one needs to measure not only overall performance but also the performance and efficiency of discrete activity areas within the airport. Thus one needs to know not only the total revenue per work-load unit (WLU) but also the aeronautical revenue per passenger or per square metre. In developing disaggregate indicators for internal monitoring of an airport's performance, most difficulties are usually surmountable. When making inter-airport comparisons this may not be so. The more disaggregate the measure the greater its value for airport management but the more acute the problems of data availability and comparability. There is thus a need to reconcile what is desirable with what is feasible.

Airport authorities appear to have woken up to the potential value of effective performance measures as management tools. The key problem lies in determining the specific indicators which are most relevant to the airport business and which can be most readily produced. In the mid-1970s the Transport Studies Group of the Polytechnic of Central London set out to develop a methodology for measuring airport performance (Doganis and Graham 1987). Using detailed operational and financial information for 1983 for a sample of twenty-four European airports, a wide range of potential performance indicators, both aggregate and disaggregate, were examined. Their usefulness to managers and their data needs were assessed. A short list of possible indicators was presented in the conclusions to the study. This only contained those indicators which were considered valuable for airport managers and which a priori appeared to be feasible for European airports in terms of data availability. The findings of that 1983 study provide the basis for the discussion which follows though the detailed performance indicators have, where possible, been updated to 1989.

The indicators proposed for use by airports, fall into six discrete areas of airport performance:

1 overall cost performance
2 labour productivity
3 productivity of capital employed
4 revenue-generating performance
5 performance of commercial activities and
6 overall profitability.

These indicators have emerged as a result of studies of European airports. While most of them would be equally applicable to airports in other parts of the world a few may not be. At the same time there may be other indicators not mentioned here which may be needed to reflect particular operating or financial features of other groups of airports such as those of the United States.

The reasons for the inclusion of particular indicators and some of their shortcomings are set out in the following sections. For most of the indicators comparative tables are produced showing how each of a sample of European airports performed in 1989. Various adjustments have been made to improve data comparability and to try to ensure that one is comparing like with like. In particular, non-operating and extraordinary costs and revenues as well as taxes have been excluded. But not all comparability problems could be adjusted for. The most critical adjustments that should be made are those needed to take account of less usual activities when performed by different airports, such as passenger handling or air traffic control. An earlier study using 1983 data did this in some detail (Doganis and Graham 1987). But this was not always feasible for 1989. As a result, in some cases, indicators are proposed for which it was not possible to produce tables because the 1989 data was inadequate. These have been included because of their potential value to airport managers and also because it was felt that the data required to calculate them could be produced relatively easily by airports if they decided to do so.

MEASURES OF OVERALL COST PERFORMANCE

It seems appropriate to start any performance analysis by looking at general overall performance indicators. To help explain these measures discrete areas must then be examined individually to gradually build up a thorough understanding of the relationships which exist within an airport.

1 **Total cost per WLU (after depreciation and interest)**
2 **Operating cost per WLU (excluding depreciation and interest)**
3 **Capital costs per WLU**
4 **Labour costs per WLU**
5 **Labour costs as percentage of total costs**
6 **Capital costs as percentage of total costs**
7 **Aeronautical costs per WLU**

Turning initially to overall cost performance one starts by looking at unit

Table 8.1 Costs per WLU[1] in 1989 for sample of European airports (£ based on purchasing power parities)

Airport	Total costs per WLU (£)	Operating costs[2] per WLU (£)	Capital charges per WLU (£)
Vienna	13.04[3]	11.46	1.58
Milan	11.39[3]	9.54	1.85
Rome	11.37[3]	10.47	0.90
Frankfurt	8.83[3]	6.97	1.86
Birmingham	8.51[4]	6.29	2.22
East Midlands	8.14[4]	6.05	2.09
Manchester	8.10[4]	6.31	1.79
Dublin	–[5]	5.93	–
Amsterdam	6.64	4.86	1.78
Belfast	6.24	5.81	0.43
Glasgow	6.21[6]	–	–
Basel-Mulhouse	6.19	4.15	2.04
London Gatwick	5.45[6]	–	–
London Heathrow	5.27[6]	–	–
Geneva	4.12	2.56	1.56
Copenhagen	3.97	2.64	1.33
Marseilles	3.29	2.33	0.96
Nice	3.13	2.12	1.01
Average	7.05	5.83	1.53

Notes:
[1] A work-load unit (WLU) equals one passenger or 100kg of freight handled.
[2] Operating costs exclude capital charges (i.e. depreciation and interest).
[3] Very substantial involvement by airport in handling activities.
[4] Substantial involvement by airport in handling activities.
[5] Dash indicates data not available.
[6] Excludes interest.

costs, that is *total costs per WLU* (Table 8.1). Seven of the European airports studied – Vienna, Milan, Rome, Frankfurt and to a lesser extent Birmingham, East Midlands and Manchester – with the highest unit costs are all involved with handling unlike the other airports. Rome and Dublin also tend to have higher unit costs because they operate the duty-free shop themselves.

Therefore ideally it would be better to exclude the costs associated with handling, the duty-free shop and air traffic control (which is another service only provided by some airport authorities). Unfortunately such detailed cost data could not be obtained for 1989. However experience of previous years has shown that the range of unit costs obtained narrows quite significantly if adjustments are made to eliminate the impact of these three activities.

To adjust for any inconsistencies arising from differences in sources of financing or in depreciation policies in different countries or between airports in the same country, one can look at *operating costs per WLU* (see the second column in Table 8.1). Operating costs are arrived at after exclusion of all capital charges, that is mainly depreciation costs and interest. For several airports the unit operating costs are substantially lower than their total unit costs, which suggests that they have relatively high capital charges.

As an aid to understanding these total cost measures one might also look at labour costs and capital charges separately. *Capital costs per WLU* are relatively easy to establish but may be less reliable because of variations between airports in the way they determine such costs. This is therefore a performance measure which should be treated with some circumspection. Nevertheless, it can give some insight into the level of investment at each airport. Where this indicator is unusually high or low it may indicate some irregularity in the handling of investments or capital charges at that particular airport which may merit more detailed investigation. In the case of the European airports sampled here it was possible to establish the capital charges per WLU for most of them (see the third column in Table 8.1). This is essentially the difference between total costs per WLU and operating costs per WLU. Birmingham had the highest unit capital costs in 1989. This was because the airport had undertaken a major expansion scheme in the early 1980s resulting in the transfer in 1984 of its activities from the old terminal to an entirely new terminal complex on the other side of the runway. The investment costs of this scheme had been very high. In contrast, Belfast airport despite its own expansion scheme had low unit capital costs of only £0.43 per WLU. This suggested that the investment was not being fully depreciated. In fact Belfast did not charge depreciation on assets financed out of European Community or other grants.

Among European airports labour costs are more significant than capital charges, representing on average about 42 per cent of total costs. They therefore merit careful monitoring. *Labour costs per WLU* among European airports in 1989 showed very wide variations (see the first column in Table 8.2). French and Swiss airports which tend to function more as landlords than operators had particularly low unit labour costs, while it was the airports most heavily involved in handling activities that had the highest staff costs, notably Milan, Rome and Vienna.

A further way of monitoring capital and labour costs and one which obviates the need to convert currencies is to express them as percentages of total costs. *Both labour costs and capital costs as a percentage of total costs* are useful measures in identifying the significance of each input for an airport's total operations.

Time series data for those indicators expressed as percentages may also be more easy to establish for individual airports since one can ignore inflation or currency changes. While percentages may not be true indicators in the sense of

Table 8.2 Labour costs and labour productivity in 1989 for selected European airports (£ based on purchasing power parities)

Airport	Labour costs per WLU (£)	WLU per employee
Milan	7.70	2,900
Rome	7.10	3,000
Vienna	6.44	3,200
East Midlands	4.31	3,600
Frankfurt	4.08	3,600
Manchester	3.20	5,700
Belfast	2.65	6,100
Birmingham	2.61	6,900
Dublin	2.42	6,600
Amsterdam	2.35	9,100
Basel-Mulhouse	1.71	9,900
Geneva	1.35	15,000
Copenhagen	1.26	10,000
Nice	1.17	14,300
Marseilles	1.06	16,000
Average	3.29	7,700

	Revenue[1] per employee (£)
Birmingham	71,700
Geneva	64,200
Amsterdam	63,200
Manchester	62,900
Nice	60,700
Basel-Mulhouse	60,600
Marseilles	60,200
Dublin	59,700
Belfast	48,500
Copenhagen	43,600
Vienna	43,200
Frankfurt	37,900
East Midlands	35,400
Rome	34,800
Milan	32,800
Average	52,000

Source: Transport Studies Group, Polytechnic of Central London.
Note: [1]Revenue excludes interest earned.

measuring input-output relationships, they are nevertheless useful in showing the relative importance of particular inputs or outputs.

Separate analyses of aeronautical and non-aeronautical costs can provide valuable insights to the roles played by the traditional traffic operations and the more ancillary commercial activities at different airports. Aeronautical costs are those costs which arise from an airport's airside facilities and operations (runways, taxiways, aprons, lighting, marshalling, etc.) including that element of terminal costs which is required for traffic handling and processing purposes – in other words from the provision of its most essential services. For this reason and because aeronautical revenues per WLU are easy to establish and monitor, it would be particularly useful to measure *aeronautical costs per WLU*. In the course of the present analysis it was not possible to separate these costs out. However, it became clear that for most airports separately identifying such costs would be a relatively easy task should the operators decide to do so. But this would involve the arbitrary allocation of some common costs, particularly in the terminal area, between aeronautical and commercial activities. While a few airport managements already do this, others feel that such arbitrariness undermines the usefulness of the results.

LABOUR PRODUCTIVITY

Since labour and capital are the two major input costs for airports, some further exploration of labour and capital productivity is justified. The following indicators can be used for monitoring labour productivity in addition to labour costs per WLU:

8 WLU per employee
9 Total revenue per employee
10 Value added per employee
11 Value added per unit of staff plus capital costs
12 Value added per unit of staff costs

The labour costs discussed previously are dependent on two separate factors, the productivity of the labour employed and the wages and salaries paid. The physical productivity of airport labour can be measured in terms of *WLU per employee*. When this indicator was calculated for the group of European airports in the sample very wide variations were found (second column in Table 8.2). When comparing labour costs per WLU with WLU per employee it is noticeable that the airports with high labour costs are generally the ones with low output per employee. Nevertheless, where labour is cheap airports may use it more plentifully in order to provide a better service. In that situation a simple indicator such as WLU per employee on its own may be misleading. In order to combine labour productivity and labour unit costs in a single measure one could also use WLU per £1,000 of labour cost (any monetary unit can be used). However, this is no more than the inverse of the labour cost per WLU.

Work-load units (WLU) measure the volume of passengers and freight handled by an airport. But airports provide a range of heterogeneous services in addition to passenger- and freight-handling facilities. These include runways for aircraft, catering services, shopping facilities, parking and so on. The level of such services is related to the volume of traffic throughput, but workload units may be a very poor measure of an airport's total output. An airport authority's total revenue or turnover may be a better indicator of its overall activity level, though these measures too have their shortcomings. Nevertheless, the *total revenue per employee* is a useful measure of the relationship between the number of airport authority employees and the revenue generated by the airport from all sources. Such revenues will come not only from aeronautical sources but from commercial activities as well. The revenue per employee in 1989 for selected European airports is shown in the third column of Table 8.2.

The interrelationship of the three labour-performance indicators discussed so far throws up some interesting insights into the labour productivity of some of the airports in the sample. The showing of Milan and Frankfurt in Table 8.2 is of particular interest. Both these airports had very low WLU per employee. It is evident that this is due to their substantial involvement in passenger, baggage and freight handling. This means more labour is needed resulting in high labour costs and low output (WLU) per employee. But these extra activities should generate additional revenue. Therefore when one looks at revenue per employee the relative position of these airports should improve. In fact it fails to do so especially in the case of Milan whose revenue per employee is the lowest in the sample. The implication may well be that Milan is grossly overstaffed though its overall revenue performance as shown later is good.

In contrast to Milan, some French and Swiss airports which act more as landlords seem to have been very successful in generating high revenues per airport employee. Geneva, in particular, stands out as an airport with very low labour costs per WLU, indicating minimal involvement in the various airport activities or functions, but with very high revenue per employee.

At some airports, the airport authority collects revenue through its charges to cover the cost of activities undertaken by others. For instance some British airports include fees for air traffic control in their own charges but then pass this revenue on to the air traffic control authorities. Charges for security may also be handled in this way. Clearly revenues arising in this way should be excluded from analyses of employee productivity since it is not the airport's own employees who are generating this income.

One could go a step further and assess the *value added per employee*, value added being the total revenue less the cost of goods and services bought in. Value added is the wealth created by the airport. This requires more detailed expenditure information but the earlier Polytechnic of Central London study

Table 8.3 Value-added ratios for European airports 1989

Staff plus capital costs		Value-added ratios per unit of: Staff costs		Capital costs	
Manchester	1.82	Nice	2.96	Belfast	12.13
Belfast	1.69	Manchester	2.84	Rome	9.23
Nice	1.59	Birmingham	2.78	Vienna	5.77
Birmingham	1.50	Marseilles	2.44	Milan	5.29
East Midlands	1.36	Copenhagen	2.37	Manchester	5.07
Marseilles	1.28	Basel-Mulhouse	2.34	East Midlands	4.16
Frankfurt	1.26	Geneva	2.28	Frankfurt	4.03
Copenhagen	1.15	East Midlands	2.02	Nice	3.42
Vienna	1.13	Belfast	1.97	Birmingham	3.27
Amsterdam	1.08	Amsterdam	1.90	Marseilles	2.70
Basel-Mulhouse	1.06	Frankfurt	1.84	Amsterdam	2.51
Geneva	1.06	Vienna	1.41	Copenhagen	2.23
Rome	1.05	Milan	1.27	Geneva	1.97
Milan	1.02	Rome	1.18	Basel-Mulhouse	1.95
Average	1.29		2.11		4.55

Source: Transport Studies Group, Polytechnic of Central London.

showed that it was possible to produce this indicator for many European airports (Doganis and Graham 1987).

An alternative approach is to produce value added per unit of cost. Value added, that is revenue minus the cost of goods or services bought in, divided by the total annual staff costs and capital charges produces the *value added per unit of staff plus capital costs*. This is more of a global measure than an indicator of labour productivity. However, this value-added ratio can be taken a step further by calculating separate value-added ratios for labour and capital. These two measures should reflect the impact of different mixes of labour, and capital inputs at the airports. Of the two, the *value added per unit of staff cost* is probably the most valuable measure in that discrepancies in measuring staff costs are likely to be less significant than those arising in relation to capital costs and charges. Some of the very wide variations in the value added per capital cost ratios found between different airports are likely to be due to differences in the methods of financing investments or in depreciation policies.

One advantage of these value-added ratios is that they can be calculated for each airport in its own currency conversions. To show how such ratios might be used Table 8.3 has been produced using the 1989 data for European airports. The table does show how airports performing well or badly can be highlighted.

PRODUCTIVITY OF CAPITAL EMPLOYED

13 Value added per unit of capital costs
14 WLU per £1,000 net asset value

15 Total revenue per £1,000 net asset value

The drawbacks of the first of these indicators has already been discussed. But both of the capital productivity measures which involve identifying and assessing the net value of assets may also pose particular difficulties. This is especially likely where the various major assets at an airport are not all owned by the airport authority itself. Despite such difficulties it is valuable to try to establish the asset values of individual airports because capital is a major factor input. Assessing the efficiency with which capital is employed must, therefore, be of importance to airport managers but also to government or other bodies which are involved in the provision of capital investment.

WLU per £1,000 (or $1,000) net asset value measures the productivity of the capital used (as seen in an airport's asset value) in terms of the traffic which is being handled. On the other hand, if one is more concerned in an airport's total 'output' from all the various activities and services being provided then *total revenue per £1,000 of net asset value* might be a better indicator of output in relation to the assets being used.

The Polytechnic of Central London study of European airports attempted to establish the net asset value of the twenty-four airports under investigation. It proved possible to do so on a more or less comparable basis for only nine of them (Doganis and Graham 1987). This was because of the problem of calculating net assets in view of the different accounting and financing practices in the countries involved. In the longer run it should be possible to ask airport authorities to estimate their asset values on a standard basis for purposes of comparative analysis. In the short run, one is forced to limit the use of capital-productivity indicators to those airports for which net asset values can be estimated with some certainty. Alternatively, one might use such indicators largely for internal monitoring rather than for inter-airport comparisons.

One aspect of these indicators which should be carefully borne in mind is that they are very much affected by the stage in the investment cycle that an airport happens to be in. Thus an airport which has just undertaken a major costly expansion providing sufficient capacity to see it through the next ten years of traffic growth will appear to be performing badly compared to one which is over-congested and urgently in need of expansion. On the other hand, the above indicators could be used to assess and compare the capital productivity of different development schemes at a particular airport.

REVENUE-GENERATION PERFORMANCE

16 **Total revenue per WLU**
17 **Adjusted revenue per WLU**
18 **Aeronautical (or non-aeronautical) revenue as a percentage of total revenue**

19 Aeronautical revenue per WLU
20 Non-aeronautical revenue per WLU

Total revenue per WLU measures the overall performance of an airport in generating revenue. The total revenue levels are affected by many factors, some of which may be beyond the control of individual airport managements. It was mentioned earlier that airport revenues may be inflated if airport authorities collect fees for others such as the air traffic control services. They will also be inflated where airports themselves undertake functions, such as handling or the operation of duty-free shops, normally provided by others. Revenues from such activities can often be easily identified and subtracted from airport's total revenue in order to provide a more comparable indicator. Thus *adjusted revenue per WLU* should be a better guide of revenue performance when making inter-airport comparisons. The adjusted revenue is after the exclusion of all revenues collected on behalf of other agencies or those arising from activities or services not normally undertaken by most airport authorities. The greater the range of adjustments that can be made the more comparable the data become.

The 1989 revenue per WLU for our sample of European airports is shown in the first column of Table 8.4. As one would expect the seven airports most involved with providing handling services themselves to have the highest unit revenues. It proved possible, however, to identify their handling revenues and to then rank the airports in terms of adjusted revenue per WLU, the adjustment in this case being the exclusion of handling revenues (second column of Table 8.4). Comparison of the rankings and unit revenues in the two columns shows that the revenue performance of those airports most heavily involved in handling, that is Vienna, Rome, Milan and Frankfurt, appears much less impressive when handling revenues are excluded. On the other hand exclusion of handling does not affect the revenue performance of Manchester or Birmingham very much even though both provide some handling services. Overall the United Kingdom airports appear to do particularly well in terms of adjusted revenue per WLU while the French regional airports are relatively poor performers.

One needs to break down total revenues further into their two main components, that is aeronautical and commercial or non-aeronautical. A first step is to express each of these as a *percentage of total revenue*. This is easy to do and can be done without the need for currency conversions if one is comparing airports in different countries. An individual airport can, for instance, assess its own aeronautical-revenue percentage both in terms of its past performance or some explicit target figure and in terms of the performance of comparable airports or the industry average.

The *aeronautical revenue per WLU* indicates an airport's success in generating revenue from aircraft landing fees, passenger charges and parking and hangarage charges. However, aeronautical-revenue performance is not entirely under the control of airport managers. It depends on the level and

Table 8.4 Total revenues[3] per WLU in 1989 for selected European airports (£ based on purchasing power parities)

Airport	Total revenue[2] per WLU (with handling) (£)	Airport	Adjusted revenue[1] per WLU (without handling) (£)
Vienna	13.63	Birmingham	10.12
Rome	11.72	Manchester	9.61
Milan	11.47		
Manchester	11.05		
Birmingham	10.43		
Frankfurt	10.39		
East Midlands	9.91		
Glasgow	9.29		
Dublin	9.10	Dublin	9.10
London Heathrow	8.39	Vienna	8.76
Belfast	7.93	London Heathrow	8.39
London Gatwick	7.81	Belfast	7.93
Amsterdam	6.96	London Gatwick	7.81
Basel-Mulhouse	6.13	Amsterdam	6.96
		Frankfurt	6.63
		Rome	6.26
		Basel-Mulhouse	6.13
Copenhagen	4.35	Milan	4.99
Geneva	4.28	Copenhagen	4.35
Nice	4.26	Geneva	4.28
Marseilles	3.75	Nice	4.26
		Marseilles	3.75
Averages	8.38		6.83

Source: Transport Studies Group, Polytechnic of Central London
Notes: [1] For those airport authorities who do not undertake handling themselves, the figure in column 2 is the same as in column 1. Only the top eight airports in left-hand column have significant handling involvement but adjustments could not be made for Glasgow and East Midlands.
[2] Excludes interest received.
[3] Work load unit (WLU) is one passenger or 100kg of freight handled.

structure of airport charges, which may be controlled or influenced by government decisions, and also on the mix between international and domestic traffic, since charges for the latter are lower. However, this indicator does tell us how much an airport collects in charges for each traffic unit or work-load unit. It may be a better guide to an airport's pricing policy in relation to that of other airports than comparisons of complex charging structures might indicate. Thus while airlines and IATA have repeatedly complained of BAA Plc's peak

Table 8.5 Aeronautical and non-aeronautical revenues of selected European airports in 1989 (£ based on purchasing power parities)

	Aeronautical revenue per WLU[1] (£)		Non-aeronautical revenue per WLU[2] (£)
East Midlands	7.18	Dublin	5.14
Birmingham	6.97	London Heathrow	4.91
Belfast	6.24	London Gatwick	4.63
Manchester	6.09	Rome	4.25
Glasgow	5.29	Amsterdam	4.19
Vienna	4.89	Glasgow	4.00
Dublin	3.96		
London Heathrow	3.47	Vienna	3.87
Frankfurt	3.28	Manchester	3.52
London Gatwick	3.18	Frankfurt	3.36
Basel-Mulhouse	2.84	Basel-Mulhouse	3.29
Amsterdam	2.77	Birmingham	3.15
Copenhagen	2.73		
Milan	2.59		
Rome	2.01	East Midlands	2.74
Nice	1.74	Geneva	2.58
Geneva	1.71	Nice	2.52
Marseilles	1.62	Marseilles	2.14
		Belfast	1.69
		Copenhagen	1.63
Average	3.81	*Average*	3.39

Notes: [1] Aeronautical revenues are after excluding handling revenues.
[2] Non-aeronautical revenues exclude interest earned.

charging structures at London's Heathrow airport, an examination of the 1989 aeronautical revenues per WLU suggests that it is the UK's regional airports which may have particularly high aeronautical charges. This is because there is relatively little control over airport charges in the UK. Conversely the Italian government controls such charges more directly, hence the relatively poor rating of Milan and Rome airports. The figures in Table 8.5 do indicate which airports have most scope for pushing up their unit aeronautical revenue either by increasing the level of charges or by attracting more international traffic.

One also needs to examine the *non-aeronautical revenue per WLU* (second column in Table 8.5). This measures the ability of an airport's management to capitalize on the whole range of commercial opportunities open to it. Once again, however, its ability to do this may be limited by factors largely beyond its control, at least in the short term. These are the size and design of the terminal building/s and the availability of land within the airport boundary.

The range of activities and services which can be developed is also a function of the total traffic being handled. Therefore it may be better to compare airports with broadly similar traffic levels. Generally, smaller airports will be more dependent on aeronautical revenues. This was the case in 1989 with Birmingham and East Midlands airports, two of the smaller airports in the European sample. Larger commercially oriented airports which may be particularly successful in generating non-aeronautical revenues may as a consequence decide to hold down their aeronautical charges. This may have been the case with Dublin or Amsterdam in the late 1980s (see Table 8.5).

The potential value of performance indicators can be gauged by looking at an individual airport in order to assess its performance in terms of revenue generation. Birmingham is an interesting case. Its adjusted revenue per WLU (Table 8.4) is the highest and in itself this is quite satifactory. But further breakdown of this total figure (Table 8.5) shows that Birmingham's non-aeronautical revenue per WLU is rather low. It is not performing well in this area and its poor performance here has been compensated for by very high aeronautical revenue per WLU. In terms of the latter indicator Birmingham out-performs most other airports.

Airport revenue data are more readily available, more accurate and pose fewer comparability problems. Because of this, revenue-performance indicators are easier to calculate than cost-efficiency indicators and greater reliance can be placed on the actual figures produced.

PERFORMANCE OF COMMERCIAL ACTIVITIES

21 Concession plus rental income per passenger
22 Concession revenue per passenger
23 Rent or lease income per passenger
24 Concession revenue per m²
25 Rent or lease income per m²
26 Airport concession revenue as percentage of concessionaires' turnover

In addition to the global indicators of revenue generations discussed above, one also needs to use disaggregate indicators to obtain a more useful insight into the performance of an airport's various commercial or non-aeronautical activities. The fact that it is easier to identify sources of particular revenue streams than to allocate costs makes disaggregate revenue analysis more accurate and more meaningful than disaggregate cost analyses. Emphasis on detailed performance monitoring in the non-aeronautical area is justifiable on two grounds. First, because airports are trying to generate an increasing proportion of their total revenues from such sources. Second, because concession and rental revenues are much more susceptible to management action than aeronautical revenues which may be controlled by governments or by the level of traffic. In other words, airport managers may have greater scope to improve performance in the commercial areas than in the aeronautical.

In the first instance one needs to monitor the commercial revenue generated per passenger handled. Since the bulk of commercial activities are orientated towards meeting the needs of passengers and those accompanying them to the airport, passenger numbers are a better measure of an airport's throughput in the commercial area than work-load units would be. The first key measure of its commercial performance which an airport should assess is the *concession plus rental income per passenger*. This measures the airport authority's revenue from all concession fees and rents per passenger handled. This overall figure can be broken down into its constituent parts namely *concession revenue per passenger* and *rental income per passenger*. The 1989 figures for all these indicators for the selected European airports for which is was possible to obtain such data are given in Table 8.6. Regrettably the BAA Plc airports are not included since data availability for these airports diminished after privatization.

It is interesting to note that despite its greater size and its reputation for duty-free shopping, Amsterdam did not perform particularly well compared to the larger of the UK regional airports, namely Manchester and Birmingham. Its overall concession and rental income per passenger was marginally higher but its concession income per passenger was markedly poorer. This is partly due to the fact that the airport has a share in the company operating the catering concession. As a result the concession fee is largely nominal but the airport benefits indirectly from its share of the concessionaire's profit. Vienna was also noticeable in having particularly low concession revenue per passenger which contrasted to its very high unit-rental income.

One could break down concession revenues further and look for example at catering concession income per passenger or duty-free income per departing international passenger.

Airports need to know how effectively they are using the space allocated for renting and for concessions. In addition to revenue per passenger, they should also be monitoring the *concession revenue per m^2* and the *rental income per m^2*. These are indicators for which it may be more difficult to make inter-airport comparisons because information on space allocated to particular activities may be hard to come by and may not be strictly comparable. But there should be no problem in using these indicators for internal monitoring.

The final key indicator of commercial performance is *airport concession revenue as a percentage of concessionaires' total turnover*. This effectively measures the airport authority's success in transferring some of the con-cessionaires' potential profits to itself. Since some of the concessionaires may have been granted a monopoly by the airport, the airport authority is effectively trying to maximize its own share of any monopoly profit.

Ultimately an airport's performance in terms of concession or rental incomes is a function of several variables (see Chapter 7). Three are

Table 8.6 Concession and rent revenue per passenger for selected European airports in 1989 (£ based on purchasing power parities)

Airport	Concession revenue plus rents per passenger (£)		Concession revenue per passenger (£)		Rental income per passenger (£)
Amsterdam	3.07	Birmingham	2.47	Vienna	2.13
Frankfurt	2.92	Manchester	2.33	Basel-Mulhouse	1.46
Birmingham	2.83	Amsterdam	2.05	Amsterdam	1.02
Manchester	2.75				
Vienna	2.40	Geneva	1.47	Belfast	0.57
Basel-Mulhouse	2.03	Copenhagen	1.25	Geneva	0.56
Geneva	2.03	Nice	1.17	Marseilles	0.43
		Belfast	1.13	Manchester	0.42
Milan	1.71			Birmingham	0.36
Belfast	1.70			Nice	0.36
Copenhagen	1.61	Marseilles	0.72	Copenhagen	0.35
Nice	1.53	Basel-Mulhouse	0.57		
Marseilles	1.15	Vienna	0.27		
Average	2.14	Average	1.34	Average	0.77

particularly important: the total space available for renting or for concessions, the marketing and selling skills of the concessionaires and the nature of the contracts between the airport and its tenants or concessionaires. To obtain an insight into its commercial performance in the light of these variables an airport should use even more disaggregated indicators. Each commercial activity or concession can be looked at separately and its performance can be assessed with measures traditionally used in the retail trades. Depending on the concession being monitored one could use some of the following measures.

To assess the skill and success of individual concessionaires one might look at:

1 turnover (or sales) per m² of shop/concession area
2 turnover per passenger (for duty-free per international passenger)
3 turnover per concessionaire's employee
4 passengers making purchases as percentage of total passengers.

To assess the amount of space devoted to different concessions and the suitability of its precise location one might examine:

1 sales area (m²) per passenger
2 percentage of passengers entering each sales area.

Finally, to evaluate the contractual arrangements between the airport and individual concessionaires one should monitor for each concession the airport's concession revenue as a percentage of that concessionaire's total turnover.

All these indicators can be applied to individual concessions, different groupings of concessions (e.g. tax- and duty-free or tax- and duty-paid), or by terminal or particular area (e.g. all airside as opposed to landside areas). However, comparisons between quite different concessions may be meaningless because of the variations in the value of and demand for their services and products.

As an example of the potential value of disaggregate indicators of commercial performance, Table 7.1 (p.156) shows the airport's share of the concessionaires' turnover in 1987–8 for a small sample of airports. The success of UK airports in generating duty-free sales was contrasted with the failure of Greek airports, while Dutch airports, amongst which Amsterdam loomed large, only extracted 22 per cent of their turnover as concession fee. The French branch of the then International Civil Airports Association carried out surveys of French airports in 1984 and 1987 and successfully produced for each airport disaggregate commercial performance indicators such as those suggested above (ICAA 1988). It can be done!

PROFITABILITY MEASURES

27 Surplus or deficit per WLU
28 Revenue to expenditure ratio

While airports can monitor their own overall performance in terms of annual profits or losses, such absolute figures may not be sufficient as management tools. They give no indication of how much better an individual airport could be doing nor how its profit record compares to that of other airports. Annual profits may be going up in absolute terms but at the same time the profit margin could be going down. Direct comparisons of the profits of different airports may also mean little if these airports handle differing traffic volumes. To overcome such problems one needs to assess the profit margins being achieved.

The *surplus/deficit per WLU* indicates the profit margin in terms of the difference between total unit costs and unit revenues at each airport. As the margin is expressed per unit of output, that is per work-load unit, it is possible to compare airports of different sizes.

Ideally profitability should be assessed in terms of the financial return of the assets employed in the business. But it has already been pointed out that trying to establish the real asset values of airports as opposed to the published values is complex and difficult. While an individual airport may be able to do this in order to assess its own rate on return of assets employed, the problems involved in making international comparisons of airport profitability are such as to suggest that an alternative measure should be used. The *revenue to expenditure ratio* (Revex ratio), which is widely used for the same reasons in the airline industry, is the total revenue expressed as a ratio (or a percentage) of the total costs after depreciation and interest (see p. 1–3 and Table 1.2). Thus a ratio of 1.01 (or a percentage of 101) would indicate that revenue exceeds costs by 1 per cent. As with some other indicators, problems of currency conversion are avoided since the ratio can be calculated in an airport's own currency. Variations in the treatment of depreciation between countries or airports will clearly affect cost levels and therefore the Revex ratio. However, such variations may be less critical if the ratio is seen to measure the degree to which each airport covers what it perceives to be its own costs.

The two profitability measures for the sample of European airports are shown in Table 8.7. It should be borne in mind when comparing different airports that their profitability is partly a function of the skill of its managers and partly a function of the profit targets set or imposed by the ultimate owners, usually central or local government, or by the board of directors. If an airport is merely required to break even it will inevitably have a low profit per WLU and a low Revex ratio.

Looking at these measures one gains an insight into aspects of the performance of individual airports that was not possible using other indicators alone. Thus, Nice which was near the bottom of the sample in terms of all the revenue indicators (Tables 8.5 and 8.6) has a rather high Revex ratio. This was achieved because its unit costs were actually the lowest (see Table 8.1). In absolute terms its profit per WLU is fairly average but since both unit costs

Table 8.7 Profitability measures for selected European airports in 1989 (£ based
on purchasing power priorities)

Airport	Revex ratio	Profit/loss per WLU[1] (£)
London Heathrow[2]	1.59	3.12
Dublin[3]	1.54	3.17
Manchester[4]	1.51	4.10
Glasgow[2]	1.50	3.08
London Gatwick[2]	1.43	2.36
Nice	1.41	1.28
Belfast	1.34	2.14
Birmingham[4]	1.29	2.43
East Midlands[4]	1.28	2.29
Frankfurt[5]	1.18	1.56
Marseilles	1.17	0.57
Copenhagen	1.10	0.38
Vienna[5]	1.08	1.06
Amsterdam	1.05	0.34
Geneva	1.04	0.16
Basel-Mulhouse	1.04	0.24
Rome[5]	1.03	0.39
Milan[5]	1.02	0.23
Average	1.26	1.61

Notes: [1] Profit per WLU includes depreciation and interest received or paid except
where shown otherwise. (WLU = 1 passenger or 100kg of freight.)
[2] Excludes interest.
[3] Excludes depreciation and interest
[4] Airport authorities with some involvement in handling.
[5] Airport authorities with major direct involvement in handling.

and revenues are low the difference between them is small. Nevertheless, in
ratio or percentage terms the profit margin is high. Geneva airport, on the
other hand, which was like Nice a low-cost, low-revenue airport, achieved only
marginal profitability with a Revex of 1.04. Another interesting point to
emerge from Table 8.7 is that those airports most heavily involved in
providing their own handling services, namely Vienna, Frankfurt, Milan and
Rome, do not appear to improve their profitability as a result. Their Revex
ratios placed them all in the bottom half of the sample in 1989.

CONCLUSIONS

In putting forward a number of performance indicators no attempt has been
made to draw conclusions on the performance, good or bad, of any of the
sample airports. It would be more appropriate that the airports themselves
should do this. But the potential value of particular indicators has been

illustrated by considering the cases of individual airports. This was done, for instance, with Birmingham when discussing revenue performance.

The indicators proposed are those which are likely to be most useful to managers for internal monitoring and for which data can more readily be obtained to allow for inter-airport comparisons. But ultimately the value of any performance indicators depends on the skill of the manager who uses them and the way in which they use them.

The aim of the present chapter has been to show that it is possible to produce for European airports at least a range of performance indicators covering many but not all areas of airport activity. Clearly the indicators are of least value where the data base is weak or uncertain. But the major conclusion of the analysis must be that, given a willingness on the part of airport authorities, it is possible to make cross-country performance comparisons on the basis of the indicators proposed. The validity and significance of the indicators will clearly increase as the quality of the basic information provided can be improved.

Chapter 9

Airports in the United States

Anne Graham

Air transport is more highly developed and more extensively used in the United States than in any other part of the world. As a result US airports dominate the world's airport industry providing, as shown in the opening chapter (pp.15–23), a very high proportion of the world's largest airports. Airports outside the United States generally have many similarities in terms of patterns of ownership, of administration and of sources of finance and revenue. Historically, however, US airports have developed particular financial and administrative structures which differentiate them from airports in other parts of the world. These differences occur, first of all, because of the particular relationships that US airports have with the airlines; second, because of the practice of renting or leasing large amounts of terminal space or even entire terminals to individual airlines; finally because the sources of finance available in the United States for airport investment are quite different from those available in other countries. These factors have given US airports unique economic and financial characteristics. It is for this reason that US practice deserves more detailed assessment.

RELATIONSHIP WITH THE AIRLINES

US airports, like airports in most other areas of the world, are publicly owned. Most are owned by cities or counties although a few are under state or federal ownership. Some of the airports are not operated directly by the government body but by a separate public organization such as a multipurpose port authority (an example is the Port Authority of New York and New Jersey) or an airport authority (such as the Metropolitan Washington Airports Authority).(Patterns of ownership are described on pp. 11–14).

What differentiates US airports is, therefore, not their form of ownership but the level of involvement of their customers, the airlines. In effect, these publicly owned airports are operated in close conjunction with privately owned airlines. This unique public/private character of the airports has a significant impact on financial operations, such as the pricing of facilities and services and on the funding of investment. At some airports, the airlines in fact share many of the financial risks of airport investment and operations.

US airports enter into legally binding contracts known as *airport-use agreements* which detail the conditions for the use of both airfield and terminal facilities. These contracts are negotiated between the airport and its airline customers. They will specify the fees and rental rates which an airline has to pay and the method by which these are to be calculated. There are two basic approaches to establishing the airport charges: *residual* and *compensatory*:

1 *Residual approach*: The airlines pay the net costs of running the airport (or airport cost centre such as the airfield or terminal) after taking account of concession and other non-airline sources of revenue. The airlines, therefore, take considerable financial risk since they provide a guarantee that the level of charges and rents will be such that the airport will always break even. This means, for example, that if the air traffic diminishes the amount of revenue generated from the airlines will still need to be sufficient to cover the agreed net costs. So the airport will not suffer any losses despite the decline in traffic.
2 *Compensatory approach*: The airlines pay agreed charges and rates based on recovery of costs allocated to the facilities and services that they occupy or use. Here the airport operator assumes the risk of running the airport, and if the traffic drops, for instance, so will the revenue from the airlines.

Table 9.1 shows in a simplified form how the two different methodologies work. There are assumed to be two cost centres, the terminal and airfield. With the residual approach, revenues from non-airline sources are deducted from the maintenance, operations, administration, debt-service and other costs. The residual cost left is then used as a basis for setting the charges. Thus the residual cost of the terminal which is $50,000 is divided between 6,500 ft² of space to produce a rental of $7.69/ft². A similar approach is used to calculate the landing fee. With the compensatory approach the airlines' share of the total costs is calculated based on actual use and then this figure is used as a basis for setting the charges. In the example in Table 9.1, the airline's share of the $100,000 terminal costs is 65 per cent or $65,000 which spread over 6,500 ft² produces a rental rate of $10.00/ft².

Airport managements have applied these two different approaches in various ways to suit the particular needs of their airport. Some airports have adopted a hybrid approach, combining both the residual and compensatory methodologies (see Table 9.2). For example, new agreements at the Washington airports have a revenue-sharing element. At the end of each year, the profit or loss from all the airport operations including commercial facilities is split between the airport authority and the airlines. The profits assigned to the airlines will be put towards off-setting the next year's fees.

Traditionally the use agreements have been long-term contracts ranging

Table 9.1 Illustrative calculation of US airline charges under residual and compensatory approaches

	Residual		Compensatory	
	Terminal ($)	Airfield ($)	Terminal ($)	Airfield ($)
Operations/ maintenance/ administration costs	40,000	40,000	40,000	40,000
Debt service/ other costs	60,000	60,000	60,000	60,000
Total costs	100,000	100,000	100,000	100,000
Revenue from non-airlines sources	–50,000	–50,000	n/a	n/a
airline share	n/a	n/a	65%	75%
Residual cost	50,000	50,000	n/a	n/a
Activity level	6,500 sq. ft^2	100,000 lb weight[1]	6,500 sq. ft^2	100,000 lb weight[1]
Rental rate^2	7.69		10	
Landing fee^2		0.50		0.75

Source: Based on a table produced by the Congressional Budget Office (1984).
Notes: [1] Gross landing weight.
        [2] Per sq. ft^2.
        [3] Per 1,000 lb weight.

between twenty and fifty years. The compensatory agreements have tended to be shorter contracts giving airports less security but greater freedom. At a number of airports in the last ten years, there has been a trend towards shorter-term contracts reflecting the airports' desire to remain more flexible in a more uncertain deregulated environment.

At many of the airports the airlines will lease or rent their terminals, with the length of airport-use agreements normally coinciding with the length of the lease agreement. The terminal space will be either assigned on an exclusive-use basis to a single airline or on a joint-use basis for several airlines. The airport usually remains in control of areas needed for international formalities if the airport has international traffic. Sometimes, such as at John F. Kennedy airport at New York, the airlines will have long-term ground leases which enable them to finance and construct their own terminals.

The use agreements often guarantee that the airlines play a significant role in the making of airport capital-investment decisions. This is specified in the *majority-in-interest (MII)* clauses of the agreements, so-called because they invole

Table 9.2 The financial management approach of large US airports 1990

Airport	Residual	Compensatory	Hybrid	MII clause?[1]
Dallas-Fort Worth	*			Yes
Detroit Metropolitan	*			Yes
Honolulu	*			No
Las Vegas McCarran	*			No
Los Angeles	*			Yes
Memphis	*			Yes
Miami	*			Yes
Pittsburgh	*			Yes
San Francisco	*			Yes
Seattle	*			Yes
Tampa	*			Yes
Atlanta Hartsfield		*		Yes
Chicago O'Hare		*		Yes
Kansas City		*		Yes
New York JFK		*		No
Phoenix		*		No
Salt Lake City		*		Yes
San Diego		*		No
Baltimore			*	Yes
Boston Logan			*	No
Charlotte			*	Yes
Denver Stapleton			*	No
Houston Intercontinental			*	No
St Louis-Lambert			*	Yes
Minneapolis			*	Yes
Orlando			*	Yes
Philadelphia			*	Yes
Washington National			*	Yes

Source: Airport Operators Council International (AOCI) 1990.
Note: [1] Majority-in-interest (MII) clauses give major airlines at airports certain powers concerning airport investment decisions.

'signatory' airlines which together carry the majority of the airport's traffic. The specific powers granted to the airlines in such clauses vary but typically the airlines involved have to approve all development plans over a certain cost. MII are far more common amongst airports which have adopted residual rather than compensatory approaches to financial management (see Table 9.2).

SOURCES OF CAPITAL INVESTMENT

Bond financing

Many airports are financed partly or largely from the private sector through the bond market. They usually raise the money through two different types of bonds: *general obligation bonds* which are backed by the issuing government and *revenue bonds* for which debt service is paid entirely out of revenues generated by the airport.

General obligation bonds are bonds issued by a government of, for example, a city, county or state. The bond payments are secured by the full faith, credit and taxing power of the issuing government body. They are secured and serviced out of general tax receipts and any other revenue of the government rather than directly from revenues generated by the airport. The airport will, therefore, be competing with other public community projects for the capital.

The bonds are sold at relatively low interest rates. This results in low debt payments for the government body. The issuing of this type of bond is limited, since usually the total general obligation indebtedness of a city, county or state is not permitted to be more than 5–10 per cent of the total valuation of the taxable property in the community. Often approval will also be needed from the voters before any bonds are issued, hence delaying the start of development works which may be urgently needed.

Revenue bonds are secured by the future revenues of the airports. The issuance of revenue bonds, unlike general obligation bonds, is not limited but they may have slightly higher rates of interest because of the perceived greater risk in being secured by future airport revenues rather than the taxing power of the relevant local government body.

For revenue bonds, the airport will pledge that its income will be sufficient to cover the cost of interest and capital repayment over the period of the bond issue. The anticipated level of coverage of net revenues to debt service (the coverage ratio) typically ranges between 1.2 to 1.5. The measure of risk reflected by the interest rate will be dependent on this coverage ratio. As with other bonds sold in the commercial bond market, most airport revenue bonds will be rated by leading investment services (e.g. Moody's and Standard and Poor's) to give a guide as to their quality. Generally airport revenue bonds are rated quite highly, especially those for the large airports. For example in 1990 a survey of thirty-one large hub airports (AOCI 1990) found that eight airports had the best possible rating (i.e. Moody's Aaa rating) and twelve had high ratings (i.e. Aa ratings).

When an airport is run by a multi-purpose authority, such as the Port Authority of New York and New Jersey, revenue bonds may also be sold. In this case the revenue of the entire authority rather than specific revenues of the airports will be pledged to pay all outstanding debt.

As well as these general revenue bonds there are other revenue bonds to suit the needs of differing airports. The most common are the *lease* or *special facility bonds*. These are used if the airport wants to build a particular facility at an airport, such as a terminal or cargo hangar. In this instance, rather than securing the bonds with the general revenues of the airport, the bonds are instead guaranteed by the future rental or lease payments of the airline or airlines who are going to use the facilities. Long-term agreements are secured with the airlines in order to provide the airport with a guarantee of future income.

Finally, there are also a few bonds which are a combination of the general obligation and revenue bond. These *self-liquidating general obligation bonds* are usually secured by the full faith and credit of the government body but are serviced from airport revenues. They, therefore, have certain of the advantages of the general obligation bond, for example low interest costs, but are not subject to debt restrictions nor are they in competition with other public works for capital funding.

One of the major advantages of all these bonds is their exemption from tax on interest paid to bond-holders. However, in an attempt to increase federal tax revenues and reduce perceived abuses of tax-exempt bonds, various tax reforms were introduced during the 1980s which made the bonds less attractive to investors.

The relative importance of these different types of bonds for large airports are shown in Table 9.3. In the past, general obligation bonds were the most common source of airport finance since airports were not considered to be self-sustaining. However, with increasing commercialization within the industry and increasing pressures on government for funding of other public projects, general obligation bonds are now far less common. It is usually only the smaller airports which rely on this type of funding. The larger airports are generally financially much stronger and are, therefore, able to compete in the commercial bond market and issue revenue bonds. For example general obligation bonds accounted for only 2 per cent of the total bonds issued between 1978 and 1982 at large airports, 14 per cent at medium-sized airports and 30 per cent at small-sized commercial airports. By contrast at general-aviation airports, 64 per cent of the bond finance came from general obligation bonds (Congressional Budget Office 1984).

Federal aid

The federal government provides airport investment funds through the *Airport Improvement Program (AIP)* which is administered by the Federal Aviation Administration (FAA). The money is provided by the *Airport and Airways Trust Fund* which is financed by the following federal user taxes on various sectors of the aviation community:

1 10 per cent domestic passenger ticket tax
2 $6 per head tax on international passengers
3 6.25 per cent way-bill tax on air freight
4 aviation fuel tax of 15 cents per gallon
5 jet fuel tax of 17.5 cents per gallon.

In 1990 the total tax revenue was nearly $4 billion with nearly 90 per cent of

Table 9.3 Airport bonds of large US hub airports 1990

	Type of bond				
	Revenue	General obligation	Special facility	Other[1]	Total
	(%)	(%)	(%)	(%)	(%)
Detroit Metropolitan	100				100
Honolulu	100				100
St Louis-Lambert	100				100
Los Angeles	100				100
Miami	100				100
San Francisco	100				100
Seattle	100				100
Tampa	100				100
Washington Dulles	100				100
Washington National	100				100
Orlando	98		2		100
Philadelphia	95	5			100
Pittsburgh	91	9			100
Las Vegas McCarran	90	10			100
Houston Intercontinental	90		10		100
Denver Stapleton	87		13		100
Salt Lake City	75	10	15		100
Kansas City	71		29		100
Dallas-Fort Worth	70		30		100
Atlanta Hartsfield	61		39		100
Chicago O'Hare	60		40		100
Charlotte	59	13	28		100
Phoenix	38	26		36	100
Memphis	21	11	51	17	100
Minneapolis	17	83			100
New York JFK				100	100
New York La Guardia				100	100
New York Newark				100	100
Baltimore				100	100
Boston Logan				100	100
San Diego		100			100
% airports using these bonds	81	29	32	23	

Source: AOCI 1990.
Note: [1] In most instances these are consolidated bonds issued by a port authority or other transportation authority.

the income (excluding interest payments) coming from the tax on domestic passenger tickets. Between 1982 and 1990, monies from the Trust Fund accounted for 57 per cent of all FAA money spent on improving and operating the airport and airspace system with the rest coming from general taxes. The Aviation Safety and Capacity Expansion Act of 1990 lays down that in future the Trust fund will provide around 75 per cent of the total FAA spending on airport and airspace improvements.

To obtain an AIP grant, the airports have to be included in the *National Plan of Integrated Airports System* (NPIAS) which, at present, contains more than 3,000 airports. Grants are payable for planning projects and development projects associated with the construction, improvement or repair of airports. They are also payable for planning and implementing noise-improvement projects. There are two types of grants. Up to 49.5 per cent of the funds are allocated according to a formula based on passenger throughput. The remainder are discretionary funds mostly allocated to small and general-aviation airports and for special needs.

In 1990 the FAA issued grants from the Trust Fund for the AIP which amounted to $1.4 billion. The Trust Fund also paid for airways facilities and equipment ($1.7 billion) and for research and development ($170 million). In addition, money from the Trust Fund contributed to the costs of operating and maintaining the airspace system ($807 million),

In recent years, because of congressionally imposed expenditure limits, Congress has annually appropriated less money for aviation projects than planned, and by the end of 1990 there was an uncommitted surplus of $7.4 billion in the Trust Fund. The result of this is that the federal budget deficit appeared smaller while the aviation users were being overtaxed.

Bonds and federal grants are the two main sources of finance for airport investment. It may be seen from Table 9.4 that on average at least twice as much money is obtained from airport bonds as from federal grants. The only exception was in the years 1986–7 just after new less attractive tax-exemption conditions relating to the bonds were introduced. In general the larger the airport the less its reliance on the AIP, usually less than 20 per cent of total funding, and the more its reliance on the bonds. It is usually the small airports, which, being unable to attract enough private lenders for bonds, are most dependent on federal aid. For them federal aid often makes up over 60 per cent of their total capital funding (Rodgers 1990).

State Finance

The state governments may also provide some additional finance for airport investment. Fuel taxes are the major revenue source for these funds with other incomes including those from aircraft registration, airport licensing, pilot registration and airport operating income tax. The exact amount of state funding varies quite considerably between states. For example, in 1988 some

Table 9.4 Bonds and federal grant financing at US commercial airports

Year	Federal grants ($ billions)	Airport bonds ($ billions)	Total ($ billions)
1983	0.4	2.0	2.4
1984	0.7	3.2	3.9
1985	0.8	2.7	3.5
1986	0.9	0.5	1.4
1987	0.9	1.1	2.0
1988	1.3	3.1	4.4
1989	1.4	2.7	4.1
Annual averages	1.0	2.2	3.1

Source: Rodgers 1990.

states such as Alaska, Florida, Maryland, Minnesota and Virginia each allocated over $10 million for airport development whilst other states such as Colorado, Delaware, Louisiana, Nevada and West Virginia provided no or very little financial assistance (Gellman 1989).

Self-generated funds

Occasionally a small amount of investment is funded by self-generated retained income, that is the airport's net revenue or surplus. In theory, the residual-cost approach is designed to guarantee that the airport will break even rather than make large profits although some airports have actually modified their approach to ensure that an adequate surplus is made. By contrast, however, those airports adopting a compensatory approach know that they may not always make a profit. However since their rents and charges are not set purely on a cost-recovery basis, substantial profits could also be made. For this reason, airports with a residual approach on the whole tend to generate lower surpluses, if any, than those airports which adopt a compensatory policy. It, therefore, tends to be the latter airports who are in a better position to use retained earnings for investments.

There are, however, legal constraints on airports that retain surpluses. Local and state legislation coupled with the fact that airports are public enterprises usually means that there will be strict limits on the levels of profit allowed. There have actually been a few cases when airlines have sued airports who have attempted to use accumulated surpluses for future investment. For example this recently occurred in 1989 when Continental and United Airways sued Denver airport for retaining surpluses for financing the new airport.

Airline and third-party sources

Finally, airlines or others may themselves undertake to invest directly in airport facilities which elsewhere would normally be provided by the airport authority itself. At many US airports, airlines have constructed their own cargo, maintenance and support facilities, usually on land leased or rented from the airport. At some airports, such as New York's Kennedy airport, they have even constructed their own terminals. In addition, other third-party investors have involved themselves in airport developments, especially in the cargo area and in the provision of fuelling systems and other technical facilities. Such direct investments clearly reduce the level of investment capital needing to be raised by the airport.

AIRPORT REVENUES

US airports generate their revenue from airport charges (landing fees, parking, etc.), rentals from airlines and other users, and concession fees from shops, restaurants and other commercial enterprises. Where they differ from airports in other countries is in the proportions of revenue generated from each of these sources.

As discussed above, the aeronautical charges and airline leases and rentals are charged on a cost-recovery basis (either residual or compensatory). Commercial rents and concession fees are generally determined by market conditions with the objective of maximizing revenues.

The landing fees will usually be established by the airport-use agreement and adjusted as agreed. At 'residual' airports, the landing fees will be the revenue source that ensures break-even since they will be based on the difference between the projected costs and other revenues. At 'compensatory' airports they will be based on an averaging out of the actual costs of airfield facilities. The landing fees are normally very simple, being a fixed rate per 1,000 lb. At some airports the signatory airlines, who have agreed to a 'majority-in-interest' clause (see pp.191), pay less.

US airports, unlike those in most other areas of the world, have not legally been allowed to levy passenger charges since 1973. This ban was introduced primarily because some of the fees levied from such head taxes were being diverted to non-airport uses. The situation regarding passenger charges has, however, changed since 1990 (see pp.203–4).

The rental charges at US airports vary considerably. Some airports break down their airports facilities into multiple categories and have a separate charge for each. Others employ a flat rate for all airport facility space. Concessionaires usually pay a variable fee, typically based on a percentage of turnover.

It may be seen from Table 9.5 that, for a sample of large US airports, 23 per cent of the revenues came from landing fees and other aeronautical charges, 23 per cent came from rents, and 33 per cent came from concessions. Compared with European airports, American airports derive a much smaller amount of revenue from landing fees and a higher amount from rents. This is because of the common practice in the United States for airlines to rent or lease areas of

Table 9.5 Revenues at large US airports 1989–90

	Revenue sources						Total revenue per WLU ($)
	Aviation		Non-aviation[2]				
	Aeronautical fees (%)	Rents[1] (%)	Concessions (%)	Car park (%)	Other[3] (%)	Total (%)	
St Louis-Lambert	37	24	21	0	18	100	2.83
Dallas-Fort Worth	36	10	12	20	22	100	3.61
Washington National	32	10	32	0	26	100	2.88
Houston Intercontinental	31	27	17	19	7	100	4.12
Denver Stapleton	29	34	29	0	8	100	4.29
New York Newark	28	30	26	0	15	100	8.60
Boston Logan	24	19	16	25	17	100	5.48
New York JFK	22	29	16	0	33	100	7.29
Atlanta Hartsfield	21	9	33	0	37	100	2.46
Portland	20	26	36	0	18	100	5.58
Washington Dulles	20	23	40	0	18	100	4.26
Baltimore	20	16	49	0	15	100	3.82
Los Angeles	17	27	54	0	1	100	3.08
Salt Lake City	16	29	29	0	25	100	3.05
Las Vegas McCarran	14	44	27	4	11	100	5.26
San Francisco	11	17	54	0	18	100	4.53
Averages	23	23	33	4	17	100	4.45
Averages of European airports[5]	56	8	16	2	18	100	13.52

Notes: [1] Normal practice outside USA would be to classify rents together with other non-aviation activities above as 'non-aeronautical'.
[2] Non-aviation revenue does not include interest earned.
[3] Excludes interest received.
[4] As a result of rounding the percentages do not all total 100.
[5] See Figure 3.5, p. 55.
Source: AAAE 1990 and airport annual accounts.

the terminal and gates for their exclusive or joint use. In Europe, where this does not happen, the airlines' payments to the airport are primarily in the form of landing fees, passenger fees and related charges rather than in the form of rents or lease payments.

While the terms 'aeronautical' and 'non-aeronautical' are widely understood and used outside the United States, American airports tend to use a different breakdown of their activities and revenues. Many split them into aviation and non-aviation. Aviation revenues not only include aircraft landing fees and fuel charges/commissions but also rents and lease revenues from land, terminal and other buildings or hangars used by airlines, manufacturers or others providing airport services. Non-aviation income would include earnings from concession fees, from car parking, car-rental concessions, recharges to tenants for electricity and other utilities and any other miscellaneous revenues. It does not usually include interest earned which for many US airports is a much more important revenue source than in Europe. Using this breakdown of activities, an analysis of sixteen airports in 1989–90 (see Table 9.5) suggests that aviation income on average was somewhat less than half the total revenues while non-aviation revenues taken together generated more than half the total (54 per cent).

In 1989–90 the average unit revenues (i.e. revenue per WLU) of US airports was $4.45 compared to $13.52 for European airports (Table 9.5 last column). This was the result of lower airport charges, because US airport operators tend not to get involved in any additional activities such as handling and because most of the passengers are domestic and therefore have a lower average spend in shops, catering and other facilities, and moreover, are unable to buy duty-free goods. The US airports with the highest proportion of domestic passengers (for example, St Louis, Washington National, Atlanta and Salt Lake City) may be seen to have the lowest unit revenues (see Table 9.5).

As regards concession revenue, many of the characteristics identified for European airports appear to apply equally for US airports. For example, the range of concessions and the revenue from concession fees increase with airport size. However, because of the predominantely domestic nature of US airports, duty-free revenues are not a very important source of concession revenue. Instead, car-parking and car-rental revenues make up a large proportion of the commercial revenues (although clearly the importance of these car-related sources will vary depending on the extent to which the airport deals with terminating rather than transferring traffic). For example, Washington Dulles airport in 1990 generated 45 per cent of its concession revenue from car parking and 18 per cent from car rental. Revenue from duty-free sources accounted for much less than 10 per cent of total concession revenues at Dulles. By contrast the BAA airports in Britain, for example, generate about half their concession revenue from duty-free sales, about a fifth from car parking and less than 5 per cent from car hire.

In the past US airports have generally tended to be less skilled in maximizing commercial revenues than the European airports. In recent years, however, various improvements have been brought about by, for example, introducing more competition amongst concessionaires, negotiating more beneficial contract terms, improving the location of commercial facilities and diversifying.

An area of growing concern as regards commercial policy is the relationship between on-airport and off-airport concessionaires. For example car-rental on-airport companies typically give the airport 10 per cent of their gross revenues. Off-airport companies pay comparatively less by having a charge which is usually just related to the costs of providing ground access. Various airports have tried to raise the off-airport rates because they are afraid of losing their on-airport operators. This move has been opposed by the off-airport operators, who claim that they need the lower fee to be able to offer lower prices, and they have sought federal help.

AIRPORT COSTS

Generally at US airports, especially the larger ones, capital charges are a higher percentage of total costs than staff costs (see Table 9.6). This is the opposite situation from what usually occurs in Europe and elsewhere. The staff costs tend to be low because the airports do not get involved in any additional activities such as air traffic control or handling. The capital costs on the other hand are high largely because bonds have to be financed whereas in other countries investment funds may often come from self-retained funds, grants or loans with very low interest rates which will reduce the capital costs. The capital costs at the Washington airports are much less than at other US airports because they used to be operated directly by the federal Government and were not dependent on revenue bonds for investment capital.

In 1989–90 the average unit costs for a selection of US airports was $3.48 (per WLU) compared to $11.37 in Europe (see Table 9.6). This difference arises largely because the airport operator gets involved in less activities and the majority of airports deal primarily with domestic passengers where the associated costs of providing facilities and services are much less than for international passengers. Additionally differences occur because of the unique relationship between US airports and the airlines. Since the airlines in many cases will rent or lease terminals, hangars and so on from the airport, the maintenance and operation costs will be the responsibility of the airline, not the airport. Where there are long-term ground leases and the airline has invested in the facility, the investment costs will also be reduced.

EFFECTS OF AIRLINE DEREGULATION

The deregulation of domestic air services in the late 1970s has created a much more risky financial environment for the airports. They can no longer rely on

Table 9.6 Costs at large US airports 1989–90

	Cost structure					Total costs per WLU
	Staff	Other operating	Total operating	Capital	Total[2]	
	(%)	(%)	(%)	(%)	(%)	($)
Washington (both airports)	46	37	83	18	100	2.88
Detroit Metropolitan	18	53	71	29	100	5.05
Chicago[1]	31	34	65	35	100	3.63
Los Angeles	17	43	60	40	100	2.51
St Louis-Lambert	14	35	49	51	100	3.25
Dallas-Fort Worth	12	26	38	62	100	5.05
Memphis	11	18	29	71	100	6.32
Atlanta Hartsfield	14	14	28	72	100	2.20
Averages	22	34	56	44	100	3.86
European averages	42	34	76	24	100	11.37

Source: Airport annual accounts.
Note: [1] 1988 data used.
       [2] As a result of rounding the percentages do not all total 100.

carriers to be always there to pay fees and charges. There has therefore been a need for a more flexible management approach. The full effect of deregulation on use agreements will not however be known until all the present long-term agreements expire, many of them in the 1990s. Nevertheless, there does appear to be a trend towards shorter-term contracts reflecting the airlines' desire to remain more flexible and the airports' need for greater control in a more uncertain environment. Several airports have also shifted away from a residual to a more compensatory approach to financial management. This type of approach becomes attractive to airports which have reached a certain level of maturity and have strong markets and which can therefore maximize their revenues rather than rely on the airlines to guarantee that they break-even.

In spite of these developmens, revenue bonds have continued to be the most viable form of finance for medium- and large-sized airports. This is primarily because investors, rather than looking to long-term lease agreements with airlines for security, are now placing greater emphasis on the local air-travel demand for the airport services. Airports with a high percentage of origin and destination passengers rather than transfer traffic are therefore in a particularly strong position. In these cases the financial failure of one carrier is not considered to be a major threat as the strength of the market will encourage another carrier. For example, the rating of the bonds at Dallas Fort Worth Airport did not change when one of its major carriers, Braniff, collapsed in 1982.

Hub airports are generally considered to be less financially secure since the failure of any one airline or the withdrawal of its services could result in permanent loss of patronage of the airport. This greater risk can have important implications for bond ratings. For example airports such as Atlanta, Salt Lake City and Nashville all had their ratings downgraded in the 1980s either because of increased reliance on hub operations or because of the poor financial performance of the airlines providing the hub and spoke services. Many of the hub airports have become totally dominated by one or a small number of carriers. A growing problem is that often these airlines gain control over the major portion of the available gates and concourse space. They can then prevent other airlines from competing by refusing access to gate and terminal space. The airport may as a consequence lose much potential traffic and revenue. Dominant hub airlines, if they are signatory airlines of a 'majority-in-interest' (MII) clause, may also be able to use their veto powers granted by the airport to forestall the capacity improvements which could bring about more competition and generate more traffic for the airport.

Since deregulation, some airport operators have tried to lessen the restrictiveness of the MII provisions. For example, some have limited MII approval only to projects of major importance, some have introduced measures which require MII disapproval rather than approval and others have increased the level of disapproval needed amongst the signatory airlines to affect any future development plans.

FUTURE SOURCES OF FINANCE

Undoubtedly the major challenge facing the US airport industry during the 1990s is how to provide all the additional airport infrastructure which is urgently needed. According to the FAA, in 1988 twenty-one US airports exceeded 20,000 hours of airline flight delays. With an average airline operating cost of about $1,600 per hour of delay, this means that each of these twenty-one airports produced over $32 million of delay costs in 1988. By 1998, the number of airports which could exceed these hours of flight delays is projected to grow to forty-one unless capacity improvements are made (FAA 1990), In 1990 the Airport Operators Council International estimated that in total $56.6 billion would be needed to meet the airports' capital needs in the following ten years (AOCI 1990).

However, many consider the existing funding sources to be inadequate and are concerned that the airports will not raise sufficient revenues to meet these investment needs. The major criticism of federal grants is that they are subject to congressional spending procedures. Additionally many believe that they would be more effective if they were allocated according to needs rather than passenger throughput. Alternatively financing through self-retained surpluses is difficult because of residual costing and legal constraints. As regards bonds, the changes in the tax laws have made revenue bonds less attractive and cities are reducing the number of airport general obligation bonds issued because of competition from other public community projects.

Privatization

Privatization of airports could bring some much-needed additional private money for investment. In the last few years, there has been much interest expressed by the private sector in either buying airports outright or entering into long-term management contracts. For example airports such as Alliance, Albany County, Greater Peoria and Atlanta have all been discussed as candidates for privatization as have several military airports due for closure. Various issues would have to be resolved if such developments were to take place. For example, would private airports still be eligible for federal aid and would the airport bonds still be exempt from tax? There is also the problem of ensuring that the airports would not abuse their monopoly power. A special task force has been formed in Washington to consider these issues.

The passenger facility charge

For a number of years US airports have demanded the right (withdrawn in 1973) to be able to levy a passenger facility charge (PFC) which would go directly to the airports rather than into federal funds to be redistributed. Airports would therefore be more certain of the availability of funds and would, by being able to pledge revenues from PFCs to pay for debt, be in a better position to borrow from private lenders. This type of funding, unlike revenue bonds, would also be largely independent of airline control.

In 1990 the Aviation Safety and Capacity Expansion Act was passed permitting such a charge to be levied as long as a national policy on aircraft noise was formally established at the same time. The FAA was expected to publish rules regarding PFCs based on this legislation in mid-1991. The major PFC provisions of the 1990 Act include:

1 The airports will be able to impose a $1, $2 or $3 PFC fee for originating and transfer passengers (with a limit of two per one-way trip).
2 The PFCs will be collected by the airlines.
3 The revenues from the PFCs must be spent at the airport or at another airport controlled by the same body which imposes the fees.
4 The fees must be used only for identified, eligible airport-related projects to preserve or enhance airport capacity, security or safety, or to furnish opportunities for enhanced airline competition, or to mitigate noise. The PFCs may be used to back bonds for such projects.

5 The Secretary of Transportation must decide whether to approve a PFC application. Airlines must be consulted but they will have no veto powers.
6 Projects developed with PFC funds may not be subject to agreements granting airlines the exclusive right to use the new facilities.
7 Large and medium hub airports which impose as PFC will forego up to 50 per cent of their Airport Improvement Program (AIP) entitlement based on their throughput formula whilst small airports will be able to keep all their federal grants.

If most of the fifty largest airports impose a $3 PFC, the revenues generated will be in the order ot $1.2 billion. However, not all these airports are likely to levy such a fee either because it will not be needed or because the regulations regarding the fee will be too restrictive. It may be seen from Table 9.7 that even if the airport's AIP entitlement is halved, the large airports will still be in a better financial position with a $3 PFC. It is also clear from Table 9.7 that PFC revenue, if used to back bonds, would give airports a tremendous potential for issuing bonds to raise capital. Concern has been voiced, however, about an airport's ability to use PFC revenues in this way if the airport already has a substantial number of revenue bonds. Higher coverage may also be needed for bonds backed by PFC revenues. Alternatively, in several cases, the bulk of the airports' investment needs could be met by PFC revenues. The introduction of the PFC will facilitate financing of investments especially at large hub airports. But small airports would also benefit indirectly since the unused AIP grants for large and medium airports could be used for greater funding of smaller airports. These latter airports would in any case be too small to benefit from levying PFCs.

Congestion-related pricing

One of the major difficulties with the present financial system is that the landing fees at the airports do not reflect the high costs of relieving the congestion that occurs during periods of peak demand. As in Europe, there has been talk for many years of peak pricing but, except for surcharges payable for general aviation, there are no peak-pricing policies in operation. If such fees were to be introduced, major obstacles, such as federal legislation stipulating that the charges must be considered reasonable and non-discriminatory and the nature of the long-term agreements with the airlines which forbid any changes in charges structure, would have to be overcome.

Boston Logan airport is one of the few airports which, having no agreed formula with airlines for setting landing fees, attempted to tackle the capacity problem with a change in pricing policy. The first phase of its Program for Airport Capacity Efficiency (PACE) was implemented in July 1988 and adjusted slightly in October 1988. This introduced a movement charge for runway use as well as a weight-based charge, and had the effect of significantly

Table 9.7 Passenger facility charge revenues at selected US airports 1990

	1989 total enplane-ments[1] (m)	AIP entitle-ments ($m)	Estimated annual revenue ($3 PFC)[2] ($m)	PFC bonding power[3] ($m)	Annual investment average investment needs[4] ($m)
Chicago O'Hare	28.9	16.0	86.8	723.6	71.4
Dallas-Fort Worth	23.8	15.8	71.4	594.7	89.2
Los Angeles	22.6	15.4	67.9	565.9	18.4
Atlanta Hartsfield	21.6	16.0	64.7	539.1	59.7
Denver Stapleton	13.7	11.1	41.2	343.3	471.2
San Juan	4.0	4.0	12.0	99.8	10.3
Portland	3.0	3.3	9.0	75.7	4.1
Dallas Love	2.8	3.0	8.3	69.2	1.0
Indianpolis	2.7	3.0	8.1	67.2	21.0
West Palm Beach	2.6	3.0	7.9	65.6	10.2

Source: Rodgers 1990, AOCI 1990.
Notes: [1] An enplanement includes originating and transfer passengers.
[2] Does not include requirement that large or medium airports give back up to 50 per cent of the AIP funds on imposing the PFC.
[3] Assumes 8 per cent interest rate and fifteen-year term to maturity. It represents total borrowing power which can be supported by PFC fees to repay debt service.
[4] As identified by the National Plan of Integrated Airports System (NPIAS).

Table 9.8 Landing charges at Boston Logan airport

	1987–July 1988	July–September 1988	September–December 1988	1989
Fee Structure	$1.31 per 1,000lb	$.54 per 1,000lb plus $91.78 per landing	$.55 per 1,000lb plus $103.55 per landing	$1.49 per 1,000lb
Resulting charge for small-sized aircraft (40,000lb)	$52	$113	$126	$60
Resulting charge for medium-sized aircraft (150,000lb)	$197	$173	$186	$224

Source: IATA annual.

increasing the landing fees for smaller aircraft, who make less efficient use of the airport capacity (see Table 9.8).

However, in December 1988, in response to complaints from airlines and other affected parties, the US Department of Transportation ruled that Logan airport had violated federal law since its landing-fee structure unjustly discriminated against smaller aircraft and represented an unscientific approach to airfield cost allocation. As a result of this, the airport resorted to its former pricing structure. Had it not done so it would have ceased to be eligible for its $10 million federal airport-improvement grants in 1989. It is interesting that when the PACE pricing mechanism was in effect, Logan rose from twenty-first to second position in terms of on-time performance on the list of the twenty-seven busiest US airports. Once the programme was abandoned, Logan's on-time performance immediately began to deteriorate and it is now bottom of the list. In May 1989 the airport lost an appeal against the Department of Transportation's ruling. Subsequently Massport, the authority which owns Boston Logan, turned to developing a new version of a congestion-sensitive, operations-based landing fee, working more closely with the Department of Transportation. If Massport's efforts are successful in getting round federal restrictions on airport charging policies, then it is likely that other US airports may also move away from average-cost pricing to more directly cost-related charges as a way of alleviating congestion.

Chapter 10

Airports in the developing world

INCREASING EMPHASIS ON PROFITABILITY

The key questions faced by government and airport directors in western Europe during the 1970s was whether their airports should be run as commercial enterprises and whether they should try to make a profit. As we have seen, many European governments concluded that the major airports, at least, should try to recover their costs from the users and should not be subsidized out of general taxation. During the late 1980s governments and airport managers in the developing world had to resolve the same issues. Up to that time little attention had been given to the unprofitability of their airports. Airports like roads were assumed to be essential public services to be provided by governments at whatever cost.

All that has begun to change. Those aid agencies which provide funds for airport developments in the Third World are increasingly insistent that airports should put their accounts in order and that they should try to meet all costs including debt or interest repayment out of revenue. At the same time there is a tendency, which is accelerating, for developing countries to set up autonomous airport authorities to manage the major airport or airports in each country. This has happened in Thailand, Nigeria, India and the Philippines. But knowledge and understanding of airport finances in the developing world has been fairly limited.

One reason for this may have been the lack of data and their unreliability when they were available. It was not until 1979 that the International Civil Aviation Organization (ICAO) produced its first circular (145–AT/50) on Airport Financial Data for the year 1976 (ICAO 1979). In this and subsequent circulars, financial data for a few airports in the developing world began to appear for the first time. Despite any reservations about the validity of some of the ICAO figures, it is, nevertheless, possible to draw some general conclusions from these data and from field research carried out by the Polytechnic of Central London, by the College of Aeronautics of the Cranfield Institute and by others.

On the basis of the published figures, of which a selection are given in Table

Table 10.1 Profit or loss of selected Third World airports (financial year 1989)

	Annual traffic (passenger millions)	Profit or loss (US$ m)	
Bangkok[1]	12.2	74.4	
Mexico City[1]	11.1	42.5	
Caracas[1]	7.2	10.6	
Rio de Janeiro[1,2]	6.5	23,9	
São Paulo[1,2]	5.6	10.3	
Bogota	4.4	14.7	
Lagos	1.9	3.0	
Buenos Aires (1988)	1.8		−5.1
Medellin (Colombia)	1.6	2.3	
Acapulco (Mexico)	1.6	6.0	
Penang (Malaysia)[1]	1.5	2.7	
Barbados	1.4	2.0	
Kota Kinabalu (Malaysia)[1,2]	1.1[3]		−0.6
Kathmandu	0.9	2.8	
Mauritius	0.8	2.4	
San Salvador (El Salvador)	0.5[3]		−1.8
Mahé (Seychelles)	0.3		−0.6

Source: ICAO 1991.
Notes: [1] Minimal or no depreciation shown in airport accounts.
    [2] 1988 data used.
    [3] Estimated data.

10.1, it would appear that most *capital-city airports* in Third World countries are profitable. Generally speaking those airports with an annual throughput of two million or more passengers are profitable while most of the unprofitable airports have a smaller traffic level. Superficially the financial performance of these developing-country airports appears to be better than that of some of their European counterparts.

Whereas the capital-city airports appear in many cases to be achieving a profit, *regional airports* in the same countries frequently do not. While regional airports inevitably have lower costs because their facilities are on the whole of a lower standard than those of the capital, their revenues are also very much lower. This is not only because of lower traffic throughput but also because, unlike their European counterparts, regional airports in the Third World have little or no international passenger traffic from which to generate non-aeronautical revenues. While largely dependent on domestic traffic, such airports generally offer substantial rebates on domestic landing fees. In the Philippines the domestic landing fee rebate is 65 per cent and in Malaysia 50 per cent. Similar rebates are widespread in other developing countries. To make matters worse, domestic passenger service charges are either set at very low levels or are not charged at all. There is in any case little scope for increasing such charges since they may already represent a significant expenditure for domestic passengers. Thus the need for improving economic performance may be greatest among regional airports. But since little data are available on regional airports, the discussion which follows concerns itself primarily with the capital-city airports.

Closer examination of the financial figures for many of the capital-city airports in Table 10.1 suggests that in many developing countries airport costs are grossly understated for one or both of the following reasons. First, because the costs of services or facilities provided to the airport by other government departments are often not included in the airport accounts. This is frequently the case with runway or apron maintenance which may be done by the Ministry of Public Works, or the Highway Authority or some such body. Terminal-building maintenance may also be undertaken by the Ministry of Public Works while some of the airports' administration or accounting may be done by employees of other ministries. The cost of all these services may be absorbed in the accounts of these other government departments. For example, at Mauritius airport, which according to Table 10.1 produced a surplus of US$2.4 million in 1989, the costs of the terminal facilities, of the hangars and of the maintenance areas were excluded from the airport accounts. They were borne by some other department. Second, many airports in the developing world do not include depreciation as a cost. This is because airport investments are not financed out of revenue but out of government funds or bilateral or international aid. Depreciation is not perceived as a cost nor is it used as a means of building up a reserve for future investments. Inevitably, this attitude stems from the fact that too many airports follow accounting practices geared to the requirements of government departments rather than to commercial or management needs.

If one were to adjust the profit and loss accounts of airports listed in Table 10.1 to allow for the understatement of costs where it occurs, the effect would be to reduce the level of profits at some of the larger airports, such as Bangkok or Mexico City, and to push some of the smaller airports like Mauritius, which appear to be profitable, into a loss position.

In some of the poorer developing countries low costs may be due to very low levels of maintenance. When airport equipment or parts break down they may not be repaired either because of lack of technical skills or because the replacement parts need to be imported. The equipment stays out of operation and deteriorates further until, hopefully, it is replaced by a subsequent foreign aid programme.

Though the overall financial performance appears to be reasonably favourable, major airports in developing countries do face some very particular problems on the financial side.

NEED FOR BETTER ACCOUNTING PRACTICES

A major problem faced by many if not most airports in developing countries is that their financial accounts are totally inadequate for management purposes and do not provide a true assessment of each airport's financial performance. There are several reasons for this.

Some airports are not self-accounting units, but are administered as part of larger government organizations such as the Ministry of Transport or the Department of Civil Aviation, or of semi-independent authorities such as the Philippine Bureau of Air Transportation or India's National Airports Authority. In all cases the airports' true costs are submerged and lost within the accounts of the larger parent organization whose responsibilities may be much wider than just operating the airport/s. In countries such as Sudan or Pakistan where the Department of Civil Aviation has been part of the Ministry of Defence problems of confidentiality further distort airport accounts.

A further problem, already mentioned, is that many services are provided at the airports by other government departments which do not then invoice the airports for the cost of these services. Such services may include the maintenance of runways, taxiways and aprons, airport cleaning and refuse collection, airport security, terminal maintenance and building work, electricity and water supply, fire services and so on. The costs of one or more of these services may not be covered by the airport or may not even be considered as a cost by the airport management.

Finally, at most developing-country airports there has been no attempt to introduce up-to-date management accounting systems. This is partly because, as previously pointed out, airport accounts are submerged in the accounts of larger government departments, and partly because airports have not hitherto been thought of as commercial enterprises. It is as a result of this that key cost items such as depreciation or interest on bank or aid loans are frequently ignored altogether. This is also due to the fact that many airports do not keep an up-to-date register of airport assets and therefore have no realistic basis on which to calculate depreciation charges. They should have a register of assets which should include the original costs of all equipment and buildings while equipment or facilities no longer in use should be deleted. In some airports, the manager does not even have a recent inventory of facilities, equipment and spare parts for which they are responsible.

Poor accounting practices also result in delays in invoicing. Cash flow at many airports could be significantly improved by speeding up the despatch of invoices to airlines and concessionaires. Frequently airline invoices are sent out several months after the landings concerned took place. This may be due to slow procedures and/or poor monitoring of landings and of other services provided by the airport.

There are still very many Third World airports, and some in Europe too, where all revenues collected go directly to the government treasury and expenses are met out of an annual budget allocation from the relevant ministry. In other words revenues are credited to one account while expenditures, especially capital investments, may be met out of a quite separate account or accounts. There is little interaction between revenues and expenditures. As a result there is no incentive for airport managers to generate increased revenues, since funds available for expenditure do not necessarily depend on revenues earned.

Because of the above shortcomings in their accounting practices and structures, airports may not be in a position effectively to monitor or control their costs or even to know what is their true financial performance. Key decisions on such questions as the level of landing fees, passenger charges or commercial rents, etc. have to be based on inadequte information. Thus a crucial first step in improving economic performance must be to ensure that each airport's accounts reflect accurately the full costs incurred by that airport. The immediate result of doing this may well be a deterioration in its financial results as costs previously excluded from the accounts are added in. But unless this is done there can be no sound basis on which, in the longer term, airport managers can set about improving their economic and financial performance.

Once their accounts are on a full and proper basis, airport managers and directors need to examine carefully both the level and structure of their aeronautical charges and their policies on commercial activities. The overall objective, according to the ICAO Council, should be to ensure that users share 'the full economic cost to the community of providing the airport and ancillary service, *including* appropriate amounts for interest on capital investment and depreciation of assets' (ICAO 1981). Moreover, under favourable conditions airports may produce sufficient revenues to provide 'reserves for future capital improvements'.

IMPROVING AERONAUTICAL REVENUES

Partly because of inadequate accounting systems and partly because they have tended to act as government departments rather than as commercially orientated enterprises, most airports in developing countries have poorly developed policies on aeronautical charges.

When one examines airport landing and related charges, almost everywhere in the developing world two characteristics emerge. First, the tariff structures tend to be very traditional and very simple. There is no attempt either to maximize revenue or even to try to relate charges more closely to costs. For example, many airports do not impose a night landing or lighting surcharge. Where a surcharge is imposed it rarely reflects the very high costs of keeping an airport open during night hours for just a handful of flights. Nor in most cases are there surcharges for the use of airbridges, when these are in short supply, so as to reflect the high cost of providing and maintaining them. Nor are there any peak-period surcharges so as to spread the peak demand for

Table 10.2 Third World airport charges compared to European February
1991: Charges for Boeing 747 with 280 passengers

| | Landing Fee (US$) | Passenger fee paid by | | Total (US$) |
		Airline (US$)	Passengers (US$)	
London Heathrow (peak)	1,672	7,341		9,013
Frankfurt	5,174	2,244		7,418
Paris	3,423	2,329		5,752
Caracas	1,134		5,167	6,301
Hong Kong (peak)	1,140		3,588	4,728
New Delhi	3,082		1,516	4,598
Rio De Janeiro	1,745		2,752	4,497
Karachi	3,115		1,269	4,384
Mexico City	1,307[1]		2,800	4,107
Singapore	2,030		1,965	3,995
Bankok	1,519		2,227	3,746
Manila	1,122[1]		2,401	3,523
Jakarta	2,041		1,347	3,388
Nairobi	495		2,800	3,295
Cairo	1,402[1]		1,648	3,050
Kuala Lumpur	1,381		1,553	2,934
Buenos Aires	2,718		77	2,795
Lagos	741		1,756	2,497

Note: [1] Includes airbridge fee.
Source: Compiled using IATA annual.

apron space and aircraft gates and thereby put off major investments. This
despite the fact that demand at some Third World airports may be very highly
peaked and at night because of the effect of time zones. Thus Bangkok has a
major traffic peak between 2100 and 2400 hours every night. Second, airport
tariffs are only changed very infrequently and usually only after several years
have elapsed. In the Philippines there was no change in the fees between 1970
and 1977 and in Algeria between 1974 and 1979.

Yet the last decade has seen a rapid inflation in airport costs. Only very
recently have Third World airports started to envisage increasing their tarrifs
every two years or even every year. Yet many of their European counterparts
have been changing their tariffs more or less annually for many years.

Most Asian and other Third World airports have not followed the ICAO
recommendation on passenger-related charges and continue to impose an
airport passenger tax direct on the passenger. This slows down the throughput
of passengers at airports and increases the demands for space. But it also
makes changes in the passenger tax difficult to impose because of public
awareness and opposition. If the passenger-related charge were levied directly
on the airlines as part of the landing fee it would be easier to increase it in
response to rising costs.

The net result is that airport charges at most Asian and other Third World airports are substantially lower than those of airports in Europe or the United States (see Table 10.2). Clearly there is scope for substantially increased revenue generation from aeronautical charges both by adapting them more closely to costs and through more frequent changes in the level of charges.

The impact of low charges is further aggravated in a number of countries where the national carrier is exempted from paying landing fees. This is the case with several airlines in the Middle East. In some countries the national carrier is invoiced for airport charges and either refuses to pay or pays only after many months delay.

An additional problem faced is the loss in the foreign-currency value of landing fees or other aeronautical charges if these are fixed in a local currency which is depreciating rapidly because of high domestic inflation. Since many airport costs may be in foreign exchange it may be necessary to increase aeronautical charges frequently if the local currency is falling in value. Frequently this is difficult because of the slow bureaucratic procedures involved in obtaining approval for increases in landing and other charges. The better alternative may be to specify such charges in an international currency such as US dollars. About thirty or so airports now do this including in China, Chile, Colombia, Jamaica, Tanzania and Uganda.

MAXIMIZING COMMERCIAL OPPORTUNITIES

Our earlier analysis of revenue structures of European airports in 1989 showed that on average about 30 per cent of total airport revenues are generated from a variety of commercial activities (rents, concessions, direct sales and car parking but excluding recharges to tenants and other non-specified aeronautical revenues). But this is an average figure and airports with well-developed commercial and shopping activities may be generating up to 40 per cent or even 50 per cent of their total revenues from such activities as was the case with Gatwick (over 50 per cent) and Amsterdam (38 per cent) in 1989. Airport managers should set themselves a target of generating about 40 to 45 per cent of their total revenues from commercial activities since a 50 per cent figure is rarely reached. Few Asian or other Third World airports achieve commercial revenue levels that even approach 40 per cent (Table 10.3). Airports such as Bangkok with non-aeronautical revenues exceeding 35 per cent of their total revenues are the exception rather than the rule.

Another way of assessing the revenue-generating performance of airports is to examine their concession and rental income per passenger. This has been done for 1989 for a selection of Third World airports for which data were available (Table 10.4). Their concession and rental income on a per passenger basis after excluding the fuel concession fees, is very low. Only Bangkok, of those sampled, had a revenue close to the European average of about US $3.55 while all the others were way below it. However, a more

Table 10.3 Concession revenue and rents as percentage of total revenue 1989[1]

	(%)	
Bangkok	36	
European average (approx)	30	
Kuala Lumpur	30	
Colombo	27	
Nairobi[2]	26	
Guadalajara (Mexico)	24	(inc. fuel charges 12.8%)
Barbados	25	
Rio de Janeiro	23	
Penang	22	(inc. fuel charges 8.1%)
Mexico City	22	(inc. fuel charges 11.0%)
Buenos Aires	14	
Caracas	13	(inc. fuel charges 2.2%)
Medellin (Colombia)	12	
Bali	9	
Lagos	9	(inc. fuel charges 2.6%)
Bogota	8	
Tehran	3	
Katmandu	2	

Source: ICAO 1991.
Notes: [1] Only airports with over 1 million passengers per annum included.
[2] 1988 data used.

Table 10.4 Concession and rental income per passenger in 1989 (excluding fuel concession income)

	(US $ per passenger)
European average	3.55
Bangkok	3.38
Barbados	1.40
Mexico City	0.77
Tehran	0.64
Bali	0.63
Penang	0.51
Caracas	0.47
Bogota	0.47
Medellin (Colombia)	0.36
Lagos	0.31

Source: Derived by author using ICAO statistics.

appropriate measure might be the concession income per international passenger.

Third World airports generally appear to have underestimated the revenue-earning potential of commercial activities, and as a result the number and range of retail outlets or other concessions is very limited. A number of problems have to be overcome if revenue generation from non-aeronautical sources is to increase.

First, even where there has been an awareness of the importance of non-aeronautical revenues, airport authorities have found that their own airport terminals were not designed with this in mind. As a result there is often inadequate space for concession areas within the terminal building. This is particularly so with airports designed in the late 1960s and early to mid-1970s. Even at some newer airports or terminals, space may be limited because the designer and the airport authority may have failed to appreciate the revenue-earning potential of commercial areas. This happened at Manila International opened in the mid-1980s and at the new Bangkok terminal extension opened in the late 1980s. Often, space for shops has been cut back to keep the overall terminal building project within a strictly limited budget even though this might endanger the overall economic feasibility of the project.

Second, the range of retail shopping concessions at many airports is very limited especially on the landside of the terminal. Too often the few shops available are almost identical in the range of goods they sell, usually a mixture of local handicrafts, watches and cameras or cheap electronic goods. One can see this in Kuala Lumpur, Bangkok and many other airports. Such shops often mirror the shops found in tourist hotels and in downtown shops. Having too many identical outlets, especially when space is in short supply, reduces the level of passenger facilities, fails to maximize the revenue-earning potential of the space available and may well reduce the profitability of each outlet for the concessionaire. Space permitting, the range of goods and shops available can be very much wider than many airport managers appreciate. Local and imported fruits and foods, sports goods, clothing and luggage should all have a place in airports catering for international passengers.

Finally, where concessions do exist they are frequently underpriced with a tendency for them to be let on a fixed rental based on area rather than a concession fee related to the turnover of the shop or concession. Fixed rentals are widespread in south-east Asian airports. The result is that airport authorities fail to benefit from any increase in concession turnover arising from traffic growth. All the benefits accrue to the concessionaire. Moreover, since the rental is fixed there is little incentive to change concessionaires. There is clearly a need at many airports to introduce a system of tenders for commercial concessions and to base concession fees on turnover.

Many Third World airports are, of course, adversely affected by the relatively low incomes of the airport users, both passengers and others, when compared to European or North American airport users. This has a twin impact. Less per head is likely to be spent at the airport by passengers or visitors and, in addition, charges for many services are likely to be lower or non-existent. It is not uncommon, for instance, to find that car parking at airports is provided free of charge.

Airport earnings from duty-free shops normally appear within concession revenues. Inevitably airports are secretive about such earnings because they are commercially sensitive. At most of the larger UK airports and at some other European airports we find that between 55 per cent and 60 per cent of concession revenue comes from duty-free concessions (see Table 6.1, p.120). For one or two airports the figure is closer to 70 per cent. This is probably the upper limit. Airport managers should be aiming at a 60 per cent target share from their duty-free shops. If duty-free shops generate concession revenue which is substantially less than 60 per cent of total concession income then there is cause for concern. But this is the case at many Third World airports. The duty-free shops do not generate their proper share of concession revenues. This is due in part to the lack of sufficient suitable terminal space, in part to the inexperience of the duty-free concessionaires and partly to the nature of the traffic handled. At the same time it should be borne in mind that in many developing countries, because of religious, social or fiscal reasons, duty-free spirits or tobacco products may be less attractive for the local market. Duty-free sales will consequently be lower unless foreign residents make up a large share of the airport's total traffic. Where this is not the case, the airports will need to be innovative in developing their airside concessions to compensate for lower duty-free income.

The concession revenues reported by many Third World airports are often heavily dependent on fuel throughput charges. This is especially so among South American airports (see Table 10.3 above). When fuel charges are included in concession revenues for these airports they may give a false impression of their success in generating concession income. The real earnings from shopping, catering and related commercial activities may still be relatively low.

LABOUR COSTS AND MANPOWER ISSUES

Developing-country airports have a major cost advantage in that the wages and other costs of labour employed at the airport are generally much lower than the labour costs of airports in the developed world. This is partly because of the lower level of wages in the countries concerned and partly because most airports have been run as parts of government departments where wages tend to be particularly low. The lower labour costs must be an additional factor in explaining the apparently favourable financial performance of many developing-country airports.

But developments are likely to erode this labour-cost advantage because the creation of independent airport authorities is giving greater scope to airport managements to break away from government or civil-service wage rates. While the lower labour costs are also reflected in the lower construction costs of terminals and runways, the cost of specialist equipment may well be very high. Equipment for air traffic control, for ground handling, airbridges, specialized vehicles and so on will invariably have to be imported. Its installation may be expensive and the problems and costs of maintenance are certain to be high. Hitherto, sophisticated equipment was generally only installed at the major airports. During the later 1980s many domestic airports began having their facilities upgraded, as has been happening in Malaysia, and the costs of operating these airports will rise dramatically.

Traditionally, governments in many Third World countries have placed greater emphasis on the technical and operational side of airport development rather than on the financial and managerial side. They have failed to appreciate the economic and developmental benefits which might accrue from sound airport management and have therefore failed to put into their airports staff of high seniority and with adequate and relevant training. They have also failed to give them adequate responsibility and power. In too many countries, senior airport staff are retired military personnel, former air traffic controllers or fairly junior government officials with relatively poor training for the job they have to do. If specialist trained staff do exist they may be transferred to other government departments or they may move to the private sector where wages are invariably higher.

The low status and limited administrative authority of airport or department of civil aviation staff means that they may well be unable to ensure the co-operation of other government departments (customs, immigration, police, etc.) or even the airlines so as to improve the operation or the economics of their airports.

Airport managers often face a major problem because their national airline will usually be much more powerful and much closer to the government than the airport director or the department of civil aviation. The airline's views and desires will often be given preference and priority irrespective of their impact on the airport/s. For instance, the government will turn a blind eye to delay or even non-payment of airport charges, increases in airport charges will be refused because of airline opposition, expensive airport equipment or facilities may be forced onto the airport, and so on.

This relative lack of power together with the failure to develop adequate expertise among airport managers and senior staff has further repercussions. It results in many countries in an over-dependence on foreign consultants and contractors. These are expensive and frequently give advice or build facilities which are poorly adapted to the real needs and financial resources of the airports and countries concerned.

The major justification for operating airports in developing countries on a more commercial basis is that the financial drain on central government resources should be substantially reduced. But for this to happen, not only should the airport authorities be given the commercial freedom to implement more profit-oriented aeronautical charging and concession policies, but they must also be given political support when dealing with airlines or government departments. Unless such support is forthcoming, attempts to run airports on a more commercial basis will founder on the opposition of other interested parties and on bureaucratic obstacles.

References

AAAE (1990) *1990 Survey of Airport Rates and Charges,* Alexandria, VA: American Association of Airport Executives.

AACC (1990) *Annual Report 1989,* Geneva: Airport Associations Co-ordinating Council.

AACI (1991) *Communique No. 27,* Brussels: Airports Association Council International.

AEA (1987) *Capacity of Aviation Systems in Europe,* London: Association of European Airlines.

Airbus (1991) *Market Perspectives for Civil Jet Aircraft,* Toulouse: Airbus Industry.

Airline Monitor (1989) (June) Ponte Verde Beach, FL: ESG Aviation Services.

AOCI (1990) *Airport Bond Financing Survey of Large Hub Airports,* Washington DC: Airport Operators Council International.

BAA (1988) *BAA News* (November).

BAA (1989a) *1989 Report and Accounts* Gatwick: BAA Plc.

BAA (1989b) *BAA News* (November).

BAA (1990) *BAA Airports: Traffic Statistics - 1989/90,* Gatwick: BAA Plc.

BAA (1991a) *1991 Annual Review,* Gatwick: BAA Plc.

BAA (1991b) *Landing, Passenger and Parking Charges from 1 April 1991,* Gatwick: BAA Plc.

Brendel, G. (1991) 'Commercial revenues: a concessionaire's view', *Airport Economics and Finance Symposium 1991,* London: Polytechnic of Central London.

CAA (1986) *Air Traffic Distribution in the London Area,* CAP 552, London: Civil Aviation Authority.

CAA (1988) *Air Traffic Management in the United Kingdom,* CAP 537, London: Civil Aviation Authority.

CAA (1989a) *Traffic Distribution Policy for the London Area and Strategic Options for the Long Term,* CAP 548, London: Civil Aviation Authority.

CAA (1989b) *Traffic Distribution Policy for Airports Servicing the London Area,* CAP 559, London: Civil Aviation Authority.

CAA (1991) *The Need for Traffic Distribution Rules,* CAP 578, London: Civil Aviation Authority.

Carré, A. - D. (1990) *Aéroports et Stratégie d'Enterprise,* Paris: Institut du Transport Aérien.

CEC (1991) *Proposal for a Council Regulation on Common Rules for the Allocation of Slots at Community Airports,* COM (90) 576 Final, Brussels: Commission of the European Communities.

Congressional Budget Office (1984) *Financing US Airports in the 1980s,* Washington DC: Government Printing Office.

Doganis, R. (1988) 'Shopping for profits', *Airline Business* (September).

Doganis, R. (1991) *Flying Off Course: The Economics of International Airlines*, Second Edition, London: Routledge.

Doganis, R. and Graham, A. (1987) *Airport Management: The Role of Performance Indicators*, London: Transport Studies Group, Polytechnic of Central London.

Doganis, R. , Dennis, N. and Graham, A. (1990) '*Interaction of airport congestion and air transport demand and supply*', London: Department of Transport Seminar Paper (unpublished).

DTp (1991) *Study on Airport Slot Allocation Final Report*, London: Department of Transport.

FAA (1990) *1990–91 Aviation System Capacity Plan*, Report No. DOT/FAA/SC-90-1, Washington DC: Federal Aviation Administration.

Gellman Research Associates (1989) *Current and Alternative Methods of Financing Large Commercial Airports in the United States: Prepared for Federal Aviation Administration*, PA: Gellman Research Associates: Jenkintown.

Graham, A. (1991a) '*The economics of European airports*', *Airport Economics and Finance Symposium 1991*, London: Polytechnic of Central London,

Graham, A. (1991b) '*Measuring airport performance*', *Airport Economics and Finance Symposium 1991*, London: Transport Studies Group, Polytechnic of Central London.

Heinzelmann, U. (1991) 'Towards optimal concession revenue and rents', *Airport Economics and Finance Symposium 1991*, London: Polytechnic of Central London.

HMSO (1977) *Agreement between the Government of the United Kingdom and the United States of America concerning Air Services*, Cmnd 7016, London: Her Majesty's Stationery Office.

HMSO (1978) *Airports Policy*, Cmnd 7084, London: Her Majesty's Stationery Office.

HMSO (1985) *Airports Policy*, Cmnd 9542, London: Her Majesty's Stationery Office.

HMSO (1988) *The Air Navigation Order 1988: Statutory Instruments*, London: Her Majesty's Stationery Office.

IATA (annual) *Airport and* En Route *User Charges Manual*, Geneva: International Air Transport Association.

ICAA (1988) *Étude sur les Commerces en Zone Publique et en Zone sous Douane sur les Aéroports: commission des recettes extra-aeronautiques (Metz Conference)*, Paris: International Civil Airports Association, French Section.

ICAO (1967) *Statement by the Council to Contracting States on Charges for Airports and Route Navigation Facilities*, Doc. 8718–C/975, Montreal: International Civil Aviation Organization.

ICAO (1971) *Annex 16 Noise (Chicago Convention)*, Montreal: International Civil Aviation Organization.

ICAO (1979a) *Development of Non-Aeronautical Revenues at Airports*, Circular 142–AT/47, Montreal: International Civil Aviation Organization.

ICAO (1979b) *Airport Financial Data, 1976*, Circular 145–AT/50, Montreal: International Civil Aviation Organization.

ICAO (1980) *Convention on International Civil Aviation*, Sixth Edition, Doc. 730016, Montreal: International Civil Aviation Organization.

ICAO (1981) *Statements by the Council to Contracting States on Charges for Airports and Route Navigation Facilities*, Doc. 9082/2, Montreal: International Civil Aviation Organization.

ICAO (1989a) *The Economic Situation of Air Transport Review and Outlook 1978 to the year 2000*, Circular 222–AT/90, Montreal: International Civil Aviation Organization.

ICAO (1989b) *Financial Data*, Digest of Statistics, Series F, Montreal: International Civil Aviation Organization.

ICAO (1991) *Airport and Route Facilities 1989,* Digest of Statistics No. 376 Series AF, Montreal: International Civil Aviation Organization.

Little, I. M. D. and Macleod, K. M. (1972) 'New pricing policy for British airports', *Journal of Transport Economics and Policy,* 6(2).

McDonnell Douglas (1989) *World Economic and Traffic Outlook,* Long Beach, CA: McDonnell Douglas.

MMC (1985) *British Airports Authority,* Cmnd 9644, London: Her Majesty's Stationery Office for the Monopolies and Mergers Commission.

NEI (1989) *The Impact of Abolishing Duty and Tax Free Allowances in the European Community,* Rotterdam: Netherlands Economic Institute.

NEI (1990) *The Impact of Abolishing Duty and Tax Free Allowances in the European Community,* Rotterdam: Netherlands Economic Institute.

Philipson, T. 'International legal obligations of airport operations', *Airport Economics and Finance Symposium,* London: Transport Studies Group, Polytechnic of Central London (unpublished).

Ramsey, F. P. (1928) 'A mathematical theory of saving', *Economic Journal,* 38:543–59.

Rogers, J. M. (1990) 'Potential changes in airport finance' Paper to American Bar Association, Washington DC: American Bar Association (unpublished).

SRI (1990) *A European Planning Strategy for Air Traffic to the year 2010,* Meulo Park, CA: SRI International.

Starkie, D. and Thompson, D. (1985) *Privatization of London Airports,* London: Institute of Fiscal Studies.

Starkie, D. (1991) 'Slot trading at United States airports,' Brussels: Commission of the European Communities (unpublished).

Toms, M. (1991) 'Towards cost related pricing', Airport Economics and Finance Symposium 1991, London: Polytechnic of Central London.

Index

68, 193–7, 203–4; rentals 128, 142;
revenues 56–8, 197–200; slot trading
109–11; *see also* Airport and Airways
Trust Fund

value added 174–7
Vancouver 4, 10, 16
Vienna 8–10, 13, 26, 28, 47, 54, 66, 76,
167; performance 2–3, 171–86
Virgin Atlantic 104

Washington: Dulles 194, 198–201;
National 4, 16–17, 102, 191, 194,
198–201
Weitnauer 145
West Palm Beach 205
Work Load Units (WLU) 20–1, 163;
performance 22–3, 171–86

Zurich 13